Barcode in Back

MW01120579

*The Dynamics
of Genre*

Victorian Literature and Culture Series
Jerome J. McGann and Herbert F. Tucker, Editors

THE *Dynamics* OF *Genre*

Journalism and the
Practice of Literature
in Mid-Victorian Britain

Dallas Liddle

UNIVERSITY OF VIRGINIA PRESS
CHARLOTTESVILLE AND LONDON

University of Virginia Press
© 2009 by the Rector and Visitors of the University of Virginia
All rights reserved
Printed in the United States of America on acid-free paper

First published 2009

9 8 7 6 5 4 3 2 1

LIBRARY OF CONGRESS CATALOGING-IN-PUBLICATION DATA

Liddle, Dallas, 1963–
    The dynamics of genre : journalism and the practice of literature in mid-Victorian Britain / Dallas Liddle.
      p.   cm. — (Victorian literature and culture series)
    Includes bibliographical references and index.
    ISBN 978-0-8139-2783-1 (cloth : acid-free paper)
    1. English literature—19th century—History and criticism—Theory, etc.
2. Journalism and literature—Great Britain—History—19th century. 3. Authors and publishers—Great Britain—History—19th century. 4. Influence (Literary, artistic, etc.) I. Title.
    PR461.L45 2009
    820.9'008—dc22

                                              2008027894

For Andrea

Contents

Acknowledgments

THIS BOOK HAS BEEN a long and evolving project, and I need to thank many people for help they gave me literally last century. Florence Boos of the University of Iowa, best of advisors and mentors, has given fifteen years of unfailing generosity and invaluable knowledge of Victorian literature and the arts. Teresa Mangum helped shape my early understanding of periodicals studies, and has helped keep me on track since. Help formulating and testing the arguments in individual chapters has come from many quarters: colleagues in the Scholarly Writing Group at Augsburg College helped with the introductory chapter, while the Harriet Martineau chapter is doubly indebted to Linda Peterson, to whose new edition of the *Autobiography* I gratefully switched as soon as it appeared, and who gave valuable feedback on a draft of the argument. Chip Tucker of the University of Virginia helped me reconceive and strengthen several parts of the manuscript, especially the chapter on Trollope. Heidi Hope Johnson and Patricia Murphy gave formative advice on the George Eliot chapter; Andrew Maunder diagnosed weaknesses in an early draft of the sensation novel chapter; while Patrick Leary generously tracked down and sent me a contemporary source I hadn't known about, and pointed out another logical gap I hope I since have been able to fill. Conferences on book history and print culture held by the English faculty at the University of Oxford in late 2005 and early 2007 introduced me to leading scholars whose generosity in commenting on my project and answering my questions matched their expertise, including Laurel Brake, Simon Eliot, Peter McDonald, and Asa Briggs, for whose kind encouragement I am particularly grateful.

The librarians of Wilson Library at the University of Minnesota have generously allowed me full access to its important collections of Victorian periodicals. Dixie Ohlander, interlibrary loan librarian of Lindell Library at Augsburg College, has tracked down many sources I had despaired of finding, while the professionalism and expertise of the librarians and staff of the British Library at St. Pancras and at the Newspaper Library at Colindale have helped me make the most of research trips. Grants to make those trips have come from the University of Iowa Department of English and from Augsburg College, which also provided the sabbatical leave that allowed me to finish the manuscript. None of these colleagues, friends, enablers, and kindly strangers, of course, can be blamed for the errors that remain.

My greatest debt is to my family, all of whom made contributions or allowances, or both, during the long months of writing, and especially to Andrea, who set her own work aside to copyedit and proofread the entire manuscript, thereby giving me new understanding of my remarkable good fortune in marrying her, just when I thought I understood it all. No greater love hath a life partner than this.

Part of my first chapter appeared as "Bakhtinian 'Journalism' and the Mid-Victorian Literary Marketplace" in a collection of papers from the Oxford First Annual Conference on Book History, published in Blackwell's online journal *Literature Compass* 4 (2007), and is reprinted here by permission. The editors of *Victorians Institute Journal* have cordially allowed me to reprint in chapter 4 an essay originally published in their vol. 26 (1998), pp. 5–37. Chapter 5 is a revised version, reprinted by kind permission of the publishers, of "Anatomy of a 'Nine Days' Wonder': Sensational Journalism in the Decade of the Sensation Novel," first published in *Victorian Crime, Madness, and Sensation,* ed. Andrew Maunder and Grace Moore (Aldershot, Hampshire: Ashgate, 2004), pp. 89–103.

*The Dynamics
of Genre*

PROLOGUE

> Why this sort of change [in the style and form of periodicals], which
> is perpetually recurring, should usually bring with it a correspond-
> ing change, and sometimes a corresponding improvement, of literary
> production, is more than any one can say, but the fact is not easily
> disputable.
>
> GEORGE SAINTSBURY, *A History of Nineteenth Century*
> *Literature* (1896)

IN THE PAST TWENTY YEARS it has become conventional wisdom among literary historians and scholars that magazines, reviews, and newspapers were the discursive context and physical medium of most important British literature in the nineteenth century. Agreement on this intimate relationship between periodicals and literary texts has become widely shared without also developing into a tool for critical interpretation, however, so perhaps it would be more accurate to say that it has become conventional without yet becoming wisdom. To claim that one discourse was the context or medium for another is more a premise for research than a conclusion, since contexts and media can have strikingly different relationships to the works they con-textualize or mediate.

This book is an attempt to study, with a new level of specificity and accuracy, the influence of the genre forms used by mid-Victorian journalists on the practices of contemporary writers of poetry, the novel, and serious exposi-tory prose. I will try to show that relationships between journalistic and liter-ary genres can be traced much more rigorously than has yet been done, and that these relationships were highly significant for literary history, altering the careers of some famous mid-Victorian writers and influencing the wider shape of mid-Victorian literary culture. Newspaper and periodical genres were capable of exerting such pressure because, of the written discourses developed in Britain by the middle of the nineteenth century, they had the most practical and immediate significance for the Victorians themselves, both for writers who depended on them for occasional or (often) primary income and for readers who relied on newspapers and magazines for news, entertainment, and basic knowledge of their own world.

As important as journalism was to the Victorians, however, it is now the area of Victorian written discourse least understood by scholars, and this may be partly because formal description of Victorian journalism—its genres, conventions, assumptions, influences, and implicit values—has still hardly begun. Historians have long been interested in the forms of past historiography, and literary scholars have a well-developed if more recent interest in the forms taken by past literary criticism and scholarship, but scholars of Anglophone journalism have come very late (if they have come even now) to any parallel interest in the historical forms and genres used in journalism. This will be less surprising if we remember that theoretical study even of modern journalistic discourse began only with the advent of university journalism programs in the twentieth century, and that the vocabulary used by specialists to describe Anglo-American newswriting genres and their elements—from "inverted pyramid" to "feature" to "nut graph"—has been created by editorial praxis and vocational pedagogy rather than by scholarly investigation.[1] Scholars of journalism are still in the earliest stages of identifying and describing the genres used in historical journalisms.[2]

The many gaps in scholarly understanding of Victorian press discourse will have to be addressed, however, because the study of Victorian literature and culture is undergoing a sea change in its methods and resources. Technology is rapidly adding thousands of pages of Victorian periodicals, some formerly available at only a few libraries (or at only one, the British Library Newspaper Library at Colindale), to the shared textual field all Victorianists can easily investigate, and to the sources all Victorianists will customarily use (Leary 79). This welcome increase in the availability of periodical texts is in part driven by, and in part drives, a new interest in journalism and periodicals from scholars of culture, history, and literature.[3] Via databases such as the now-venerable Internet Library of Early Journals (ILEJ), academic projects such as Laurel Brake's Nineteenth-Century Serials Edition (NCSE), and for-profit ones such as the 19th Century British Library Newspapers managed by Gale and the British Periodicals collections from ProQuest, research into Victorian periodicals is becoming radically easier to do just as this subfield is gaining the attention of a rising generation of scholars who admire the interdisciplinary successes of Victorian Studies (both the interdisciplinary enterprise and its eponymous journal) and who can take advantage of thirty years of pioneering academic study of periodicals, including such triumphs of individual and collaborative scholarship as the *Wellesley Index* (1966–89, CD-ROM 1999) and the *Waterloo Directory* (1976, CD-ROM 1994, online from July 2001).

While some recent work has used this expanding access to Victorian periodical texts to aid traditional research projects such as reception history and the tracing of textual references (Leary 74–77), scholars have also begun to use these texts in more ambitious attempts to remap and revalue the nineteenth-century literary and cultural marketplace,[4] and sometimes to suggest that recovered or rediscovered periodical texts by major writers should be added to those writers' artistic oeuvres or even to the canon, as Marian Evans's 1856 review essay "Silly Novels by Lady Novelists" has been added to the *Norton Anthology of English Literature*.

Two problems of methodology arise for the scholars who use periodical texts in these ambitious ways. The first, a descriptive problem, involves figuring out what we are reading, exactly, when we read a periodical text; it turns on our unmet need for a usable guide to the conventions of text, style, and genre that governed thousands of different periodical forms extant at any given historical moment. It also includes related problems of defining what should count as "text" in the scholarly study of periodicals, and of theorizing, attributing, and assessing authorship, which in a periodical text is always both mediated by and opposed to editorship. Some of the challenges in this area have been well described by Lyn Pykett and Margaret Beetham.[5]

The second problem of methodology is more epistemological—it concerns how scholars can connect evidence from the periodical press rigorously enough to the ambitious interpretive claims we so often try to make about specific Victorian authors, editors, and publishers, and (still more broadly but also more commonly) about British social formations of class, culture, and historical contingency. Should a text created in a periodical's mostly non-literary genre forms—often in the expectation of anonymity, and altered to an unknowable extent by an editor—be considered valid documents of an author's literary intentions and career? What interpretive tools can enable us to read a periodical text originally created to influence or manipulate its readers' opinions as evidence of what those opinions originally were? Such problems go to the core of what many literary scholars and book historians hope to accomplish using periodical texts. Is it even possible for scholarly use of periodicals to fulfill the hope Michael Wolff expressed in 1971, in a landmark article: that periodical archives could be treated by scholars as "repositories of the general life of Victorian England" (26), and that the individual issue of the Victorian periodical might become "the basic unit for the study of Victorian cultural history" (27)?

I think these methodological problems are solvable, both in theory and in practice, but the most important challenge for scholars at our historical moment seems to be that much of the practice of periodicals-based research remains surprisingly unengaged with its own methodology.[6] Many scholars do not seem to see that using periodical texts as primary sources for literary or book history imperatively raises both the problems I have described, and that studies that ignore these issues compromise the validity of their own conclusions. In the absence of basic descriptive knowledge about Victorian periodical genres (or even of an agreed framework for developing such knowledge[7]), for example, many scholars still assume that periodicals did not have separate or significant genre forms of their own. Rather remarkably, many critics trained to recognize the finest grains of formal and generic structure in poetry and the novel, and to interpret their influence with theoretical sophistication, still treat periodical "sources" as if they expect such texts to provide transparent access to the thoughts of their writers—or, still more oddly, to the thoughts of their original readers.[8] Such unexamined assumptions have hampered the work of Victorianists since our earliest attempts to understand the forms of Victorian prose nonfiction.[9] And while specialists in periodicals studies have made progress in cataloging the larger physical forms of periodical publication—review and magazine, tabloid and broadsheet—they have to date made little headway in describing and theorizing even the everyday genre forms in which Victorian journalists cast their articles: the bread-and-butter genres and subgenres of "leading article" and "slashing article," "middle" and "review."

It may be because of these missing links in our understanding of the Victorian press that so many scholars still approach periodical articles assuming that text created using a journalistic form (say, a Marian Evans article in the *Westminster Review*) can be evaluated and placed with respect to its author's

5

other work through a reading of its content alone, as if a text in a journalistic genre were capable, at least in principle, of encoding and conveying all the same philosophies, projects, and authorial intent as a text by the same writer in a literary genre (say, *Middlemarch*). Such projects rely on the always-unspoken assumption that the content of a text and its genre form are sufficiently separable that "meaning" can be translated or transferred from one genre into another intact.

According to the Russian literary theorist Mikhail Bakhtin, however, any literary practice that assumes that meaning can readily be abstracted from genre is premised on a flawed understanding of genre. Bakhtin has shown that meaning and genre form resist separation in much the same way that meaning resists translation from one language to another, because genre is a necessary component of meaning as well as a medium for it.[10] In his essay "Discourse in the Novel," Bakhtin sometimes uses the term "genre" as a synonym for or subcategory of "language" itself, because he sees that genres perform primary functions of language in reflecting, representing, and helping to constitute particular worldviews. A text without genre is as difficult to imagine, and would be as difficult to interpret, as speech without language.

Because genres contain and encode meaning, for Bakhtin they necessarily mediate and help to constitute the meaning of all the text they contain. In very highly conventional genres, such as the modern romance or horror novel, genre conventions alone may well determine the meaning of an entire work.[11] But although Bakhtin does say at one point that "form and content in discourse are one" (*Dialogic* 259), his ideas are not simply a recasting of Marshall McLuhan's famous formulation, in which the genre has now become the message. Rather, for Bakhtin, genres perform the complex and language-like function of limiting and shaping the terms and available meanings of texts, enhancing some and muting others through an "overall accentual system" (*Dialogic* 288) unique to that genre at that historical moment. Genres operate strongly on meaning at the level of connotation and subtext, working to make the text they contain reflect the genre's own worldview.[12]

Much of this Bakhtinian understanding of genre's function is probably not hard to accept—especially for anyone who has put a manuscript into the mail. Most working writers understand that genres and meanings are on some level inextricable; those who write professionally must choose genres appropriate for the meanings they want to convey, or, still more commonly, choose meanings to match the genre to which they have been assigned. Just as the education of most modern professionals consists largely of acquisition of their profession's discourse genres (and the values and worldview acquired along with them), much of the actual composition of published texts, even academic ones—even this one—is a discursive negotiation in which the writer translates a specific body of information into the shaping conventions and available meanings of an existing genre. The genre itself—business memo, mystery novel, academic paper, or news report—provides rich resources of meaning that increase the sophistication and depth of certain kinds of communication between a competent writer of that genre and a competent reader, even as it renders other kinds of communication and ranges of meaning more difficult to convey. Furthermore, by predeciding (almost automating) many of a writer's most difficult creative choices, genres dramatically speed both the writer's work of composition and the reader's work of comprehension. This practical function of genres becomes particularly important when discourses must be produced on a tight schedule to meet a preexisting set of readerly or market expectations, since the more rapidly the discourse must be composed (or will be read), the more writers will need to rely on genre conventions to accomplish quick composition.[13] We could predict that genres that have been designed or have evolved specifically to enable rapid composition—the military order, the police log entry, the modern journalist's "hard news" report—will tend to be more standardized and conventionalized than others, to the point that it can be difficult to tell, from the finished product, whether the writer has expressed herself through the genre or the genre has been expressed through the writer.

Poets and novelists, philosophers and familiar essayists, obviously also compose in genre forms. But Bakhtin notes (and other genre theorists including Alastair Fowler and John Frow have also noted[14]) that artistic users of language are more conscious of their tools and more deliberate in their relationship to genre. "For the writer-craftsman the genre serves as an external template," writes Bakhtin, "but the great artist awakens the semantic possibilities that lie within it" (*Speech Genres* 5). English comic novelists from Fielding and Sterne to Thackeray and Dickens are some of Bakhtin's best examples, in the essay "Discourse and the Novel," of authors who engage in deliberate play with the variety of literary, nonliterary, and speech genres they invoke and employ (*Dialogic* 301–7). Such artists may even choose their genres subversively, intending the "parodic destruction" of a genre's discursive world (309), as Miguel Cervantes famously did with the chivalric romance. Bakhtin's ideas also seem to apply to a writer's adaptation of existing popular genres to more complex artistic purposes (as Mary Shelley adapted the Gothic tale) or to the blending of genres to synthesize or contrast their conventions (as Charlotte Brontë blended the Gothic novel, fairy tale, and bildungsroman). For Bakhtin, the great and defining triumph of the novel as a genre is what he termed its "polyvocal" (*Problems* 3) ability to do its destruction, adaptation, and blending of discourses on all levels, from sentences to themes, by incorporating into its own text a "heteroglossia" of its own society's multiple and competing languages.

Some of Bakhtin's concepts about language, such as the heteroglossia of a culture and the polyvocality of the novel, are today widely accepted and increasingly used in the praxis of literary scholars, but the full implications of his idea that genres themselves are different languages in constant and active mutual interaction, and that this dynamic interaction both determines and constantly modifies the meanings they can convey, has yet to be put to useful work even in the way scholars approach the traditional artistic genres, much less in any attempt to understand the relationship of artistic genres to what Bakhtin called the "extra-artistic prose" discourses (*Dialogic* 279) that surround and penetrate them.[15] Still less have we pursued Bakhtin's most intriguing and challenging formulation about genre: that the full story of the interplay of genres—their competition and struggle—properly understood, *is* the history of literature. Struggles between literary schools and trends, Bakhtin argues, are "peripheral phenomena and historically insignificant" compared to "the deeper and more truly historical struggle of genres, the establishment and growth of a generic skeleton of literature" (*Dialogic* 5). Bakhtin sometimes uses the term "Galilean" to try to convey his conception of a decentered and complexly interacting universe of discourse ("There are many linguistic worlds, none of which is at the center," gloss commentators Gary Saul Morson and Caryl Emerson [299]), and in his revised conclusion to *Problems of Dostoevsky's Poetics*, Bakhtin foresees that an appreciation of this level of complexity in discourse must one day inevitably replace scholars' and critics' current, largely pre-Galilean expectations: "In the realm of *artistic* cognition people sometimes continue to demand a very crude and very primitive definitiveness, one that quite obviously could not be true" (*Problems* 272).

A more Galilean model that tries to trace the decentered and dynamic relationships between literary and nonliterary forms, informed by Bakhtin's ideas about genre, may be particularly useful for the study of Victorian discourse. In addition to the many other ways they helped to create modernity, Victorian men and women of letters inhabited and helped to create the first real-time shared "world of books." With a vastly expanded range of venues for published writing (both signed and anonymous), and relatively free from expectations that authors should be genre specialists, British writers of the nineteenth century may have been, as Alastair Fowler has suggested, the most dazzlingly multigeneric that any period of literary history has produced.[16] Victorian working authors not only produced text simultaneously in many discrete publishing genres, more than had ever before existed at one time, but experimentally recombined or reinvented genres and publishing forms as part of their regular professional practice—as Walter Scott famously did with *Waverly* and Dickens with *The Pickwick Papers,* but also as John and Leigh Hunt less famously did with the *Examiner,* William Cobbett with the *Weekly Register,* A. J. Beresford Hope with the *Saturday Review,* and George Smith and William Makepeace Thackeray with the *Cornhill Magazine.*

This study does not attempt a definitive history even of the dozen years of mid-Victorian genre struggle I will be considering. Even so, I try to suggest that real understanding of many interpretive problems posed by Victorian literary authors and their projects will not be possible until scholars learn to see, as Bakhtin advised, within and through the perspectives of more of its multiple genres and spheres of discourse—and become able to recognize the tones, assumptions, worldviews, and influences of nonliterary genres with which literary genres interacted. My *Canterbury Tales* chapter titles, with the competitions and negotiations they imply between different subject positions, are intended to help suggest that larger project. Victorian writers of the 1850s participated in their diverse world of books in ways analogous to those Chaucer's pilgrims used to negotiate and promote their own positions within their diverse discourse community, choosing language and genre forms to express, modify, and contend for competing visions of social reality and human nature. The assumptions and worldviews coded into the genre forms chosen by these tellers are integral to our understanding of the meanings of their tales.

My first chapter, "The Poet's Tale," uses some penetrating observations on genre offered by Elizabeth Barrett Browning in *Aurora Leigh* as the starting point for an exploration of the relationship between journalistic and literary forms that had developed in Britain by the mid-1850s. I suggest that this relationship put significant pressures on mid-Victorian literary artists such as Barrett Browning—pressures scholars have found difficult to recognize partly because our theoretical tools for understanding genre have not been calibrated to read how and when genres struggle. I suggest that seeing the relationship between the genres of mid-Victorian culture as Bakhtin recommends, however—not as complementary forms to be categorized, but as contending and competing worldviews—may help us productively rethink some familiar passages in mid-Victorian literary history.

In the body chapters that follow, I apply Bakhtinian readings of the dynamic relationships between genres to interpretive problems posed by mid-Victorian writers including Harriet Martineau, Anthony Trollope, George Eliot, and the school of 1860s "sensation novelists." The chapters on Martineau and Trollope are intended to be parallel and complementary: both writers had relationships with the genre forms of contemporary journalism that have been missed or misinterpreted by many biographers, and both also reward closer reading by offering valuable analyses of journalistic genres that add to our understanding of the dynamic pressures within mid-Victorian discourse. Harriet Martineau is a particularly interesting example of a skilled prose writer who, over the course of a varied career, wrote in almost every extant fiction and nonfiction genre, and even invented a successful hybrid genre of her own. Despite the sophistication and creativity she displayed in her writing practice, however, Martineau's most-read and most-used text today, the *Autobiography,* consistently disclaims any deliberate manipulation of genre forms. Scholars have tended to take her at her word, interpreting her career according to what she claims to have intended, and treating the *Autobiography* as a literally factual account, not as a generic artifact shaped at a particular historical moment to a particular ideological end. My chapter rereads the *Autobiography* in its historical context as a document of 1855, and suggests that it offers clues to the decision Martineau had recently made at that time to suspend much of her work as an independent author to devote herself to anonymous newspaper journalism.

Anthony Trollope is another author whose complex relationship with journalism has yet to be explored in the critical literature. In addition to his famous tally of nearly fifty novels, Trollope wrote nonfiction of all genres and lengths, including review, magazine, and newspaper journalism, but his career-long theoretical interest in the dynamic discursive community that journalism created in Britain, informed by his participation in these different generic projects, has been difficult for modern scholars to recognize. Dickens and Thackeray are the acknowledged Victorian commentators on the professional world of Victorian letters, but Trollope's less well-known analysis of journalistic discourse in Victorian society offers insights to the modern reader that can complement and help clarify their portraits of the press. Dickens and Thackeray were former press apprentices themselves, and both tend to see Victorian journalism from a writer's-eye view. In Trollope's fictions of journalism, we are less likely to see the writer of press discourse at all, and much more likely to see careful tracings of just the kind of generic interplay modern book historians are increasingly interested in reconstructing: how journalistic discourses interact and ramify within society as they are read and shared, begetting still other discourses and changing the lives of the people they touch.

In two more paired chapters, I consider cases in which scholars have observed relationships between literary and journalistic writings, but have been led by incomplete understanding of Victorian journalism to similarly incomplete conclusions. Scholars who look at Marian Evans's journalistic writing of the mid-1850s for the *Leader* and *Westminster Review,* for example, often assert that Evans drew on an "apprenticeship" in review journalism under John Chapman to create the authoritative narrating persona of George Eliot. I try to show that confusing the forms and goals of George Eliot's art with those of Marian Evans's journalism—something the novelist herself pointedly resisted doing—may have led to years of misreading of the shape of, and early influences on, George Eliot's early career. Similarly, students of the British literary world of the late 1850s to middle 1860s have long believed that "sensational journalism" and the "sensation novels" of Wilkie Collins, Mary Elizabeth Braddon, and others were parallel attempts at the same historical moment to do the same cultural work. Assumptions that the novelistic and journalistic "sensation" genres shared common goals and philosophy may have hampered scholarly understanding of sensation fiction's discrete generic project, however, and notably fail to explain another fact scholars often remark: the hostility of many periodical reviewers to the sensation novel form. In this chapter I use a real point of contact between genres—a "true" sensational crime story from the newspaper press of early 1868—to suggest that sensation fiction and journalism may have been much more ideological and generic opponents than allies.

While these four chapters focus on case-study relationships between literary writers and genres and their journalistic or periodical contexts, two final sections return to problems of theory and method. Chapter 6 reviews the current state of theory in the study of the periodical press, in which two levels appear to operate. The most influential global theories are those of social scientists Pierre Bourdieu, Jürgen Habermas, and Benedict Anderson, but these writers offer little direct guidance for literary scholars or historians in how to interpret individual periodical texts, and none about what should count as the unit of periodical "text": is it the article, the issue, the individual editorship, or the run of the journal as a whole? Scholars who have attempted to help solve problems of periodical studies at this more concrete level of research praxis include Laurel Brake, Margaret Beetham, Lyn Pykett, and Michael Wolff, who for their part have attempted little higher-order modeling. I suggest that Bakhtinian theory may be able to bridge the gap, enabling us to read historically specific genres of Victorian journalism simultaneously as competing worldviews, as large historical phenomena, and as recognizable patterns and elements within individual texts.

In a short epilogue, I show how the mid-Victorian dynamics of genre between journalism and literature traced in this book had begun to operate less strongly even by the mid-1860s. I return to the theoretical issues of the first chapter to suggest their value in helping to develop a generically conscious method usable within the context of the history of the book, the interdisciplinary subfield now developing from previous models of literary history and literary historicism, and the potential value of a Bakhtinian view of literary history that would recognize competitive and cooperative relationships between generic forms as well as between individual texts, schools, and writers.

1 THE *Poet's* TALE

Literature, Journalism, and Genre in 1855

> Throughout the entire development of the novel, its intimate interaction (both peaceful and hostile) with living rhetorical genres (journalistic, moral, philosophical and others) has never ceased; this interaction was perhaps no less intense than was the novel's interaction with the artistic genres (epic, dramatic, lyric).
>
> MIKHAIL BAKHTIN, "Discourse in the Novel"

AS BOOK 3 OF ELIZABETH BARRETT BROWNING'S verse novel *Aurora Leigh* (1856) opens, its poet-protagonist is a moderately successful woman of letters in mid-nineteenth-century London. Aurora Leigh's reflections on her early professional career are often celebrated as among the first artistic portrayals of a British woman writer, but one passage in particular is remarkable for the way Barrett Browning paints the problems of the mid-Victorian author. Her protagonist's dilemma at this point is not between action in the world and poetic discourse, though that might have been expected after the *agon* between Aurora and her cousin Romney in book 2. The poet's more recent struggle has been between two kinds of discourse. As she moves with uncharacteristic hesitancy to identify the second discourse, however, Aurora seems to have something on her mind—or conscience.

> The midnight oil
> Would stink sometimes; there came some vulgar needs:
> I had to live that therefore I might work,
> And, being but poor, I was constrained, for life,
> To work with one hand for the booksellers
> While working with the other for myself

And art: you swim with feet as well as hands,
Or make small way. I apprehended this,—
In England no one lives by verse that lives;
And, apprehending, I resolved by prose
To make a space to sphere my living verse. (3: 299–309)[1]

Like her distant literary cousin Moll Flanders, also a single woman in London, Aurora prefaces an embarrassed confession of the expedient she has used to survive with a string of explanatory or exculpatory clauses. Although Aurora's vocation is poetry, in mid-Victorian England the market for poetry is too small to provide primary income even for a single poet: "No one lives by verse that lives."[2] The literary artist who needs income must also participate in more flourishing markets. Aurora has therefore written "prose"—a kind of text booksellers will pay for. The full secret is not yet out, however. As Aurora reveals in the next lines, the booksellers have dictated more than her prosody; under their direction she has learned and practiced highly specific forms and genres.

I wrote for cyclopaedias, magazines,
And weekly papers, holding up my name
To keep it from the mud. I learnt the use
Of the editorial "we" in a review
As courtly ladies the fine trick of trains,
And swept it grandly through the open doors
As if one could not pass through doors at all
Save so encumbered. I wrote tales beside,
Carved many an article on cherry-stones
To suit light readers,—something in the lines
Revealing, it was said, the mallet-hand,
But that, I'll never vouch for: what you do
For bread, will taste of common grain, not grapes,
Although you have a vineyard in Champagne;
Much less in Nephelococcygia
As mine was, peradventure.
                    Having bread
For just so many days, just breathing-room

For body and verse, I stood up straight and worked
My veritable work. (3: 310–29)

Her veritable work may be that of a poet, but Aurora reveals here that she
has solved one pressing problem—and created another—by also becoming a
professional journalist. She has written extensively for multiple venues in the
periodical press ("cyclopaedias, magazines, and weekly papers"), returning to
her poetry in precious intervals when she has written just enough to pay for
food and shelter a few days ahead. But Aurora's distaste for her own periodical
writing is clear. At best she regards it with arm's-length amusement, at worst
with revulsion: "The midnight oil would stink."

The distancing Aurora does here seems based in a conviction that in producing periodical text she has not in some sense really been writing at all, but
only reproducing the preexisting forms and voices of the periodicals themselves. Some of the conventions she participates in, such as the anonymity
that was still in 1856 almost universal for periodicals, seem to have relatively
little impact on her text itself—and unlike some contemporary journalists,
Aurora does not consider anonymity a hardship; she takes credit herself for
"holding up my name / To keep it from the mud." Much more troublingly,
however, the periodicals have prescribed her persona and tone, requiring her
to use a written voice foreign to her own personality, values, and artistic sense.
She has had to use the Victorian journalist's editorial "we" in review writing,
for example, and has even carried it off "grandly," although she considers the
convention comically archaic and pretentious. Periodical writing has limited
her similarly on the levels of topic and theme: her nonfiction articles have
been carved "on cherry-stones / To suit light readers," cleverly but shallowly
made to suit an audience expecting only entertainment. To write for periodicals, in this passage, has not meant adapting Aurora's own ideas and words
for a different mode of external publication, but alienating herself from her
own voice and intellectual ability to take on the voices prescribed by the genre
requirements of the periodical press.

Aurora's attempt to explain how so much of her own writing has therefore
not really been her own writing finds expression in this passage in a cascade of
metaphors and images that come close, in their paradoxical power, to Iago's "I
am not what I am." Eight separate metaphors in twenty-nine lines both define
and help to widen the distance between Aurora's journalism and her poetry.

The two kinds of writing are done with different hands (lines 303–5; perhaps with an ironic echo of Matthew 6:3[3]) or journalism is done with feet instead of hands (305–6). If verse is life, journalism is only the shelter Aurora builds to protect life (309); if the poet's name is clean, journalism is mud (311–12); if poetry is sculpture, journalism is folk carving (318–19); if poetry is wine, journalism is bread (321–25); if poetry is written standing tall, journalism is done in a slump or stoop (328); if poetry burns the midnight oil, journalism burns oil that stinks (299–300).

Barrett Browning's purpose here seems to be to draw a distinction between poetic discourse and journalistic discourse so fundamental that these genres will be shown to differ not only in quality but more fundamentally in kind. And while it might be a mistake to attribute Aurora's analysis of journalism uncritically to Barrett Browning (who was known to write the occasional review and *Athenaeum* article herself, and not under pressure of starvation), it seems significant that when Barrett Browning wrote in April 1853 to Anna Jameson that the long poem she projected would be "intensely modern, crammed from the times," she immediately added in parentheses, "(not the 'Times' newspaper)" (*Letters* 2: 112).

As a representation of and commentary on the mid-Victorian writer's life, this passage raises issues that go well beyond the beliefs of Aurora Leigh or the critical interpretation of *Aurora Leigh*. If Elizabeth Barrett Browning does not intend Aurora's conflict to seem unique—and nothing in the passage marks this working writer's circumstances as different from those of any other contemporary working writer—Barrett Browning is diagnosing an important conflict in the mid-1850s between poetic or literary discourse and journalistic discourse *as discourses*. But such a diagnosis would be at odds with at least two major elements of the modern conventional wisdom about the relationship between mid-Victorian periodicals and literary authors.

First, modern scholars have never recognized a distinction—or dilemma—that seems painfully clear to Aurora: that writing for mid-Victorian periodicals meant joining a different discursive marketplace and employing different genres or groups of genres than did writing in artistic genres, even in nonfiction prose genres. Instead, they have represented periodicals as broadly continuous with, if perhaps also somewhat influencing the development of, already-existing genres such as the familiar and personal essays. Recent studies have tended to minimize the significance of the conflicts Aurora describes at this mid-century era, depicting the separation of "popular" and "art" literatures as more a phenomenon of later-Victorian and even post-Dickensian decades. T. W. Heyck, for example, has argued that between 1830 and 1860 the broad term "men of letters" was a "respectable sobriquet, including a very wide variety of writers—poets, novelists, journalists, biographers, historians, social critics, philosophers and political economists" who were seen as sharing a common occupation and function (24), and John Gross's classic study *The Rise and Fall of the Man of Letters* begins by defining the term "man of letters" itself "fairly broadly, so that it covers a major figure like Carlyle . . . [,] one or two poets and novelists in the less familiar role of critic," and a larger number of "journalists and reviewers, teachers and interpreters" (xiv). Heyck and Gross thus assume that British producers of literary and journalistic text in this mid-century period shared a relatively inclusive and homogenous professional identity, one not due to subdivide until the 1870s and after. Such scholars do not, of course, claim that no distinction was made in this period between text that was art and text that was not, but they rarely draw the distinction by *genre*, preferring other markers such as author's reputation (Dickens's name versus G. P. R. James's), publisher's reputation (Moxon versus the Minerva Press), "differences of moral weight" (Heyck 24) in individual works themselves, or other cues built into the publication, reception, and content of texts. But Aurora's very different analysis suggests that a working writer in 1856 might already have perceived a larger conflict between genres of literary and periodical writing *as* genres, and that a writer at this mid-Victorian period might also have perceived a troubling ascendancy of the periodical genres, to the cost and detriment of the literary ones.

Second, students of the periodical press have long believed that whatever factors may have lowered the intellectual caliber of journalism later in the century (from the time Matthew Arnold began to mock the *Daily Telegraph* through Stead's "New Journalism" and on into the darkest days of the Edwardian press barons), through the 1850s and into the 1860s journalism was a relatively substantial, thoughtful, and even intellectually serious form of discourse. In *Literature and the Press* (1960), Louis Dudek, though no fan of later-century newspapers from the New Journalism onward, has only praise for the "large intelligent public" of mid-Victorian newspapers, and characterizes "the best papers of this [mid-century] period" as "a high point of serious and respectable newspaper writing," believing that, at least for some part of

the mid-century, "contact between journalism and literature was advanta-
geous to both walks of life" (76, 79). The belief that participation in journalism through the mid-century could serve as valuable training or apprenticeship for literary authors is still widely held by literary biographers, and one
scholar has gone so far as to criticize those who would treat periodical writing,
especially when done by women, as *merely* apprenticeship, suggesting that it
be seen instead as a full-fledged "overlapping" career for women authors that
allowed them to "develop wide-ranging intellectual interests as critics, poets,
novelists, and social theorists" (Easley, *First-Person Anonymous* 8, 1). But in
Aurora's account, contemporary journalism does not even rise to the status
of an apprenticeship. It is only an expedient, giving Aurora nothing of value
except a paycheck precisely because, as she represents it, writing in periodical
genres can have no other benefit for a poet. Aurora's journalism is neither professional training in letters nor an intellectually stimulating career, but only a
distraction, an embarrassment, and a burden.

Together, these aspects of the experiences and reflections Barrett Browning gives her fictional mid-century woman of letters suggest an important
challenge to the received reading of the relationship between mid-Victorian
periodicals and literature. They suggest that competition between genres of
writing that were valuable as market commodities and genres that were valuable as art was a powerful factor in the mid-Victorian writer's life, and that to
some writers this competition must have been career-shaping, or even career-
defining. The struggle is partly economic, but also significantly discursive and
ideological, for Aurora shows it going beyond issues of physical survival to
those of artistic survival. To be able to write as a poet at all, Aurora must learn
and extensively practice a kind of discourse based on principles opposed to
those of her poetic craft, and she must learn to keep every element of this
journalistic practice carefully separated from her artistic writing. Ironically,
and oddly, in this passage an important obstacle to the young Aurora's mas-
tery of poetic discourse turns out to be her success at mastering journalistic
discourse. Even starvation (traditionally the British poet's archenemy, along
with madness and the occasional ill-timed visitor from Porlock) is less a threat
to Aurora Leigh's art here than journalism seems to be.

In the first major section of this introductory chapter, I investigate the
disparity between the modern assumption that mid-Victorian journalism
and literature were complementary, and Barrett Browning's representation of

them as conflicting. I want to see if other evidence supports Aurora's portrait of a mid-Victorian world of discourse ideologically and artistically divided by genre, in which periodicals were not only a different venue for publication of existing genres but also a strong generic force in their own right, and in which artistic writers were compelled to participate in alien markets and produce alien genres that seemed to be winning a dangerous ascendancy over literary forms. In the second section I will suggest a theoretical approach that might help turn recognition of this generic and ideological competition into a useful tool for literary historiography and interpretation.

Books versus Periodicals at the Mid-Century

In most modern accounts of mid-Victorian publishing, books and periodicals are shown as sharing in a single general prosperity. Nigel Cross, who divides the history of nineteenth-century authorship into three periods, characterizes the middle one as serenely satisfactory to all: "The years 1840 to 1880 saw the book and newspaper trade settling down into general profitability, except for some bumpy patches in the transitional 1840s. The majority of writers were able to make ends meet as they and their middle-class publishers produced just about the right quantity of reading matter to satisfy the middle-class reader" (Cross 5). Richard Altick, in the section of his landmark *English Common Reader* that deals with the 1850s, is still more positive in asserting that the "fifties, which saw the spread of [W. H.] Smith's stalls to almost every principal railway line in the country, were also the period when the sales of books and periodicals reached unprecedented levels" (302).

Both these statements may be true, however, and yet not be the whole or most important truth of the situation from the point of view of individual writers. Altick's assertion, though accurate, is subject to important qualifications—for example, that with respect to books it seems to apply only to the very earliest years of the 1850s. Simon Eliot's *Some Patterns and Trends in British Publishing, 1800–1919* shows that, although periodical publishing did continue to thrive throughout the 1850s, book publishing had a more uncertain decade. British book production in the mid-1850s, after hitting a peak in 1851, was relatively or even absolutely flat or declining for an extended period, not really recovering until even the late 1860s. In 1856, the year of *Aurora Leigh*, the trade magazine *Publishers' Circular* listed 3,939 book titles published, down from 4,599 in 1855, which was already a decline from 5,117 in 1854—two successive years of significant decrease according to that industry measure. The year 1857 saw the number come up only slightly, to 4,178. As Eliot says of the table showing this data, "Figure 1 reveals a profile which the whiggish among us might not have expected. There was no steady, constant incline leading from the slough of early industrial times to the sunny uplands of the almost fully-literate early twentieth century" (8). Cross-checking the data against the other leading contemporary trade publication, *Bent's Monthly Literary Advertiser,* confirms the trend: Eliot's data show that the flat book production is confirmed by *Bent's* largely parallel figures for the same years: 4,100 titles published in 1853, 3,757 in 1854, 3,653 in 1855, 3,888 in 1856, and 3,900 in 1857. A flat output of books, rather than an increase, in the 1850s and into the 1860s is further confirmed by Eliot's reading of book registrations recorded in this period by the British Library (12).

There was apparently no corresponding sluggishness in the market for periodicals. Eliot finds that in "the eleven years between 1854 and 1864 the number of newspaper ('journals') titles doubled" from 624 to 1,250 (Eliot 82; see also his table E3), while new periodicals of all types established in the 1850s "register a 51% increase over the 1840s," with 1,564 new titles established (84). Figures for paper production in the 1850s, which rose over 50 percent between 1850 and 1859, seem to corroborate that it was expanding publication of high-volume, paper-consuming periodicals—or perhaps in some cases inexpensive novel reprints with large print runs—that drove this large increase in paper use (Eliot 24). Eliot himself calls the surprisingly flat mid-Victorian market for books—the unexpected "'plateau of production' between 1858 and 1872, visible in many of the annual book production figures and in certain periodical statistics as well"—perhaps "the most improbable finding, and therefore the most suspect" (106) of his book. But if his data suggest the unexpected conclusion that in the decade after the middle 1850s, book publication suffered while periodicals throve—and perhaps suffered *because* periodicals throve—there are also many contemporary observers who both confirm and attempt to explain his unexpected result.

As early as 1833, Edward Lytton Bulwer was warning seriously in *England and the English* that the success of new-model periodicals such as the *Edinburgh Review* was being won at the expense, both economic and intellectual, of traditional literary forms. An important consequence of the critical and intellectual triumph of quarterly reviews such as the *Edinburgh* (1802) and *Quarterly* (1809), Bulwer wrote, was that "instead of writing volumes authors began pretty generally to write articles, and a literary excrescence monopolized the nourishment that should have extended to the whole body." Bulwer warned that these periodicals had succeeded, and were in his time continuing to succeed, directly at the cost of book publication: "From the commencement of [the *Edinburgh Review*], which was the crown and apex of periodical reviews, commences the deterioration of our standard literature" (262). By attracting and then virtually monopolizing the nation's intellectual talent, the reviews had reduced the number of British writers able and willing to produce rigorous and thoughtful work in history, science, and scholarship. Ideas that should have been developed in major works were instead published in abbreviated and incomplete review article form, with their value diminished or lost in the translation. Writing for periodical publication had made even "the profoundest writers" less valuable, Bulwer wrote, since such writers had perceived

> that the period allotted to the duration of an article was scarcely sufficient inducement to extensive and exhausting labour; (even in a quarterly review the brilliant article dazzled more than the deep: for true wisdom requires time for appreciation,) and, though still continuing the mode of publication which proffered so many conveniences, they became less elaborate in their reasonings and less accurate in their facts.
>
> Thus, by a natural reaction, a temporary form of publication produced a bias to a superficial order of composition; and, while intellectual labour was still attracted towards one quarter, it was deteriorated, as monopolies are wont to be, by the effects of monopoly itself. (263–64)

Bulwer charged that the economic and intellectual success of periodical discourse had made all writers who took up this "superficial order of composition," even the most knowledgeable and talented, "less elaborate in their reasonings" and "less accurate" than they would have been if writing for book publication. The result was a national literature that, while still rich in talented writers, had become relatively impoverished of developed and substantial intellectual products.[4] He argued that the interests of books and periodicals had come to be directly opposed in what was, if not quite a zero-sum game, at least a competition in which successes of periodical publication impaired the interests of book publishing, and that this competition was driven in part by the opposing expectations and standards built into these different modes of publication.

The same points were made in other articles throughout the mid-century period, in terms that make clear that the intellectual dangers periodical writing posed for books were an active topic of contemporary conversation.[5] A writer in the *Rambler* of 3 March 1849 observed how among writers "one great mind after another [is] absorbed into the deep-rolling stream" of periodical literature. "To what fatal extent this tendency of our day may hereafter be carried, it is hopeless to inquire. Whether or not it has already gone too far, so that too large a proportion of the intelligence of the country is now employed in journalism, it is certain that it may go much further still, and that *the book* may become practically extinct beneath *the newspaper* and *the magazine*" (475). The argument that this fatal tipping point had already been reached was developed almost as a formal proof in an 1861 article in *Bentley's Magazine* by novelist and editor W. H. Ainsworth. Ainsworth's troubled assessment of the repercussions of periodical literature's success begins with the first words of his article. "The present may fairly be regarded as the golden age of the professional literary man," he writes:

> Every month sees the birth of some new periodical, and the competition among publishers is so great, and perhaps suicidal, that the writer who has in any way gained the ear of the public is sure to obtain work, not only profitable but tolerably regular in its nature. At the same time, however, it cannot be denied that the character of our literature has degenerated, and that the books are rare which will be remembered by our successors, while those that have a chance of living are, with few exceptions, the productions of amateurs, who have time and money to bestow on their favourite employment. Why this is a necessary evil connected with the literature of the day it is our purpose to investigate. (215)

According to Ainsworth, the striking success of periodicals in what Wilkie Collins had recently (in 1858, even before the advent of the successful new shilling-monthly magazine form) dubbed "this age of periodicals" had indeed expanded the market demand for writing—but only for writing in forms that could be published *in* periodicals. Publishers and editors hoping for a striking success—such as those recently achieved by, for example, Dickens's *Household Words,* Smith's *Cornhill,* Beresford Hope's *Saturday Review,* and Macmillan's *Macmillan's*—were willing to pay even marginal writers and editors remarkably well to produce text for periodicals rapidly and in volume. If the pay scale for writers had been transformed for the better, however, that transformation had also rendered periodicals the main and almost sole source of professional writers' incomes, and that shift had induced writers to become factories for the quick manufacture of saleable copy: "The quantity of copy produced by a writer in vogue is something astounding, and what is published with his name is not a tithe of what he turns out under the protection of the anonymous" (217).[6] Though it is not clear that Ainsworth wants us to take "tithe" quite literally, his estimate that a successful mid-Victorian writer produced ten times more text for periodical publication than for any other genre form is striking.

Like Bulwer's, however, Ainsworth's real fears were for the intellectual consequences of this transformation. The premium journalism had placed on speed and volume of composition, and on language and ideas that would be accessible to the casual readers of periodicals, had, he believed, encouraged serious intellectual and stylistic vices. Authors forced to write quickly substituted cleverness and cheap effects for substantial research or reflection, and modern periodical writing had as a result become more verbose, shallow, and gaudy: "The popular author beats out his gold to the thinnest dimensions, and trusts to the ornamentation to distract attention from the intrinsic value of the metal" (217). By setting up its economics to reward literary composition that "requires knack, and not thought" (216), the British literary marketplace had rendered itself virtually incapable of fostering intellectual or artistic value; only amateurs insulated from market pressures were now producing text worth reading.

Ainsworth and Bulwer, though periodical editors themselves, were originally and primarily novelists. A number of mid-century writers who identified themselves primarily as journalists are also on record in this same period describing a similar dynamic of periodical genres displacing traditional literary forms. The journalists' accounts, however, tended to be celebratory. While Bulwer and Ainsworth diagnosed intellectual weakness in periodical writing and mourned its growing ascendance, the journalists triumphed at the public vindication of their commonsense worldview and widely accessible writing. James Fitzjames Stephen opened his 1862 *Cornhill* article "Journalism" with the satisfied prediction that periodical discourse "will, no doubt, occupy the first or one of the first places in any future literary history of the present times, for it is the most characteristic of all their productions."[7] And although Walter Bagehot seemed implicitly to accept Bulwer's argument that the style and values of modern periodical writing were incompatible with the care and rigor of "the scholar," in Bagehot's analysis—published in the *National Review* in 1855—the comparison between scholar and journalist strongly favored the journalist. "There is exactly the difference between the books of this age, and those of a more laborious age, that we feel between the lecture of a professor and the talk of the man of the world," wrote Bagehot;

> the former profound, systematic, suggesting all arguments, analyzing all difficulties, discussing all doubts, very admirable, a little tedious, slowly winding an elaborate way, the characteristic effort of one who has hived wisdom during many studious years, agreeable to such as he is, anything but agreeable to such as he is not—the latter, the talk of the manifold talker, glancing lightly from topic to topic, suggesting deep things in a jest, unfolding unanswerable arguments in an absurd illustration, expounding nothing, completing nothing, exhausting nothing, yet really suggesting the lessons of a wider experience, embodying the results of a more finely tested philosophy, passing with a more Shakspearian transition, connecting topics with a more subtle link, refining on them with an acuter perception, and what is more to the purpose, pleasing all that hear him, charming high and low, in season and out of season, with a word of illustration for each and touch of humour intelligible to all, fragmentary yet imparting what he says, allusive yet explaining what he intends, disconnected yet impressing what he maintains. This is the very model of our modern writing. The man of the modern world is used to speak what the modern world will hear; the writer of the modern world must write what that world will indulgently and pleasantly peruse. ("First Edinburgh Reviewers" 256)

The journalist E. S. Dallas, writing in *Blackwood's* in 1859, went so far as to predict that in the "modern world" currently being created in Britain, a separate "literary class" of authors would ultimately die out, and authorship would cease to become a profession or specialty of its own, to become merely the shared accessory skill and public voice of all professions and interests.

To successful journalists the displacement of traditional literary practices and forms by an expanded journalism might well have seemed both plausible and attractive in 1862, when the market for periodicals had never been so large, diverse, or flourishing. In financial terms, in discursive reputation, and in independence, every style and form of periodical at this point in the mid-century seemed capable of striking public success. As Stephen was writing for the *Cornhill Magazine,* his periodical was still basking in the success of its extraordinary debut and inspiring a host of shilling-monthly imitators, some of them, such as *Temple Bar,* also notable hits. Among the quarterly reviews, the new *National Review* and renewed *Westminster Review* had (re) joined the ranks of high-status periodicals whose intellectual superiority had been established over the last thirty years by such writers as Francis Jeffrey and T. B. Macaulay. Among weeklies, conspicuous new success was being won by the smart and acerbic *Saturday Review;* in newspapers, the *Times* still held much of the lordly reputation and reputed political power (if not quite the circulation) it had won during the Crimean War, even as penny papers such as the *Daily Telegraph* seemed also to be winning success and large readerships on their own terms.

New Genres, New Writers

Evidence that mid-century periodical publishing was succeeding at least partly at the cost of draining writers and readers away from the market for books is of course not yet a full case for Aurora Leigh's argument—and mine—that Victorian journalism had developed separate genres of its own, and that those genres competed ideologically as well as economically with preexisting literary forms. The differences between these modes of publication may have been confined to their distribution systems and economics, not really affecting them on the level of discourse form—even though Ainsworth, Bulwer, and Bagehot did seem convinced both that periodicals had evolved substantively different discourses and that different standards of literary and intellectual value drove the journalistic forms.[8] Some modern scholars have been inclined to read the changes that clearly did take place in content, tone, and style between eighteenth- and mid-nineteenth-century periodical forms as a seamlessly gradual evolution of genres that nonetheless remained common to both literature and journalism, such as the familiar or personal essay and the moral or didactic essay. Alastair Fowler's *Kinds of Literature,* while noting that every genre is constantly changing—indeed, that "the character of genres is that they change" (18)—much prefers models of genre change that involve "internal, mediated, or literary causes" (277) to evolutionary ones that attribute formative power over genres to external pressures, or to struggles among rival forms.[9] Lee Erickson, looking at this period in particular in his strikingly original *Economics of Literary Form,* asserts that the essay-length nonfiction of the mid-Victorian periodical remained fundamentally the same genre, albeit somewhat "evolved," as the essay "of Montaigne, Bacon, Addison and Johnson." "What had been a modest experiment in skepticism and judgment became the dominant form of intellectual discourse," Erickson writes; "the Johnsonian essay of moral judgment was replaced by the familiar essay, which sought to please the reader. . . . This accommodation also required the development of a slower intellectual pace characterized by repetitive amplification and lengthy quotation and by more easily accessible prose styles in which anticlimax was the rhetorical rule" (73–74).

But were the main essay genres of Victorian periodicals—the journalistic essay or review essay—really just more aesthetically evolved or consumer-friendly or forms of the familiar essay, standing in direct descent from Johnson and Bacon? Aurora Leigh, as we have seen, thought that mid-century periodical writing had established fundamentally different characteristic genres. One way to resolve the disputed generic paternity of mid-Victorian journalism might be to more carefully retrace its descent from periodical writing of the eighteenth century, when there does indeed seem to have been little division between the prose forms used in periodicals and books, and when their economic interests were also more closely linked.

The periodical essays of Addison, Steele, and Johnson, as Erickson has observed, were independently published in periodical form "as speculations" on which booksellers hoped "to make money afterwards by gathering them together in a book," as Samuel Johnson's bookseller did with the *Rambler* of 1750–52 (Erickson 92–93). Marilyn Butler and others have pointed out that throughout the eighteenth century British periodicals did not publish genre forms peculiar to themselves. The first "magazines" were, as their name indicates, containers for heterogeneous texts in preexisting generic shapes:

"Within the covers of a single unbound periodical readers encountered a lively, eclectic mix of fables, dreams, letters, poems, travels, natural science, history and biography," gathered in an fragmentary way that "did not distinguish one field above another or otherwise attempt to group, still less to hierarchize, knowledge" (Butler 122). And while writing for periodicals in this era was a source or even a major source of income for literary writers (including Defoe, Fielding, and Johnson), when these writers contributed to periodicals, they seem to have retained a high degree of creative and artistic control over the forms taken by their texts. As a result, periodical and book genres in the eighteenth century do seem as artistically continuous as scholar Lennard Davis suggested when he proposed that newspapers and novels were co-participants in an "undifferentiated matrix" he calls the "news/novels discourse" (Davis passim). When no clear genre lines separated even factual and fictional forms, much less their publication venues in periodicals or books, the talents and interests of individual writers would have exerted the most important influence on which genre forms could be published in the periodicals to which those writers contributed.

Even political writers for British daily newspapers, at least until the advent of the new "leading article" form early in the nineteenth century, had had wide latitude in deciding what genre forms to cast their political commentary, and seem to have sometimes chosen forms partly in order to demonstrate their own literary ability and versatility. William Hazlitt was doing a bit of this kind of self-display when, in his first year writing for James Perry at the *Morning Chronicle* in 1813, he wrote to Perry that "I should be very glad to write an answer to the Russian paper of 21st July as from a foreign journal" (*Letters* 135). Caleb Whitefoord's 1799 parody pamphlet *Advice to Editors of Newspapers* gives practical hints on how to make a wide range of this sort of journalistic fabrication convincing, but Whitefoord emphasizes that journalistic success of all kinds depends on the talent and literary acumen of the newspaper's main writer: "The Leading Article is that which, of all others, requires most genius and talent," Whitefoord's editor notes, but as "you, perhaps, have neither," he proceeds to offer a helpful list of unethical shifts and expedients (11). Up through the period following the French Revolutionary and Napoleonic wars, when political commentary gradually became a more regular and regulated feature of the British daily newspaper, newspaper proprietors who wanted to print political articles had to invest in, and rely on, well-educated literary writers who had already mastered the various forms in which political discourse could be cast. Alliances between writers in the top tiers of literary authorship and daily newspapers were as common in this era as they were to be exceptional half a century later. Dan Stuart of the *Morning Post* and *Courier* hired both Charles Lamb and S. T. Coleridge as newspaper writers. As Zachary Leader has detailed, Coleridge ultimately submitted a generic rainbow of poetry, "non-political essays, profiles, leading paragraphs, even parliamentary reports" to Stuart (23). William Hazlitt, Thomas De Quincey, Henry Crabb Robinson, William Cobbett, John and Leigh Hunt, and many other major Romantic-era authors also worked as regular staff writers for, or even actually conducted, daily and weekly newspapers.

Beginning with the *Edinburgh Review* in 1802, however, a developing theme of the new century's periodical press seems to have been that periodicals themselves would increasingly define the genre forms they published, and would require writers to adapt to and adopt increasingly specific conventions. The creation of what we now recognize as the Victorian periodical press may almost be dated from the successful experiments that fixed the forms periodical articles would take in the new century. Editors thereafter increasingly enforced house forms and styles, often by rewriting contributions to bring them into line with the identity of the periodical. A pioneer of this article-level tinkering with consistent voice and persona, Francis Jeffrey, was later identified by Walter Bagehot as the man who "invented the trade of editorship. Before him an editor was a bookseller's drudge; he is now a distinguished functionary" ("First Edinburgh Reviewers" 276).[10]

The development and institutionalization of new genre forms for British periodicals early in the nineteenth century seem to track closely with their increasing financial success, making it difficult to tell if one of these phenomena was directly responsible for the other, or whether (as seems more likely) the development of genre forms well-adapted for the production economics and target readerships of specific periodicals formed a feedback loop with their success. T. B. Macaulay's letters to his *Edinburgh Review* editor Macvey Napier between 1829 and 1843 show him sensitive to the irony that his historical essays, with their new, rather breezy style, were succeeding partly because of qualities that would damn them as seriously intended historiography. "The tone of many passages, nay of whole pages, would justly be called flippant in a regular history. But I conceive that this sort of composition has its own character and its own laws," Macaulay told Napier, in a letter in which he attributed (blame or credit for) the actual invention of the new genre to Robert Southey. "You will however perceive that I am in no danger of taking similar liberties in my history" (qtd. in Davis 15). On the first page of a well-known 1824 essay in the *Westminster Review,* James Mill similarly attributed the success of the *Edinburgh Review* on its appearance in 1802 to an innovative if not admirable recombination of genre elements—"mixing disquisitions of the reviewer with the notice of books" and seasoning the combination with a "tone of severity naturally piquant" (223)—that made the new periodical genre as disastrous intellectually as it was successful financially. Mill considered quarterlies such as the *Edinburgh* to be virtually prohibited by the economic realities of periodical publishing from printing any work of "real merit," because every "motive . . . which prompts to the production of any thing periodical, prompts to the study of immediate effect, of unpostponed popularity, of the applause of the moment," making periodicals "the natural enemy of the most important and beneficent class of opinions" (207, 209).[11]

As the success of generic experiments in the periodical press gave periodicals and their editors increasing income and financial stability, however, the relationship—we might almost say the balance of discursive power—between periodicals and their writers seems also to have changed. The generous rates of pay established by the *Edinburgh* greatly benefited many writers (Erickson 71, 100), giving some who wrote for periodicals the incomes of gentlemen and making it possible for the first time in Britain to speculate that "literature" might become one of the recognized professions.[12] But these increasingly large and financially stable periodicals also gained the ability to recruit writers not only into high-status roles as contributors or consultants but also into staff-level positions, where they could be assigned to produce increasingly conventionalized textual forms.

The standardization of genre forms appropriate for early-nineteenth-century journals must indeed have been one of the developments that ultimately made possible the remarkable achievement (considered as an accomplishment both of discourse and of engineering) of the metropolitan broadsheet newspaper. Already by the 1840s, the "daily miracle" was an octavo volume's worth of closely printed text—forty-three columns of it in the four-by-three-foot sheet of the *Times*—almost all of which had been written, typeset, cast, and printed in well under twenty-four hours. As modern journalism scholar Tim Vos has remarked of twentieth-century journalism, one way to create a pool of workers able to produce readable text in the volume and at the speed required to match this demanding production schedule is to develop genre forms that are simple and teachable, and that can quickly come to seem intuitive to a large body of contributors. Twentieth-century newspaper reporters, Vos notes, came to rely on "the inverted pyramid as a tool to cast consistent, uniform news stories out of the confusing chaos of reality. The use of news forms meant news stories could be standardized and could be produced by an interchangeable work force" (Vos 303–4). Today in the United States most bright nineteen-year-olds can—and thousands do—acquire the inverted pyramid news genre in a few weeks, and write publishable journalistic text before the midterm exam of a college journalism course. Comparable acquisition of the genre forms of Victorian periodicals by young writers—at least some of it apparently happening on a subconscious or preconscious level—is well attested in letters and articles throughout the mid-century period. Young W. M. Thackeray wrote to his mother from Paris that "this system of newspaper writing spoils one for every other kind of writing. I am unwilling, now more than ever, to write letters to my friends, and always find myself attempting to make a pert, critical point at the end of a sentence" (quoted in Elwin 55). Walter Bagehot remarked in 1872 on the "curious process" by which a successful innovation in writing "soon assimilates other writers," sometimes by "conscious imitation," but more often unconsciously: "Everyone who has written in more than one newspaper knows how invariably his style catches the tone of each paper while he is writing for it, and changes to the tone of another when in turn he begins to write for that" (*Physics and Politics* 31).[13]

In the eighteenth century, papers had taken the tones of their writers, not the other way around—writers such as Defoe, Fielding, Addison, and Johnson had been adepts and experts in literary discourse who brought their own literary genre repertoires into their work for periodicals. By a few decades into the nineteenth century, however, a changed and narrowed genre repertoire was being prescribed to writers mainly by the periodicals themselves. As David Masson wrote in 1855, "It is the capitalists embarked in this species of commerce that watch the market; the authors are but their workmen, receiving their orders, and producing the required article according to pattern" (168). This may be why the well-read Aurora Leigh, when she takes up journalism, must still learn "the use of the editorial we in a review" (lines 312–13), acquiring this and the other specific forms and conventions she needs—but despises—directly from her periodical employers, and then turning out well-defined literary commodities to those employers' orders: tales, reviews, and articles for "light readers." Although essay, expository, and short-fiction genres had all obviously existed before the rise of Victorian periodicals, the specific subgenres and conventions (of tone, diction, topic, length, theme) that made publishable text easy for a mid-Victorian journalistic newcomer to step in and begin producing were new—to within the last generation—and specific to periodicals themselves.

The development and standardization of its genre forms must have been a technology as vital to the creation of the Victorian periodical marketplace as we know it as cheaper paper, good shorthand systems, and the steam-powered press. But major innovations in production methods also change the relationship between workers and the product they create—and usually change the size, composition, and skill set of the workforce itself, as British handloom weavers were unhappily discovering at about this same period. The more standardized and conventional periodical writing became, the more its writers could be recruited not only from the ranks of literary authors, or even from among the gentleman-scholars such as Macaulay and Southey who wrote for the early *Edinburgh* and *Quarterly,* but just as easily—and often more optimally for the periodical's purposes—from anyone able to write clear English in a periodical's house style. That hiring pool included the university communities, all of the educated professions, and an increasing number of the middle and even lower classes.[14] With most creative decisions about the form and voice of articles already made by conventions of genre, periodical writers no longer needed the creative abilities or wide reading of literary authors to complete periodical assignments. In fact, writers with literary or artistic training could be *less* effective at (re)producing the standardized voices, genres, and amounts of text periodicals now required than educated professionals, who could conform without question to the conventions they were given. This is certainly the opinion of the writer of "Philosophy of Journalism" in *Chambers's Edinburgh Journal,* who notes that "Coleridge and Campbell both wrote for the *Morning Chronicle,* but with the usual ineffectiveness of mere literary men, who want the readiness demanded by journalism" (405). The writer expands the point of principle on the next page: "Mere literary men ... [,] unless possessing unusually observant minds and plastic pens, are always bad journalists; for their papers are exponents of their own idiosyncrasies, not of the public thought" (406). Nonliterary writers in journalism could congratulate themselves, as this one does, on specialist skill in periodical forms, and on their relative freedom from intellectual interference from nonperiodical influences. The ideological divide between two broad views of the proper nature and goals of discourse brought by contributors to periodicals, the journalists, and the literary authors, may explain the interesting hints of rivalry and even of hostility we have already seen expressed by some of the journalists, such as Bagehot, toward scholarly writing, and the evident satisfaction of Fitzjames Stephen and E. S. Dallas at the idea of journalistic forms expanding at the expense of literary ones.

All four parts of Aurora Leigh's analysis thus seem to be corroborated by the available evidence: that periodical writing and literary writing in 1855 had become generically separate markets and enterprises, that the periodicals had developed specific new genres of their own, that at least some literary writers working in these genres felt alienated from and co-opted by the values of periodical culture, and that British culture as a whole seemed to be favoring the periodical forms at the expense of the literary ones. But if this analysis is correct, it seems strange that so significant and large-scale a conflict within Victorian print culture has not been more clearly observed and described before now.

Here again, I think, *Aurora Leigh* can help us. In the introspective passage in book 3, the writer's struggle is described in terms that are entirely—and, perhaps, necessarily—internal. Aurora may fight Romney in full voice and *en plein air* over the nature of women, the value of poetic art, and whether he can make her accept a valuable legacy from her aunt, but the battle between Aurora's artistic discourse and her journalistic discourse is fought in internal reflection and retrospection, in a nighttime scene at her desk. As her quasi-paradoxical sequence of metaphors helps to show, Aurora's evolving understanding of the nature of these two discourses does not come about through external collisions, but in the space of Aurora's own creative consciousness. And here again Elizabeth Barrett Browning seems to have framed this struggle correctly, for what Mikhail Bakhtin has called the "intense" and "intimate interaction" of literary and rhetorical genres is not, for the most part, contested openly between individual and committed opponents; the dynamic interactions, pushes and pulls, between discourse forms occur, as Bakhtin realized, not mainly *between* writers but *within* them, almost between the very words on their pages. Although mid-century Britain certainly had arch-journalists such as Fitzjames Stephen, declared despisers of many current literary authors including Dickens, and arch-poets such as Elizabeth Barrett Browning, open despisers of most contemporary journalism and its works, the complex structure of the Victorian literary marketplace tended to remind most participants of the attractions and successes of both sides, holding out financial and creative incentives for journalists to write novels as well as for novelists to write in journals. Most Victorian writers and publishers, therefore—even Stephen and Barrett Browning—found themselves at different times in their careers taking different views of periodical discourse. Publishers shifted from taking more direct interest in their periodicals or their catalogs of books, and, especially in the 1860s, many successful authors moved to take on the salaries and cares of periodical editors. As real as it certainly was, then, the mid-Victorian competitive dynamic between genres worked its most important work on the level of the individual creative consciousnesses of writers. This process, even when it happened simultaneously to hundreds or thousands of writers at the same time, has been relatively invisible to traditional literary methodology. The dynamic struggle between Victorian discourse genres may therefore be one of the most significant influences on British literature ever *not* to have been recorded.

If the effects of this struggle between genres were as elusive and intangible as the struggle itself, however, it would be hard to see why literary historians or even book historians should take an interest in it even now. No reading of generic competition within the Victorian print marketplace offers any incentive to rewrite Victorian *literary* history unless it can be shown in some rigorous—or at least plausible—way to have had an effect on literary texts. In the second section of this introductory chapter, I want to move in that more concrete direction, drawing further on Bakhtin's theory of genre to show that the mid-century's economic and ideological competition between artistic and journalistic genres did indeed affect mid-Victorian literature in ways that can be observed and measured.

Bakhtinian "Journalization" in Mid-Victorian Literature

Mikhail Bakhtin's theoretical writings on genre might initially seem an odd tool to use to investigate a complex problem in the interpretation of historical discourses. In one of the first major articles in English to evaluate Bakhtin's theoretical approach to literary genre, in fact, Clive Thomson pointedly put the word *theory* itself in quotation marks. "If we mean by a 'theory' of genre a coherent abstract system which would account for a wide variety of literary practices," wrote Thomson, "then it would seem to be misguided to seek such an abstract system in the work of Mikhail Bakhtin" (29). Bakhtin's reading of genre does initially seem to lack general applicability to literary history, partly because Bakhtin was so specifically interested in the single and arguably unique phenomenon of novelistic discourse as to make application of his ideas to other genres and to specific historical moments problematic.[15]

Even if the novel is the only genre he studied closely, however, Bakhtin's concept of novelization still has implications for what he elsewhere describes as the "Galilean" relationship among genres, and therefore for the specific histories of genres other than the novel. When he discusses in "Epic and Novel" the tendency of the novel to parody and co-opt other forms, for example, he writes: "Historians of literature sometimes seem to see in this merely the struggle of literary tendencies and schools. Such struggles of course exist, but they are peripheral phenomena and historically insignificant. Behind them one must be sensitive to the deeper and more truly historical struggle of genres, the establishment and growth of a generic skeleton of literature" (*Dialogic* 5). The operative mechanism Bakhtin sees at work when genres struggle is illustrated in this essay, where he describes as being "of particular interest . . . those eras when the novel becomes the dominant genre. All literature is then caught up in the process of 'becoming,' and in a special kind of 'generic criticism.' . . . In an era when the novel reigns supreme, almost all the remaining genres are to a greater or lesser extent 'novelized'" (5–6).

In Bakhtin's account, the influence he calls "novelization" happens at historical moments when the novel demonstrates some of its discursive advantages over other genres: it is aware of process in ways other genres are not, is characterized by unfixed openness, and can easily and deftly incorporate multiple voices and generic forms. The resulting artistic and popular success leads to periods of crisis in which other genres notice the newcomer's success and react to it by adopting novelistic features and approaches to language where they can.[16] If they cannot do this, they risk marginalization: "Those genres that stubbornly preserve their old canonic nature begin to appear stylized" (6). Thus, Bakhtin writes, "the novel sparks the renovation of all other genres, it infects them with its spirit of process and inconclusiveness. . . . In this lies the exceptional importance of the novel, as an object of study for the theory as well as the history of literature" (7).

But if novelization is Bakhtin's only case study of the workings of a Galilean interaction among genres, it surely still implies parallel cases. If Bakhtin is right about the effects of the novel on other genres and the reasons for those effects, then in other literary markets and at other historical moments we should expect similarly striking success by one genre to result in writers adjusting their practices in other genres to reflect the new strengths they perceive in that genre. This prediction is particularly important because for Bakhtin genres are more than outward conventions; they are "form-shaping ideologies" that carry within themselves historically accumulated knowledges and ways of thinking. For writers to adopt, or adapt, new genres requires them to change not simply the outward forms of their discourse, but also its attitudes, assumptions, and worldview.

I want to hypothesize that Bakhtin's model of genre interaction may also have the potential to illuminate the mid-Victorian moment of literary history we have been considering, and that journalistic forms, rather than novelistic ones, may in this case have been the change-provoking or catalyzing genre. I want to ask whether Bakhtin's account of how one strikingly successful genre influences others might explain some of our observations about mid-Victorian literary culture more convincingly than the causative factors more typically adduced by literary historians, such as the competition of artistic or ideological schools, the psychology of individual artists, or the influence of culture-wide events. For the purposes of this specific analysis, the periodical genre I want to investigate is the anonymous review essay, which in its various subtypes ("leader" and "middle," as well as review) had grown in the early nineteenth century into the Victorian journalistic genre par excellence.[17]

For a few years in the mid-1850s, a specific set of historical circumstances, including the growing influence and virtual monopoly of the London *Times*, its peak in reputation and political influence at the time of the Crimean War, and the proliferation of new newspapers and journals after the final removal of the stamp tax in 1855, seems to have combined to push the reputation of newspaper journalism for power within British culture extraordinarily—if briefly—high. One index of this sudden increase in cultural centrality is that in 1855 the opinion-leading quarterly reviews, almost without exception, published major articles about the periodical press in general or the newspaper press in particular. In January 1855 David Masson in the *British Quarterly Review* pessimistically assessed "The Present Aspects and Tendencies of Literature"; in June the *Quarterly Review* deconstructed the genre of the newspaper advertisement; in July the *Westminster Review* took on the "London Daily Press"; and in October both Walter Bagehot in the *National Review* and W. R. Greg in the *Edinburgh Review*[18] analyzed the current and theoretical relationship between periodical writing and public opinion, with Greg warning of the potential despotism of an almost universally read newspaper like the London *Times*, which, he said, "inquires, reflects, decides for us . . . and presents us with ready-made opinions clearly and forcibly expressed" (477–78). Among weekly and daily newspapers themselves, the new *Saturday Review* ran a series of scathing articles condemning the theories and practices of the *Times*, which included the assertion in November that "no apology is necessary for assuming that this country is ruled by the *Times*. . . . It is high time we began to realize the magnificent spectacle afforded by British freedom—thirty millions of *Cives Romani* governed despotically by a newspaper" ("Our Newspaper Institutions" 3).

Nor were such claims about the remarkable political influence of journalism in 1855 made only by periodical writers, who, as we have seen, may have had reasons of their own to magnify the importance of their own discourse. No less careful an observer than John Stuart Mill wrote in *On Liberty*, which he began in 1855, that "the mass do not now take their opinions from dignitaries in Church or State, from ostensible leaders, or from books. Their thinking is done for them by men much like themselves, addressing them or speaking in their name, on the spur of the moment, through the newspapers" (131).

I should note that it's not clear to modern historians that newspapers actually did exercise any unusual or determinative power over political decision making in 1855. Parliamentary historians divide sharply over how "public opinion" influenced the MPs and ministers of the 1850s, if at all, in the face of their own agendas and alliances,[19] while even the puissant *Times* is frequently now little more than a footnote in political histories of the period. But it does seem clear that there was widespread perception in the mid-1850s among professional writers that the influence of the "public writing" published in the major quarterly, weekly, and especially daily journals was at a sudden and unexpected high point. There was also strong agreement that it was not the specific abilities or talents of any particular writers that were generating all this discursive power; the power was held to be a function of the genres journals used, a result of combining genre elements including brevity, clarity, authoritativeness of tone, persona, a rather breezy attitude toward connecting argument with evidence, and anonymity. Walter Bagehot's November article in the *National Review* is an extended analysis of the history, distinguishing features, and reasons for effectiveness of the main form of authoritative periodical writing, through which "the modern man" was to "be told what to think," which Bagehot memorably and accurately named in genre terms as the "review-like essay and the essay-like review" (256).[20]

Bakhtin's understanding of the mechanisms of generic interaction seems to predict that under such circumstances journalism and its review-essay form should have become keenly interesting to writers in other genres, and there is some evidence in the literary productions of the mid-1850s that this did happen. Before this period it was rare for a British novelist or poet to represent journalism or journalists as subjects of his or her work, although there were a few famous exceptions. Neither journalists nor even literary authors were customary subjects of literary representation before the 1850s, and the idea that those who wrote literature should also become its subjects struck one observer in 1851 as a faintly comic development ("Sayings" 428).

In 1855, however, journals and journalism suddenly appeared as subjects across a wide range of British literary writing, proliferating throughout the range of published genres. In the novel, Anthony Trollope's *The Warden* (1855), J. M. Capes's *Rambler* magazine serial "Compton Hall" (1855), and F. W. Conybeare's *Perversion* (1856) all contained detailed and realistically intended portraits of modern journalists, supplemented in all three cases with extended reflections on journalism itself, either dramatized as discussions between characters or made directly by a narrator, or, as in *The Warden*, both. In poetry in or around 1855, not only Elizabeth Barrett Browning but Robert Browning as well created journalists as characters in their poetry. Barrett Browning's modern woman of letters was of course Aurora Leigh, who, as we have already seen, supports herself in London with extensive writing as a journalist, while Robert Browning's 1855 dramatic monologue "Bishop Blougram's Apology" dramatized an encounter between two types of modern periodical writer: Blougram, the genteel and well-connected amateur (who writes "my articles / On music, poetry, the fictile vase / Found at Albano, chess, Anacreon's Greek" [lines 913–15]), and Gigadibs, the professional but minimally talented staff writer for *Blackwood's*. In life-writing, Harriet Martineau's *Autobiography* (written in 1855) was a journalist's bildungsroman that culminates with Martineau's 1854 decision to become an anonymous editorial writer for the liberal *Daily News*.

The simultaneity and sheer number of these treatments, given the literary importance of most of their authors, is already interesting. But more seems to be changing in them than a raw count of fictional journalists—the importance of journalists as characters and of journalism as a subject seems to have increased suddenly in the mid-1850s as well. In the few British novels before this period that do treat journalism, the journalistic episodes are relatively limited and peripheral to story and theme. Dickens's invention of the *Eatanswill Gazette* and its editor for chapter 8 of the *Pickwick Papers* (1837) is one brief episode in a brilliant string of them. Journalism is an almost invisible episode in Dickens's quasi-autobiographical *David Copperfield* (1849–50) and occupies only a few chapters for G. H. Lewes's man of letters Percy Ranthorpe in *Ranthorpe* (1847). Even Thackeray's gentleman of letters Arthur Pendennis in *Pendennis* (1848–50), one of the most famous of British fictional journalists, moves quickly out of hack reviewing and into *Keepsake*-style poetry and genteel fiction, hardly touching political journalism at all. In these earlier texts journalism is not a serious career or profession; it is most often handled parodically, as with the Eatanswill editor, and rarely represented as having real political influence.

By the time of *Aurora Leigh* a few years later, however, most British writers' valuation of periodical writing had clearly altered. Journalism was now a far more important discourse—a necessary evil, a professional writer's dark side with which the protagonist must reach a careful accommodation. In the mid-century novels I have mentioned, a powerful national newspaper causes the crisis in *The Warden,* a newspaper writer is the Machiavellian villain of *Perversion,* and another newspaper writer is the flawed protagonist of "Compton Hall." In Martineau's *Autobiography,* however, newspaper leader writing is the perfect vocation discovered, almost too late, at the end of the writer's lifetime journey. Representations of journalism by writers in other genres thus seem to have shifted suddenly in the mid-1850s away from episodic and peripheral representations toward more central ones, from local/historical contexts to national/contemporary ones, from parodic treatments to more realistic ones, and from relative insignificance to more central thematic significance.

Changes in a number of major writers' view of journalism seem to be reflected not only in their texts but also in significant career decisions some of them made just at this time, decisions to which an altered evaluation of contemporary journalistic and periodical discourse seems to have been crucial. It was in the mid-1850s that Marian Evans began to extract herself from her career as a professional writer and editor of review essays: in 1854 she quit her job as John Chapman's editor for the *Westminster Review,* and in 1857 she became the novelist George Eliot and formally abjured journalism, refusing to write another review essay to the end of her career.[21] It was in 1855 that the previously minor novelist Anthony Trollope had his first success with the (remarkably polyphonic) novel *The Warden,* approved by Longman's reader specifically for its treatment of newspapers and journalism. It was in 1854, also, that Harriet Martineau traded much of her independent career as a writer of essays, stories, and book-length nonfiction for anonymity as a full-time newspaper leader writer for the *Daily News.* For one measure of the literary significance of the competition between journalism and other genres, perhaps we need only consider the parallel literary history had these journalism-driven career decisions not been taken: the 1860s and 1870s with many more books by Harriet Martineau, but without those of George Eliot and Anthony Trollope.

But do we need Mikhail Bakhtin to explain this sudden and simultaneous literary interest in journalism in the mid-1850s? Literary history and genre theory have to date hardly glanced at the generic nature of journalism, but have always had tools to address the appearance of a cultural phenomenon within literary works, even within a number of them simultaneously. Journalism was part of a broader cultural conversation in which all mid-Victorian writers participated, and since, as W. H. Ainsworth pointed out, it was economically necessary for most mid-century novelists and poets to be at least occasionally journalists, this common experience alone might seem to account for the widespread mid-Victorian use of journalism as topos.

To understand what explanatory power Bakhtin brings to our reading of this phenomenon that other genre theories do not, we should note how Bakhtin's theories differ from these approaches. For Bakhtin, genre is not merely a literary category, but an inherent element in the way all language is created and used. Even everyday conventions of oral speech, such as greetings and conversational formulae, he argues, should be thought of as "primary" discourse genres. Secondary genres, which include all literary forms, are for Bakhtin complex syntheses and recombinations of the primary genres. The forms of secondary genres are therefore not monolithic, natural, or inevitable, but historically accumulated assemblages of particular features, voices, references, and effects built into them by writers and literary history up to that time.[22]

Second, and as a result, Bakhtin sees genres as much more actively meaningful than traditional genre theorists have generally seen them. Genres are not empty vessels into which a given author pours meaning; the historical processes of genre formation have already filled literary genres with a large reserve of meaning. Even before a given author decides to use them, he writes, the genres themselves are "heavily laden with meaning, filled with it" (*Speech Genres* 5), and this preexisting content both limits and potentially enriches what any given writer can express through a given genre. To work in a genre, for a writer, thus requires some level of assent to, or negotiation with, its meanings and worldview. To write *in* a genre is at least partly to think the thoughts *of* that genre.[23]

Third, Bakhtin sees all the discourse genres used within a given culture in a constant and dynamic interaction, a Galilean relationship of shifting and reciprocal influences. It is this last insight that is most revolutionary and perhaps most valuable in Bakhtin's rethinking of genre. Traditional genre theories emphasize differences and boundaries between genres, while systemic or classificatory theories from Aristotle to Northrop Frye also by their nature tend to depict cooperation among these forms, with each genre discretely responsible for a territory of prosodic features, voice, themes, seasons, and kinds of excellence. But as Bakhtin scholars Gary Saul Morson and Caryl Emerson have noted, systemic genre theories purchase their clarity about the ways genres coexist in harmony at the cost of almost complete deafness to the potential for generic *dis*harmony (300). It is this disharmony, a largely competitive but also partly cooperative tension grounded in the constant reality that writers using one genre will see, analyze, and perhaps resent or covet the successes of other genres, that Bakhtin captures and illustrates with his account of novelization. Fixed systems of genre find changes in generic relationships difficult to explain, but for Bakhtin change is the ongoing and natural condition of a genre's existence. And if genres are indeed related to each other in a Galilean system, then any large new gravity well can be expected to change a lot of other orbits.

Bakhtin's model of novelization therefore seems to authorize us to expect a kind of "journalization" in mid-Victorian letters, in which the sudden and dramatic increase in the reputation and economic power of review-essay journalism in the mid-1850s should have provoked an immediate, simultaneous, and to some degree imitative reaction from novelists, poets, and writers in nonfiction genres. As we have seen, a strong surge of literary interest in journalism at this time apparently did occur. But in other respects the form taken by the 1854–56 literary response to journalism does not so clearly follow the pattern Bakhtin's model seems to predict, at least not the largely imitative pattern described in "Epic and Novel."[24]

Here we must note one way in which Bakhtinian novelization and my proposed "journalization" might not be as directly parallel as I have so far suggested. In novelization the discursive strengths and advantages of the novel are real; that is why genres that do not learn from them risk seeming stylized and artificial. The novel has clear advantages over other genres as art, as use of language, and as representation of individual and social reality. But one of the observations many British writers made in the mid-1850s, often in the very texts I have named, was that the supposed intellectual and persuasive advantages of journalism did *not* appear to be real. The high level of cultural and political reputation review-essay journalism had achieved in 1855 did not seem to be supported by any corresponding greatness in depth of thought or analysis, accuracy, empathy, honesty, or artistry. In fact, advantages in all those areas seemed to lie with other genres.

So in addition to feeling generic pressure, British nonjournalistic writers of the mid-1850s must have faced a common generic puzzle. The marketplace and a public chorus of conventional wisdom, echoed of course by many periodicals themselves, declared review-essay journalism politically, economically, and psychologically more effective than their own preferred genres. "The man of the modern world is used to speak what the modern world will hear," declared Walter Bagehot of the review-like essay; "the writer of the mod-

ern world must write what that world will indulgently and pleasantly peruse"
(256). But the review-essay genre was also by any reasonable artistic standards
a weaker kind of discourse.

In *Aurora Leigh*, Elizabeth Barrett Browning seems to have been considering both parts of this puzzle. Interestingly, Aurora polyphonically acknowledges the existence, presumably within her literary circle, of an argument
opposed to her own position that journalism does not overlap with art.
Although she has "carved many an article on cherry-stones / To suit light
readers," she has heard from friends or critics ("it was said") that "something
in the lines" of her own writing in these light efforts has revealed "the mallet-
hand" of her own true artistry. Her own voice responds by explicitly rejecting
this reading, asserting that writing done for pay, even by a poet of real talent,
will only "taste of grain," not the "grapes" of artistic inspiration.

Another clash of competing theories of journalism—also one that ends
up damning journalism by comparison with other discourse genres—occurs
in 1855 in the conversation between Robert Browning's character Gigadibs,
a writer for *Blackwood's*, and his tormentor Bishop Blougram. Believing that
Gigadibs considers his work as a public writer at *Blackwood's* more intellectually honest than Blougram's own worldly and half-hearted espousal of Cathol-
icism, Blougram rather cruelly turns the tables on Gigadibs by pointing out
that there is no ennobling inspiration, artistic or otherwise, behind the kind
of modern journalism that Gigadibs produces. Although willing to admit that
there are indeed "privileged great natures that dwarf mine" (lines 934–35),
including "A poet just about to print his ode" (937), Blougram points out to
Gigadibs that "you,—you're just as little those as I":

> You, Gigadibs, who, thirty years of age,
> Write stately for Blackwood's Magazine,
> Believe you see two points in Hamlet's soul
> Unseized by the Germans yet—which view you'll print—
> Meantime the best you have to show being still
> That lively lightsome article we took
> Almost for the true Dickens,—what's its name?
> "The Slum and Cellar, or Whitechapel life
> "Limned after dark!" it made me laugh, I know,
> And pleased a month, and brought you in ten pounds. (943–53)

So thoroughly does Blougram demolish Gigadibs's view of his professional practice as a journalist that a narrative epilogue to "Bishop Blougram's Apology" shows Gigadibs giving up periodical writing entirely to begin an agricultural career in Australia.

Not all mid-Victorian dialogic encounters between journalistic and non-journalistic forms demonstrate such open ideological conflicts, or end in such a decisive victory for one side; the situations and conclusions are varied. An analytical comparison of journalism with its generic others also occurs in Harriet Martineau's reflections in her *Autobiography* on her new life as a newspaper leader writer, but Martineau characterizes the journalist's life differently than had either Elizabeth or Robert Browning, and journalism even provides Martineau's bildungsroman with its happy ending: "As for me,—my life was now like nothing that I had ever experienced. I had all the benefits of work, and of complete success, without any of the responsibility, the sense of which has always been the great drawback on my literary satisfactions, and especially in historical writing" (616). Anthony Trollope's clever polyphony in *The Warden* builds an analytical case study of how many contemporary worldviews and discourse genres—including print forms such as the newspaper journalism of the *Times* ("the Jupiter"), the social criticism of Carlyle ("Dr Pessimist Anticant"), and the sentimental fiction of Dickens ("Mr Popular Sentiment")—would variously interpret and represent the same situation and characters. Trollope shows each form wielding its different form of discursive power in different ways, to different degrees of success.

While these mid-Victorian writers are clearly reacting to the phenomenon of journalism and to the power of its specific modern forms, the common project in their nearly simultaneous works of the mid-1850s is just as clearly not to "journalize" their own writing, in the sense of adapting it to another genre's model or infecting it with another genre's tropes. In fact, what they are all doing is *theorizing* journalism, and at the same time comparatively theorizing journalism's discursive others—usually the very genres in which they themselves are writing at that moment. This observation foregrounds a phase of genre interaction that is only implicit in the essay "Epic and Novel," but becomes much clearer in the conclusion Bakhtin later wrote to the revised edition of *Problems of Dostoevsky's Poetics*—that part of the process of generic interaction will necessarily be a moment in which other genres analyze the new genre's features, and evaluate their uses and effectiveness against their own. In more measured language than he had used in "Epic and Novel," this later Bakhtin writes that

> no new artistic genre ever nullifies or replaces old ones. But at the same time each fundamentally and significantly new genre, once it arrives, exerts influence on the entire circle of old genres: the new genre makes the old ones, so to speak, more conscious; it forces them to better perceive their own possibilities and boundaries, that is, to overcome their own *naivete*. Such, for example, was the influence of the novel as a new genre on all the old literary genres: on the novella, the narrative poem, the drama, the lyric. Moreover, a new genre can have a positive influence on old genres, to the extent, of course, that their generic natures permit it; thus, for example, one can speak of a certain "novelization" of old genres in the epoch of the novel's flowering. The effect of new genres on old ones in most cases promotes their renewal and enrichment. (271)

If Bakhtin has indeed here predicted that writers under strong pressure from a successful new genre will necessarily theorize before they novelize (or journalize), and that the result of their theorizing is less likely to be actual adoption of the new genre with which they are contending than to be a "more conscious" reexamination of their own genres, his model may both explain the sudden mid-Victorian literary interest in journalism and offer insight into its causes.

In the mid-century works I have noted—*Aurora Leigh,* "Bishop Blougram," and *The Warden,* as well as others—mid-Victorian writers do offer thoughtful and focused analyses of journalism, its generic traits, its influence on politics and literature, and its relationship to other genres. In Bakhtin's terms this is precisely what should have occurred, but not for the reasons literary historians usually assign—that journalism was topical, or fashionable, or even thematically interesting at that particular historical moment. It should have happened, for Bakhtin, because the introduction or sudden ascendancy of a new genre necessarily reopens for working authors the very question of what genres do and how they see. New genres raise new possibilities and offer new methods and worldviews, first for the writer's critical and professional inspection, and only after that for possible adoption. The new genre helps the old genres to see their own work and possibilities more clearly.

In all but a few of the cases I have found (Martineau's will be examined closely in the next chapter), the generic investigators of 1855 seem to have come, albeit by different analytical routes, to some form of the conclusion that journalism was not a generic model to be adopted directly. Their characters behave accordingly: Aurora Leigh writes her way out of journalism and back into her poetic vocation, Gigadibs abandons *Blackwood's* for a farm in Australia, and Trollope's John Bold grows disenchanted with Tom Towers and the "Jupiter." Interestingly, these characters' analyses match but greatly precede that of wider Victorian culture, which was to take ten more years to revise and deflate the outsized reputation of the journalistic review essay.

For a few years in the mid-1850s, however, that genre's cultural and discursive reputation was very large, and during that time journalism seems to have had something like a catalyzing influence on contemporary practice in poetry, biography, history, and the novel. Traditional accounts of genres as complementary systems, or as artistic or thematic choices made by writers, don't seem to explain such a broad effect, but a Bakhtinian view of novelization, or journalization, may explain how a genre with a brief but outsized reputation might exert powerful pressure on a diverse group of writers in other genres at a single historical moment. Bakhtin's concept of novelization may offer literary historians a way to conceptualize how the brief hegemony of a nonliterary genre could spark creative renewals in other genres, not by encouraging them to imitate *it*self, but by provoking them to be more consciously and fully *them*selves.

In the next chapter, I will take up the case of one mid-Victorian writer for whom the discourse of journalism in the 1850s seems to have been most attractive—one who seems to have been convinced, at least for a time, that the genres created by mid-1850s British journalism were indeed a fundamental breakthrough in the creation of a successful and authoritative public voice.

THE *Authoress's* TALE

The Triumph of Journalism in Harriet Martineau's *Autobiography*

> For this reason it is important to know the possible generic sources of a given author, the literary and generic atmosphere in which his creative work was realized. The more complete and concrete our knowledge of an artist's *generic contacts,* the deeper can we penetrate the peculiar features of his generic form and the more correctly can we understand the interrelationship, within it, of tradition and innovation.
>
> MIKHAIL BAKHTIN, *Problems of Dostoevsky's Poetics*

IN HER RECENT REVIEW ESSAY on new books about Harriet Martineau, scholar Deirdre David is positive, but pensive. Something is missing in the available accounts of this remarkable Victorian woman of letters, she writes; of the four books she reviews, "none deals quite fully enough with that aspect of her work for which the definitive reading of Martineau would need to account: she was first, last, and always a writer, regardless of what she was writing about" ("George Eliot's 'Trump'" 88). David is surely right that Harriet Martineau was "first, last and always" a writer, and that a definitive reading of her career will so see her. But there may be good reason the book David hopes for has not yet been written. For modern readers, Martineau the writer is a more puzzling and less sympathetic figure than Martineau the feminist who advocated women's education and opposed the Contagious Diseases Acts, the sociologist who analyzed racial and gender oppression in the United States, the successful and independent professional woman, or the political writer whose leading articles in the *Daily News* during the U.S. Civil War countered the pro-South prejudices of the London *Times* and, according to W. E. Forster, "alone kept public opinion on the right side" (quoted in Arbuckle xii).

While Martineau's positions on women's issues, class issues, and international politics now seem mostly admirable, many of her statements about the theory and practice of writing are difficult even to quote or reference without seeming to intend ridicule. Martineau is a theorist of composition whose *Autobiography*, composed and printed in 1855 but not published until 1877, asserts that revision is an unmixed evil for both style and substance ("Great mischief arises from the notion that botching in the second place will compensate for carelessness in the first" [*Autobiography* 114][1]), and a novelist who both declares it impossible on principle for a human being to create a plot ("A mind which can do this must be, in the nature of things, a prophetic mind, in the strictest sense; and no human mind is that" [189]) and tells of declining in high dudgeon a publisher's request that she would write a serial story because of the impossibility—again, on principle—for serial fiction to succeed as art ("Whatever other merits it may have, a work of fiction cannot possibly be good in an artistic sense which can be cut up into portions of an arbitrary length" [409]). There is an unfortunate touch of Lady Bracknell in these wrongheaded categorical declarations that make them painful reading for admirers of Martineau's career as one of the first and greatest Victorian women of letters.

It is probably not surprising, then, that Martineau's pronouncements on writing are often passed over by scholars with the discretion appropriate to a great author's quirks, and that commentators have tacitly agreed to ignore (or silently amend) some of her most problematic texts about writing. But in this chapter I am going to suggest that well-intended discretion may have helped to hide some of the data we most need to account for Harriet Martineau's literary career. Martineau's pronouncements about writing in her *Autobiography*, even the apparently absurd ones—especially the apparently absurd ones—show integrity and consistency to a particular set of beliefs and view of writing that were at a peak of cultural influence in the year of the work's composition, 1855. Critics have not yet found a fully successful key to Martineau's career as a whole in her own psychology, in her quasi-feminist politics, in her gender or in her culture, and in this chapter I will suggest that this may be because its real mainspring may have been, as Deirdre David has suggested, in her relationship to discourse itself. If the key to Harriet Martineau's career is her relationship to writing, I will argue that this relationship can only be understood in the context of the competing worldviews and genre forms specific to mid-Victorian discourse.

To begin to put Martineau's statements about writing in the *Autobiography* into this kind of interpretive context, I would like to reexamine the most famous anecdote in the *Autobiography:* the story of Martineau's debut as a published writer.

Writing in Principle and Practice

The tale of Martineau's "first appearance in print" begins in period 3, section 2, of the first volume of the *Autobiography,* when its protagonist is nineteen years old. The narrating Martineau admits at the outset of this story that her younger self had harbored childhood aspirations toward authorship even before this, but says that her ambition was squelched by a sister's ridicule, and "seems to have disappeared from that time; and when I did attempt to write, it was at the suggestion of another, and against my own judgment and inclination" (110). In October 1821, she writes, her beloved younger brother James, finding her upset by his departures for college after term vacations, "advised me to take refuge, on each occasion, in a new pursuit; and on that particular occasion, in an attempt at authorship. . . . He desired me to write something that was in my head, and try my chance with it in the 'Monthly Repository,'" a Unitarian periodical. "What James desired, I always did, as of course" (110–11), and the young Martineau therefore obediently wrote, "in my abominable scrawl of those days, feeling mightily like a fool all the time," a manuscript titled "Female Writers on Practical Divinity," and submitted it in late September of 1821 (*sic*). "I took the letter V for my signature,—I cannot at all remember why," she writes.

> The time was very near the end of the month: I had no definite expectation that I should ever hear any thing of my paper; and certainly did not suppose it could be in the forthcoming number. That number was sent in before service-time on a Sunday morning. My heart may have been beating when I laid hands on it; but it thumped prodigiously when I saw my article there, and, in the Notices to Correspondents, a request to hear more from V. of

Norwich. There is certainly something entirely peculiar in the sensation of seeing one's self in print for the first time:—the lines burn themselves in upon the brain in a way of which black ink is incapable, in any other mode. (111)

In Martineau's account, though, even this fine double compliment from the *Monthly Repository*'s editor—the implicit one of immediate publication, the explicit one of a request for further submissions—was outdone later that same day when Thomas Martineau, the eldest brother whom she held in awe, read parts of the article aloud in company after chapel and praised it without knowing it was hers.

> After glancing at it, he exclaimed, "They have got a new hand here. Listen."
> After a paragraph, he repeated, "Ah! this is a new hand; they have had noth-
> ing so good as this for a long while." (It would be impossible to convey to
> any who did not know the "Monthly Repository" of that day, how very
> small a compliment this was.) I was silent, of course. At the end of the first
> column, he exclaimed about the style, looking at me in some wonder at my
> being as still as a mouse. Next (and well I remember his tone, and thrill to it
> still) his words were—"What a fine sentence that is! Why, do you not think
> so?" (111–12)

After a bit more of this unintentional, awkward, but thrilling interrogation, young Harriet confesses: "I replied, in utter confusion,—'I never could baffle any body. The truth is, that paper is mine.'" Thomas reads the rest of the piece in silence, but then "he laid his hand on my shoulder, and said gravely (calling me 'dear' for the first time) 'Now, dear, leave it to other women to make shirts and darn stockings; and do you devote yourself to this.' I went home in a sort of dream, so that the squares of the pavement seemed to float before my eyes. That evening made me an authoress" (112).

This story of how Martineau became an "authoress" is a fine anecdote on its own account—enduringly popular among Martineau scholars, and under-standably compelling reading for anyone who hopes to be published[2]—but it also seems to perform an important function in the *Autobiography* in preview-ing and forecasting the specific kind of authoress Martineau would become. The narrating Martineau is quite deliberate about this, using the story as the preface to a long and specific account of particular career-long writing practices. The story also seems intended to teach or illustrate (as we might expect of the didactic author of the *Illustrations of Political Economy* and *Principle and Practice*) at least five specific points about Martineau's writing—points that seem to rise to the level of principles, and to which she will be unswervingly consistent in the remainder of the *Autobiography*.

First, Martineau's writing projects will never be undertaken from motives of self-interest, but only from necessity, or at the direction of—or in response to the needs of—others. In the vocation story, as we have seen, she takes up writing "against my own judgment and inclination," only because James (who apparently must be obeyed) tells her to; she is authorized to take up her vocation as an authoress when Thomas tells her to "devote yourself to this." Later in the first volume, she perseveres with the *Illustrations of Political Economy* because "the people wanted the book; and they should have it" (138). She leaves for London to seek a publisher for the *Illustrations* when her brother Henry tells her to ("then he turned to me, and said oracularly, 'Go!'— I sprang up" [140–41]), and still later is on the point of taking a periodical editorship because friends support the idea, then turns it down when James advises against it (405). The frequently quoted passages of the *Autobiography* where Martineau says that she wrote "because I could not help it" are not declarations of her own will to authorship, though they might seem to be; they are uniformly couched in the language of self-abnegation or even of self-sacrifice. One such passage makes this clear: "Authorship has never been with me a matter of choice. I have not done it for amusement, or for money, or for fame, or for any reason but because I could not help it. Things were pressing to be said; and there was more or less evidence that I was the person to say them. . . . What wanted to be said must be said, for the sake of the many, whatever might be the consequences to the one worker concerned" (155). In this passage and similar ones Martineau denies not only personal motives but even personal volition: her reasons for writing are either completely external (an inescapable duty or responsibility) or so deeply internal as to be beyond her power to regulate or control ("I could not help it"). In the *Autobiography,* whether or not to write never seems a choice Martineau has independent or conscious power to make.

The second point the story seems intended to illustrate about Martineau's writing is her entire innocence of professional calculation or strategy. She does not choose a topic for its possible appeal to this particular Unitarian periodical's editor or readers, but simply writes "something that was in my head" and submits the resulting text to the *Monthly Repository,* without input from friends or any preliminary query, correspondence, or proposal to the editor. Nothing occurs through back channels, and there is hardly a word in the entire transaction of submission and publication that is not printed in the *Monthly Repository* itself, open to any reader to see. Again, this theme will continue throughout the *Autobiography.* Martineau's relations with publishers and editors are always, and apparently on principle, markedly open, with no strings pulled, deals cut, or connections used. Martineau repeatedly denies career-mindedness or manipulation, at one point even asserting (a claim not supported by many other contemporary accounts) that personal connections and recommendations are valueless in the world of literature and publishing.[3] Far from seeking fame or to advance her own career as a writer, she says, she has five times published works in the full belief that they would cause enough harmful controversy to end her professional literary career.[4]

The third point made in the vocation story is the inability of Martineau to keep her authorship a "secret." "I never could baffle anybody," she tells Thomas in her confusion, but in the context of the story itself, this seems rather an odd thing for her to say, and to specifically remember saying thirty-four years later. If this story of her first publication seems to suggest anything about Martineau and secrecy, indeed, it is surely that she had a knack for it, having kept her first attempt at authorship completely private (in a family of ten) through what were surely the hardest parts of the project to accomplish secretly: the writing, mailing, and waiting. Again, however, the point Martineau insists on, that she could "never baffle anybody," appears repeatedly throughout the *Autobiography.* Reminders that she "never had a secret" (the exact words occur twice in volume 1, as well as in variations such as "of all people in the world, I have perhaps the fewest reserves" [110]) become a minor motif of the book, and one upon which the narrator insists even as she provides apparently contradictory evidence. Although *Life in the Sick-Room* (1844) was published anonymously, for example, as were the three hundred some leading articles she had already written for the *Daily News* by 1855, and virtually all her other writing for periodicals, Martineau consistently if improbably claims throughout the *Autobiography* that none of her unsigned writing was truly secret, since her authorship was always immediately recognized. In the case of *Life in the Sick-Room,* she tells of being "instantly and universally detected" (449) within days of the book's publication, and in her account of beginning to write anonymous leading articles regularly for the *Daily News* in 1852, there is a similar story of being unmasked: "All the early attempts at secrecy were over. Within the first month, I had been taxed with almost every article by somebody or other, who 'knew me by my style,' or had heard it in omnibuses, or somehow. . . . Mr. Hunt [the editor of the *Daily News*] wrote me that all concealment was wholly out of the question, and that I need not trouble myself further about it" (613).

A fourth point the vocation story makes is to foreshadow Martineau's approach to composition, which in the *Autobiography* will always be a compound of complete intellectual freedom concerning subject and treatment with disciplined but relatively easy one-draft writing. "I have always used the same method in writing," she says early on: "I have always made sure of what I meant to say, and then written it down without care or anxiety,—glancing at it again only to see if any words were omitted or repeated, and not altering a single phrase in a whole work" (113–14). She commits to this approach almost from the beginning of her career, and tells of being pleased to discover long afterward that it was William Cobbett's method as well: "to know first what you want to say, and then say it in the first words that occur to you" (113). Both elements of the method, the unfettered freedom and the single spontaneous draft, seem equally important. The freedom is inaugurated in the vocation story when James tells her *to* write, but not *what* to write, in fact explicitly instructing her to write only her already-existing ideas: "something that was in my head." Later in the *Autobiography,* Martineau's refusal to allow even the smallest interference from any "second mind" with her topics, treatments, or manuscripts will be further formalized in strongly worded statements of principle.[5] The value of the single draft is established in the commentary on her own writing practice that follows the vocation story, where Martineau condemns revision as a vicious habit for any writer, injurious to form, style, and content. The best kind of writing, the *Autobiography* insists, is uninfluenced by any other mind, and not revised or edited even by its own writer. Even when writing fiction, in this case the *Illustrations of Political Economy,* Martineau tells of following the same method of spontaneous composition that she claims to have applied to all written forms: "As to the actual writing,—

I did it as I write letters, and as I am writing this Memoir,—never altering the expression as it came fresh from my brain" (160).

The fifth major point the vocation story makes is the enthusiastic reception gained by Martineau's writing. It is hard to imagine a completer *succès d'estime* than the one young Martineau achieves in this story over two imposing judges—the *Monthly Review* editor, "the formidable prime minister of his sect,—Rev. Robert Aspland" (111), and the eldest brother of whom she was in awe. Both pronounce unambiguously and enthusiastically in her favor, and under circumstances that allow no suspicion of their praise being motivated by personal kindness or anything but unbiased intellectual and professional judgment, since Aspland knows her only as "V. of Norwich," and her brother is unaware of her authorship when he praises her work. Her success flows from her merits alone, and this motif of unqualified and untainted public success by merit also appears repeatedly in the *Autobiography,* to the point of rather exaggerating Martineau's historically verifiable reception history.[6]

Rereading the *Repository*

Martineau's story of her own first publication in volume 1 of the *Autobiography* thus becomes not only the origin but also the exemplum of Martineau's professional practice, and it is appropriate that it is one of the episodes most frequently quoted and retold by scholars and students of her work. But no modern commentator I have seen has called attention to the fact that the evidence surrounding that first publication, preserved in the *Monthly Repository* and elsewhere, does not quite bear out Martineau's thematically charged account.[7] This does not mean that previous scholars have omitted to check primary sources. On the contrary, most scholarly commentators on the *Autobiography* within the last twenty-five years are demonstrably aware of at least some of the discrepancies between the account Martineau gives and the actual publication of her first article. To take an example: in the *Autobiography,* Martineau dates her article tentatively ("I think it must have been") to October 1821, and claims to have chosen the initial "V" as her pseudonym. The article was actually published a year later in October 1822, however, under a somewhat different title from the one she gives, and not over "V," but with the Latin pseudonym "Discipulus." Most scholars today handle these small

discrepancies by not directly quoting from these parts of Martineau's narrative, and by giving the correct date and pseudonym themselves in paraphrase
without drawing attention to Martineau's incorrect ones. The inaccuracies
do hardly seem worth mentioning, especially in the light of Martineau's own
assertion in the *Autobiography* that she had not looked at the piece again in
the thirty years since it was published: "I am so heartily ashamed of the whole
business as never to have looked at the article since the first flutter of it went
off" (111). It is understandable, then, that modern critics have not called attention to the issue, but let Martineau's account of the incident stand for the
themes Martineau gives it.[8]

I call attention to the counterfactual parts of the narrative now not to pick
up the fallen tomahawk of Martineau's nemesis, John Wilson Croker of the
Quarterly Review, but because there are other and more significant parts of
her story—parts with implications for the points about her writing that Martineau uses this story to illustrate—that are also unsupported by the historical
and textual record. Martineau's statements that she heard nothing from the
Monthly Repository until its simultaneous publication of her article and request
for further submissions, and that this double event occurred within a month
of her original submission, for example, are also strictly incorrect. A month
before "Female Writers on Practical Divinity. No. 1. Mrs. MORE" appeared in
the October 1822 *Monthly Repository,* Martineau would have seen her chosen
pseudonym "Discipulus" (Latin for a male apprentice or student) addressed
somewhat abruptly in the September notes to contributors: "When we have
received another communication or two from *Discipulus,* we shall be better
able to judge of his proposal; but our Correspondents are none of them of
the description that he seems to suppose." (For the *Monthly Repository's* full
editorial correspondence with "Discipulus," a sample of pseudonyms chosen
by other contributors, and a sense of the brusque tone the *Monthly Repository*
editor typically used for such communications, see appendix A.) The editor's
remark, though a bit opaque, makes it clear that Martineau's contact with the
Monthly Repository had been initiated at least a month earlier than she claims,
probably in August rather than September, and that at this point Martineau
had not sent only a manuscript, but also (or instead) a proposal that her first
submission be published as the first in a series, as it was indeed finally printed.[9]
The editor seems to have wanted more information or text before he would
make such a commitment. The evidence of the publication itself also shows

that "Female Writers on Practical Divinity" was not the title of her first article at all, but the title of the proposed *series* of articles the young Martineau had ambitiously offered to make a regular feature of the *Monthly Repository*. Martineau had not made this proposal under the genderless (although, by 1855, powerfully gender-marked) initial "V," but under a grammatically male Latin tag, "Discipulus."

Furthermore, the October 1822 *Monthly Repository* that did publish Martineau's article did not contain any simultaneous "request to hear more" from Discipulus, or any correspondence to him at all. The closest approximation came in the November issue, when the correspondence section noted, "The continuation of *Discipulus* has come to hand. His other proposed communications will probably be acceptable." This is certainly (qualified) approval, and must have pleased the young Martineau very much. But it also indicates that Martineau had again taken the initiative, before or just after her first publication, to write and send a second installment of the series, which the editor was here acknowledging. In other words, the nearest thing to a "request to hear more from V. of Norwich" that the historical Harriet Martineau could have read in the historical *Monthly Repository* was an acknowledgement that the "more" she had already sent had been received, and that further articles she had herself already proposed to the editor would "probably be acceptable." The will and volition that pushed Martineau's writing career forward during and after that first publication, in other words, demonstrably did not originate in demands either from the *Monthly Repository* editor or from Thomas Martineau. It can only have come from Harriet Martineau herself.

Fact-checking the evidence external to the *Autobiography*'s narrative, in fact, puts a different interpretive face on almost every aspect of Martineau's vocation story. The opening premise of the anecdote—that it was James who convinced her to start writing one September after repeatedly noticing how unhappy she became when he returned to college after vacations—does not seem strictly possible, partly because the piece must already have been submitted or at least proposed in August, and partly because (according to the *Dictionary of National Biography*) James Martineau did not even begin to attend Manchester College in York *until* the year of this publication, 1822. If the story of James's specific prompting is an invention, the project of publishing in the *Monthly Repository* is still more likely to have been Harriet's own idea from the beginning, a conclusion reinforced by the fact that what she sent to Aspland was not a single article but a proposed ongoing series. (This alone surely signals healthy authorial ambition, and is hard to reconcile with unwilling obedience to a brother's suggestion that she send "something.") The evidence of the editor's replies to her correspondence also shows that in addition to ambition, Martineau had good strategic sense even at the outset of her writing career. Instead of expecting her submissions to speak for themselves, she had actively negotiated for them.

What I have described as Martineau's inventions and additions to her own vocation story may even now seem not quite to justify the fuss I am making about them. Surely the main facts in Martineau's account, at least, are correct? She did write the piece in the early 1820s, it was published in the *Monthly Repository,* she did use a pseudonym, and the piece was favorably received by the editor. If any of this is headline news, I imagine some readers thinking, a headline such as "Writer's Autobiography Slightly Alters Facts" is surely appropriate only for the American parody newspaper *The Onion.*

The point I am trying to make is that Martineau's modifications to her own vocation story are worth attention because the elements that seem to have been invented are precisely and only those that support the larger thematic glosses the *Autobiography* works to impose on every account of Martineau's own writing praxis: her intellectual liberty and public obedience, her innocence of all premeditation, manipulativeness, and careerism (both the *Autobiography* and the auto-obituary she also wrote in 1855 make her younger self seem more of an ingenue by claiming that she published at nineteen instead of twenty), and the unalloyed public triumph her writing enjoyed. If the counterfactual parts of the story are separated from the rest, it begins to seem as if two Harriet Martineaus, with very different values and expectations for writing, have struggled over interpretive control of this anecdote. The 1855 narrator-Martineau explains her own authorial debut as a duty undertaken at another's request, conceived without strategy or manipulation, fully and even naively transparent in its openness, nonprofessional in form and content, written in a single draft without interference by other minds, and received with a cascade of public and professional approval. But the record outside the *Autobiography,* somewhat subversively supported by elements of the story itself, shows a younger Martineau who is both more self-motivated and more consciously and successfully strategic in her approach to that first professional success. Among the story elements that suggest a more consciously ambitious Martineau are the concrete descriptions of her younger self's emotional responses—what American composition teachers might call the "showing"— which repeatedly come into conflict with, even falsify, the language the narrator uses to name and summarize their meaning—the "telling." The heart that thumps mightily and thrills to Thomas's tone, the ink that burns into the young writer's brain, the paving squares that float before her eyes, are images of gratified ambition and glory in an intellectual triumph. The narrator's interpretive and summarizing language, however, is in a different register entirely: "I am so heartily ashamed," "feeling mightily like a fool," "against my judgment and inclination," "never could baffle anybody."

On one level, of course, we remember Paul de Man's insight that no text can ever successfully summarize its own meaning. On another, we have to admit that the gap between what *this* text explicitly claims to mean, and what the story it tells seems to mean on its own terms, is particularly wide. The historically verifiable parts of the story seem to show an ambitious and internally driven young writer displaying early talent in manipulating language to enter the professional sphere of letters (employing, among other tactics, a slightly pretentious Latin pseudonym). Recounting this story in 1855, however, a later version of Harriet Martineau seems to have gone to some trouble to prevent the reader from drawing exactly these conclusions. What scholars have assumed were minor inconsistencies or faults of memory seem in fact to have been highly consistent revisions (in the full sense of *re-seeings*) and reinterpretations of Martineau's debut as a writer. The *Autobiography* invents new circumstances, suppresses original ones, and adds a layer of commentary, all apparently intended specifically to defeat the understanding of Martineau's literary debut that its own original documents most strongly suggest.

All autobiographies, of course, necessarily construct a literal fiction as they make *sjuzhet* out of *fabula,* and all of any autobiography's characters are literary creations rather than people. But some autobiographical fictions and characters are more constructed than others, and the more obviously a factual account has been recast to be made consistent with a particular set of themes or principles, the more incentive we surely have to find the sources of the themes and understand their importance to the writer. If Martineau's account is factually inaccurate, but also highly consistent with a coherent set of beliefs about writing, it is worth investigating the nature and original sources of those beliefs. In the next part of this chapter I will suggest that the five-point theory of authorship represented in the *Autobiography*—the set of views that seem to have been imposed only in retrospect on the young protagonist of the *Monthly Repository* story—was not unique to Martineau, but was held in exactly her terms by many contemporary professional writers, both men and women, who were, like Martineau in 1855, regular users of the discursive genres of newspaper journalism.

The Journalist's Creed

In 1855, the year Martineau wrote the *Autobiography,* she had been a writer of leading articles (editorials) for the London *Daily News* for some three years, and estimated that she had already written three hundred of these articles. Her account in the second volume of the *Autobiography* of being hired by Frederick Knight Hunt as a leader writer for a metropolitan daily glows with intellectual excitement, as her account of her subsequent working life does with satisfaction. Martineau represents her career at the *Daily News* as the simultaneous perfection of her professional, intellectual, and personal lives:

> As for me,—my life was now like nothing that I had ever experienced. I had all the benefits of work, and of complete success, without any of the responsibility, the sense of which has always been the great drawback on my literary satisfactions, and especially in historical writing,—in which I could have no comfort but by directing my readers to my authorities, in all matters of any importance. Now, while exercising the same anxious care as to correctness, and always referring Mr. Hunt to my sources of information, I was free from the responsibility of publication altogether. My continued contributions to the "Westminster Review" and elsewhere preserved me from being engrossed in political studies; and I had more leisure for philosophical and literary pursuits than at any time since my youth. Two or three hours, after the arrival of the post (at breakfast time now) usually served me for my work; and when my correspondence was done, there was time for exercise, and the discharge of neighbourly business before dinner. (616)

Martineau's satisfaction is understandable, for the work she was now doing was some of the most politically and culturally influential of her career.[10] No previous account of the *Autobiography,* to my knowledge, has pointed out that the book is the work of a professional newspaper leader writer, and that it was written at the leading article's climactic point of both reputation and cultural influence.

Harriet Martineau's timing in joining a London daily newspaper as a leader writer on the eve of the Crimean War had been exquisite. Times of war are always heady for newspapers, but in 1854 the special correspondent W. H. Russell's firsthand accounts of government mismanagement of the Crimean War and the suffering of British troops, backed up by acrimonious leading articles in the *Times,* captivated the country and launched daily newspapers into what was widely believed to be the forefront of political influence. Even half a century later, Walter Besant was to estimate that the "influence and weight" of newspaper editorial writing had "culminated" during the Crimean War (212). Journalist James Fitzjames Stephen observed in 1862 that leading articles of political and current events commentary such as those written by Martineau were not only the most important kind of journalism, "the part of the paper by which its standing and influence are determined," but also perhaps the most important written discourse in British culture. They were read by the highest and most influential ranks of society, especially by political and economic decision makers; they formed, Stephen wrote, "the greater part of the reading even of the most educated part of the adult members of the busy classes" ("Journalism" 53). The newspaper leader was also the most concentratedly and pointedly authoritative genre in British society—for that matter, probably one of the most authoritative ever created off the slopes of Mount Sinai—and it meted out daily advice, guidance, and instruction in magisterial tones on every conceivable topic of contemporary social, economic, and political life. It was by the leading articles of the *Times,* as Anthony Trollope wryly remarked in *The Warden* of 1855, that "bishops are to be guided, lords and commons controlled—judges instructed in law, generals in strategy, admirals in naval tactics, and orange-women in the management of their barrows" (118). It would seem to have been just the discourse genre and historical moment for which a naturally authoritative polymath such as Harriet Martineau had been created—a woman, an hour, and a genre had all found one another.

In the last chapter I noted that the sudden increase in the reputation of journalism in 1855 seems to have made it highly interesting for novelists and poets to investigate. But we have also seen that journalists felt a different dynamic—not the pressure of another powerful discourse genre on theirs,

but the sudden and surprising apotheosis of their own. Many London newspaper writers in 1855 must have felt they had dreamed of real political influence and awoken to find it true, as Trollope's fictional journalist Tom Towers in *The Warden* walks the streets "studiously striving to look a man, but
knowing within his breast that he was a god" (125). Writers for the periodical
press at all levels, from newspaper leader writers to quarterly reviewers, seem
to have responded with an outpouring of interest in journalistic discourse
itself, creating self-reflexive theories and manifestos of journalism. The *Times*
reflected on its own might, virtue, and weighty public duties in leading articles
throughout 1855, and only waxed the greater as an icon of discursive power
and topic of public debate when other contemporary papers such as Benjamin
Disraeli's gadfly *Press* and A. J. Beresford Hope's new *Saturday Review* devoted
themselves to sustained attacks on its motives, influence, and authority. The
apparent shift in the British balance of political power toward the newspaper
press seemed significant enough for the *Edinburgh Review* to publish a major
study of daily journalism that October (it drew a peppery response from the
Times). Analyses of the theory and practice of periodical writing were proposed and argued by such heavyweight reviewers as Walter Bagehot in the
National Review and David Masson in the *British Quarterly Review*. Even the
Westminster Review published a historical account of British newspaper journalism, using, as the pretext for its review-like essay, a volume on press history
published five years earlier.

If the particular combination of beliefs and principles about written discourse that Martineau espouses in the *Autobiography* has proven difficult for
scholars to see or interpret, it may be because the full significance of the *Autobiography*'s status as the life story of an authoress-turned-journalist, composed
specifically in 1855, has not yet been assessed. As the positions of a professional Victorian newspaper writer at the mid-century, articulated at the height
of a particularly critical public controversy about the press, the beliefs about
writing that Martineau adapts her life narrative to illustrate should suddenly
seem much more familiar and comprehensible.

One of the passages scholars and critics usually let pass in silence, for
example, is the exposition of her lifelong writing methods, with their atten-
dant theory of revision, which immediately follows the vocation story in the
Autobiography. As we have seen, Martineau insists that both as principle and

as practice she has always written only single drafts. Almost from the outset of her career, she says,

I found that it would not do to copy what I wrote; and here . . . I discontinued the practice for ever,—thus saving an immense amount of time which I humbly think is wasted by other authors. The prevalent doctrine about revision and copying, and especially Miss Edgeworth's account of her method of writing,—scribbling first, then submitting her manuscript to her father, and copying and altering many times over till, (if I remember right) no one paragraph of her "Leonora" stood at last as it did at first,— made me suppose copying and alteration to be indispensable. But I immediately found that there was no use in copying if I did not alter; and that, if ever I did alter, I had to change back again; and I, once for all, committed myself to a single copy. I believe the only writings I ever copied were "Devotional Exercises," and my first tale;—a trumpery story called "Christmas Day." It seemed clear to me that distinctness and precision must be lost if alterations were made in a different state of mind from that which suggested the first utterance; and I was delighted when, long afterwards, I met with Cobbett's advice;—to know first what you want to say, and then say it in the first words that occur to you. (113)

Linda Peterson, commenting on the competing role models in this passage, has deemed it most important to Martineau's meaning that Edgeworth is a woman and Cobbett a man. Martineau chose, Peterson writes, "to dissociate herself from female scribblers and a feminine tradition of the novel, and to align herself with male writers and a masculine tradition of serious nonfictional prose" (173). But the more important alignment in the passage may be to genre rather than to gender: Edgeworth the reviser is a novelist, Cobbett the nonreviser a journalist. In fact, for Martineau's journalistic contemporaries and colleagues, one-draft composition was less a compliment to any particular role model than an absolute necessity of professional practice. It was impossible to compose long essays to short deadlines by any other method. Journalist James Macdonell, a leader writer for the *Daily Telegraph* and *Times* whose career overlapped Martineau's at the *Daily News,* was described by his biographer as regularly writing 1,200–word leading articles for the next day's *Times* in a single draft and in only three hours. After a quarter hour of difficulty, "he would make a satisfactory start, and after that work proceeded without a pause. He rarely consulted any book or made any stop. His head was bent over the writing hour after hour, while he laboriously filled sheet after sheet with neat writing. Sometimes he would complain of feeling exhausted, and be refreshed by a slight stimulant. He made no plan of work, no notes. He wrote smoothly and without a break. . . . About eleven o'clock the leader was finished and sent to the office" (Nicoll 289–90).

Martineau's self-reported productivity—a career average of twelve pages of manuscript per six-hour workday, at thirty-three lines per page—is impressive by any standard, but the ranks of mid-Victorian journalism furnish many peers for her speed, sustained time on task, and daily productivity. Before Macdonell gained his relatively easy berth at the *Times,* he was in 1872 "writing, besides five or six leaders a week for the *Daily Telegraph,* articles for the *Levant Herald* and the *Leeds Mercury,* frequent contributions to the *Spectator,* and occasional articles in the *Saturday Review, Macmillan,* and *Fraser.*" Like Martineau's, Macdonell's working day in 1872 contained six to seven hours of actual writing, in his case spaced into periods from 11 AM to 12:45 PM, then from 3 PM until 6 or 7, then after dinner until 11 (Nicoll 271). The *Daily Telegraph* at one point expected leader writers to produce full leading articles in only two hours (Scott 29–30), while Alfred Spender of the later-century *Westminster* could "get the 1,200–word leading article of the *Westminster* finished within the allotted time of an hour and a quarter" (quoted in Scott 31), and if working in partnership with colleague Charles Geake, could produce a full-length leading article in just twenty-five minutes (Scott 29). Like Martineau as well, journalists who produced text at high rates of speed and almost by stream of consciousness not only defended this practice as a professional necessity but also extolled and valorized such text, written spontaneously and without premeditation "in the first words that occur to you," as generically preferable to more deliberate and conscious composition. "It is a vice to bring a prepared mind to this kind of writing," wrote Spender. "A man may be an essayist or a philosopher and not be a journalist. If any journalist tells you that he knows what he is going to write about tomorrow you may have serious doubts about his capacity" (quoted in Scott 29). But as Martineau's reference to the "prevalent doctrine about revision and copying" makes clear, Martineau was well aware that among contemporary writers of nonjournalistic "serious nonfictional prose," revision and recopying were indeed the norm. She knew her friend Thomas Carlyle to be a careful and extensive reviser, not only of his manuscripts but even—to the exasperation of his printers—of his page proofs (293), while John Stuart Mill notes in his own *Autobiography* that he always composed two complete drafts of every major work (169–70).

Characteristic also of mid-century journalists is Martineau's claim to be in full command of her own powers, and to be able to write successfully at any time, like James Macdonell, within a quarter of an hour of starting:

> I have also found that sitting down, however reluctantly, with the pen in my hand, I have never worked for one quarter of an hour without finding myself in full train. . . . When once experience had taught me that I could work when I chose, and within a quarter of an hour of my determining to do so, I was relieved, in a great measure, from those embarrassments and depressions which I see afflicting many an author who waits for a mood instead of summoning it, and is the sport, instead of the master, of his own impressions and ideas. (156–57)

The sturdily self-disciplined approach to the production of text Martineau expresses here is indeed uncommon among mid-Victorian literary writers (with the notable exception of Anthony Trollope),[11] but normative for mid-Victorian journalists, who seem as a group to have preened themselves on just this ability. In a book on his correspondence with Elizabeth Barrett Browning, the poet and man of letters Richard Horne reports a mid-century exchange about writing between journalist Robert Bell and novelist W. M. Thackeray:

> "Are you a writer of 'moods'?" said Bell one day to Thackeray. "Yes, assuredly," was the answer; "and often not in the best moods." "Then, sometimes you can't write at all?" "Of course not; or not fit to be read." "That's strange," said Bell. "Now, I can take out my watch—lay it down upon the table—and write, within a line or two, the same quantity in the same given time." (124–25)

Fictional journalists of this period display this same pride in the ability to write readable prose on demand to almost any extent, further suggesting that it was part of the recognized ethos of the mid-Victorian journalist. The protagonist of J. M. Capes's 1855 magazine serial "Compton Hall" is a journalist who characterizes himself in the first number of his story partly with the boast, "I can write, at any hour of the day or night, on any subject whatever, and always seem to be perfectly acquainted with all its bearings" (27). As Wilkie Collins's Count Fosco in *The Woman in White* (1859–60), who has written Italian newspaper serials, is preparing to write a confession of his crimes, he tells the hero Walter Hartright that "habits of literary composition are perfectly familiar to me. One of the rarest of all the intellectual accomplishments that a man can possess is the grand faculty of arranging his ideas. Immense privilege! I possess it. Do you?" Fosco proceeds to write his confession on "a heap of narrow slips, of the form used by professional writers for the press," tossing them aside as he fills them with writing. "Slip after slip, by dozens, by fifties, by hundreds, flew over his shoulders on either side of him till he had snowed himself up in paper all around his chair" (612–13).[12] To confirm that Collins is describing (in the extravagant terms appropriate to Fosco) a standard method of rapid one-draft journalistic composition at this period, we can compare Captain Shandon in *Pendennis,* who writes the "Pall Mall Gazette" prospectus "with a desk on his knees, at which he was scribbling as fast as his rapid pen could write. Slip after slip of paper fell off the desk wet on to the ground" (404). In a Victorian newspaper office close to deadline, these slips would have been carried away to the printer's chapel as they were filled, so that working journalists frequently had to complete articles not only in a single draft but also without being able to refer to what they had already written.

Some of the other beliefs about writing that Martineau develops and illustrates in the *Autobiography* initially seem harder to reconcile with the genre ideology of mid-Victorian journalism. For example, her paired assertions that she insisted on perfect intellectual freedom for herself, and that she abnegated self-interest and ambition in favor of the interests of others, seem highly individual and even psychologically driven in their apparent contradictions. Martineau scholars have traditionally interpreted these passages of the *Autobiography* in the context of Victorian ideologies of gender, with their expectations of female devotion and self-sacrifice,[13] but recently both Amanda Anderson and George Levine have offered another context for them within intellectual history, through separate but complementary analyses of Victorian beliefs about the ways objectivity, self-suppression, and intellectual detachment could provide routes to knowledge.[14] Even if Victorian intellectuals shared an ideal of empowerment via self-abnegation, however, that ideal seems to have had a specifically journalistic version, and Martineau's position in the *Autobiography*, which repeatedly emphasizes duty to readers, takes a characteristically journalistic form. Her claims that insistence on perfect intellectual freedom for herself was consistent with perfect selflessness—more accurately, with perfect replacement of her own interests with those of her readers—in fact articulates a fundamental principle of mid-Victorian newspaper journalism.

The journalist E. S. Dallas, writing a few years later in 1859, attempted his own colorful explanation of how the custom of newspaper anonymity brought out the personal and public-spirited best sides of a journalist—in this case, a hypothetical Mr. Smith—by this same mechanism of simultaneous empowerment and suppression. Anonymity freed Smith to speak only the truth as he, Smith, saw it, Dallas wrote, and at the same time erased all strictly personal influences from Smith's work. Make Smith an anonymous writer, and

> he ceases to be a private individual, his egotism is of no use to him, what he has to write he must write on public grounds; it is no longer Smith who writes, but Smith divested of his egotism—Smith, who is compelled by his invisible cap to forget that part of his nature which is peculiar to himself and essentially private—Smith, who is forced to regard only that part of his consciousness which identifies him with every other member of the community—Smith, no longer the individual unity, but the representative man. (187)

In 1852 the London *Times* published two elaborate leaders explaining its own successful discourse practice as the same enabling combination of perfect independence of judgment with perfect identification with the public good, and the combined position was so much a part of the *Times*'s public ideology that it was incorporated into Anthony Trollope's parody of the *Times* as "The Jupiter," in *The Warden* (1855) and *Barchester Towers* (1857).[15]

All five of the declared principles of authorship and composition promoted in the *Autobiography*, though they seem heterogeneous and inconsistent to modern eyes, are elements of a well-integrated set of genre ideals, mutually consistent and logically interdependent, upon which mid-Victorian journalists based their discursive practice. We may have wondered at the *Autobiography*'s odd (and apparently counterfactual) insistence that Martineau was constitutionally unable to keep a secret, but freedom from secret keeping, although it initially also seems gender-inflected, is a point of journalistic ethics that the London *Times* particularly insisted on in 1852: "For us, with whom publicity and truth are the air and light of existence, there can be no greater disgrace than to recoil from the frank and accurate disclosure of facts as they are" (6 Feb. 1852: 4). (Compare the message and voice of Martineau: "There is nothing in money that could pay me for the pain of the slightest deflexion from my own convictions, or the most trifling restraint on my freedom of thought and speech" [210].) Even Martineau's emphasis on, and exaggeration of, the critical and public success of her own writing may not reflect personal ego so much as the journalistic principle that the public's response is the crucial evidence validating the journalist's claims to a public mission. The London *Times* made many declarations in the 1850s that referenced its own high circulation as evidence of its success in reflecting its readers' hopes and needs, such as this one (which strikes the no-secrets note for good measure): "Like ANTAEUS, the press gains fresh strength from the bosom of its mother, the people. It seeks information and nourishment from the public at large and from its own resources. . . . In a word, it adores publicity and abhors secrets. The nation delights in it because it finds in it the reflection of its most earnest feelings, its highest inspirations, and its largest hopes" (15 Oct. 1855: 6).

I am certainly not arguing here that Martineau had no beliefs or opinions of her own—that her career is defined or exhausted by the conventions of a genre. My goal is not to essentialize the *Autobiography*, much less Martineau herself, but to historicize the work, and to identify its generic sources and relationships. In fact, my position is closer to Mikhail Bakhtin's suggestion, the epigraph to this chapter, that we will best understand this or any author's distinctive contribution and beliefs when we understand the contemporary genres she chose as the best expression of her worldview at various points in her career. Bakhtin points out that genres are historically developed and internally consistent ways of using language that are intimately interdependent with—and even actually constitute—particular ways of seeing the world. In any genre, language formations and worldviews authorize and valorize each other, the worldview working out its best expression in the genre, the genre tending to encode, represent, and discursively re-create the worldview. The evidence in the *Autobiography* that Martineau was particularly in tune with the worldview and discourse of journalism as it was practiced in 1855 may go a long way toward solving the puzzle of why an independently successful authoress would move to the relative obscurity of editorial writing and remain there for more than ten years, making her stint as a *Daily News* leader writer the longest single episode of her career.

But although I have been arguing that the genre ideology of mid-Victorian newspaper journalism is a valuable and hitherto unused key to the interpretation of Martineau's *Autobiography*, I don't want to be thought to argue that Martineau was a lifelong journalist at heart, and that journalism is an interpretive key to her larger career as well as to this particular work. In fact, the most important conclusion we can draw from the remarkably clear articulation of mid-Victorian journalistic ideology by the Martineau of 1855 may be that her *Autobiography* is not in fact the story of Harriet Martineau's life *up to* 1855, as scholars have not unreasonably assumed, but rather the story of her life as she wanted to represent it *in* 1855: a snapshot (if that term can possibly apply to a two-volume, thousand-page narrative) of her beliefs about discourse at one highly charged moment in the discursive history of Victorian Britain. In the brief hiatus she took from leader writing in early 1855 to write the *Autobiography*—with, as she then believed, almost her dying breaths—Harriet Martineau may well have decided that her readers would be best served not by a portrait of public writing as she had originally practiced it, but by an illustration of the principles of discourse she had most recently come to use and believe in, and that seemed to her in 1855 to have emerged triumphant.

Genres of Ideas

Considering the *Autobiography* as the document of a particularly charged and intense moment of conflict between discursive genres—a book that represents Martineau's beliefs about writing specifically *in* 1855 and *of* 1855—may also help us move toward a better approach to explaining and relating the different parts of Martineau's career as a writer. It seems clear, for example, that her beliefs about fiction in 1855 were not those of the Martineau of 1832. One of the journalist-Martineau's tenets in 1855 is the essential valuelessness of fiction: there is hardly a major or minor work of her own fiction that the *Auto-biography* does not either dismiss with a word of derision ("Christmas Day" is "trumpery" [113], *Principle and Practice* and similar works "fiddle-faddling" [124]) or else damn with faint praise, as she does *The Hour and the Man* ("a work which I regard with some affection, though, to say the truth, without any admiration whatever" [439]) and *Deerbrook* ("true to the state of thought and feeling I was then in, which I now regard as imperfect and very far from lofty" [409]). The *Autobiography* throughout sees Martineau's own fiction with the values of a journalist, not with those of a fiction writer. It describes *Deerbrook* as an "expression" on "one or two moral subjects," figuring the novel as a fictionalized set of opinions or teachings rather than a work of art. The *Autobiography* even devalues the successful and much-loved *Illustrations,* which the *Autobiography*'s narrator claims to not now even have the "courage" to look at, "convinced that I should be disgusted by bad taste and metaphysics in almost every page" (203). She characterizes the writing of these tales as a purely mechanical process devoid of imagination or art: "The next process was to embody each leading principle in a character: and the mutual opera-tion of these embodied principles supplied the action of the story." In this account, nothing in the *Illustrations* mattered but political economy, and none of the fiction had value: "It was necessary to have some accessories,—some out-works to the scientific erection; but I limited these as much as possible; and I believe that in every instance, they really were rendered subordinate" (159).

In the preface Martineau originally wrote for the *Illustrations* in 1832, how-ever, the use of fictional discourse is the whole beauty of her scheme. In the preface to the first volume, Martineau explains that she is writing to fill a pub-lic need for information, since few books are available "which teach the sci-ence [of political economy] systematically as far as it is yet understood," and even those systematic texts "do not give us what we want—the science in a familiar, practical form. They give us its history; they give us its philosophy, but we want its *picture*" (*Illustrations* xi). She has rejected expository non-fiction and chosen narrative fiction instead "not only because it is new, not only because it is entertaining, but because we think it is the most faithful and the most complete. There is no doubt that all that is true and important about any virtue . . . may be said in the form of a lecture, or written in a chap-ter of moral philosophy; but the faithful history of an upright man, his sayings and doings, his trials, his sorrows, his triumphs and rewards, teaches the same truths in a more effectual as well as a more popular form" (xiii). This is exactly the genre ideology of the value of narrative and characterization that the essayist and future historian T. B. Macaulay had famously applied to history in his 1828 *Edinburgh Review* essay "History" a few years before, in which he had imagined a new kind of historiography that would learn the lesson of Sir Walter Scott's success at conveying a vivid sense of historical reality through fiction. Macaulay's language in this essay, as he envisions a historical discourse that conveys factual truth to the reader's heart using novelistic storytelling and characterization, is almost a paraphrase of Martineau's: "The instruction derived from history thus written, would be of a vivid and practical character. It would be received by the imagination as well as by the reason. It would be not merely traced on the mind, but branded into it. Many truths, too, would be learned, which can be learned in no other manner" (367).

Martineau scholars have hypothesized structures for the *Autobiography* that understand the narrative of changes in Martineau's writing practices from fiction to nonfiction as philosophical evolution, as personal maturation, or as an attempt to represent the Comtean evolution of her own mind toward robust intellectual freedom. Surely, however, the specific timing of the changes in Martineau's discourse practices needs to be plotted as well: not only the order in which she developed her beliefs but also the historical moments at which she adopted each new genre into her own discursive practice. In the later 1820s and early 1830s, when leading intellectual voices such as Macaulay's were valorizing fiction as the great discourse of ideas, Martineau's *Illustrations* and her preface show her becoming both a practitioner and a theorist of a fiction of ideas, in the same way that in the mid-1850s, when she adopted that historical moment's most powerful discourse of ideas—journalism—she also in the *Autobiography* became a theorist and advocate of journalism's worldview and approach to discourse.

In fact, although a tracing of Martineau's relationship to genres over her entire career is beyond the scope of this chapter, it should be clear by now that I believe that Martineau's use of the Victorian genre repertoire, and the history of the most authoritative British genres of ideas in the same period, will ultimately be found to track closely together. Born in the same year as the genre-altering *Edinburgh Review*, Harriet Martineau began to publish review essays in the 1820s as Macaulay was enhancing his own reputation and that

of the review essay simultaneously. She wrote in the genres of "useful knowledge" with Marcet and Brougham in the 1830s, wrote sociological travel books
in the later 1830s and early 1840s contemporary with those of Charles Dickens,
Frances Trollope, and Alexis de Tocqueville, and went on to become a newspaper leader writer in the great heyday of the leader in the mid-1850s. Her
attraction to the most currently powerful genre of ideas seems sometimes to
have been quite conscious: in the *Autobiography*, she tells of an early abor-
tive attempt at "a sort of theologico-metaphysical novel, which I entered upon
with a notion of enlightening the world through the same kind of interest as
was then excited by Mr. Ward's novel, 'Tremaine,' [1825] which was making
a prodigious noise" (112), and in an 1858 letter to Florence Nightingale she
explicitly compares her current use of journalistic genres to her previous work
in fiction as both a more intellectually advanced discourse than fiction and
as a superior way to reach a contemporary audience: "Society has outgrown
illustration by fiction, it appears to me: & I am quite sure that I have outgrown
the power of doing it. I don't believe that any one who has successfully written
History & "leaders" in a London "daily" cd ever again write fiction" (quoted
in Frawley 437).

Whether her gift for genres was exercised consciously or instinctively,
however, Martineau's career seems to show a canny ability to identify and
then interpolate herself into the most effective genres of ideas being written
and read at each historical moment. What may make Martineau most valuable
to modern students of Victorian genre discourse, however, is that she did not
only practice the genres of writing she acquired; she also analyzed and theo-
rized each genre, implicitly or, more often, explicitly, as she was using it. The
pattern seems to have been for her to choose a culturally successful discourse
genre and then—before, during, or after starting to write in it herself—to
form a theory of its value and write an apologia for it. Just as at the beginning
of her career she followed up her individual studies of "Female Writers on
Practical Divinity" with her own book of practical divinity, she prefaced the
Illustrations of Political Economy with a theory of the teaching value of fiction;
supplemented her book on America with *How to Observe Morals and Manners*,
a theory of sociological investigation; and discursively justified and analyzed
her own discourse as a journalist within the *Autobiography*.

Martineau's own self-evaluation, in the *Daily News* obituary she composed
for herself in 1855, that she had only ever been a "popularizer" of other think-

ers' ideas, has more or less been accepted ever since by scholars.[16] But that
term does not capture her real discursive gifts, which seem to have been those
of a remarkably skilled adapter of discourse genres—so skilled that she could
catch the essential elements and tropes of a genre and reproduce them so that
her versions were often better and fuller exploitations of the genre's potential
than her models. Bakhtin points out that each discourse genre "possesses its
own organic logic which can to a certain extent be understood and creatively
assimilated on the basis of a few generic models, even fragments" (*Problems*
157), as Dostoevsky assimilated the Menippean satire—and as Martineau's
popular *Illustrations* both assimilated and transcended the weaker useful-
knowledge writing of her models Marcet, Charles Knight, Lord Brougham,
and the Society for the Diffusion of Useful Knowledge.[17] Martineau seems to
have experimented throughout her career with finding the most powerful and
authoritative genres of ideas extant in her culture—adopting new ones nearly
as fast as the discourse culture around her could invent them. Not actually a
specialist for long in any one genre, whether "sage writing" or "wisdom writing" or "rhetoric," fiction or journalism or sociology, she was rather a generic
virtuoso who perceived and intuited the contemporary power of different
discourses, and somehow always managed to be present where, to borrow
an image from Walter Pater, the forces of language to convey knowledge and
intellectual authority were at that moment united in their purest energy.[18]

This aspect of her ability as a writer has been difficult for modern scholars
to see, mainly because a map of Victorian discourse genres that would have
allowed us to track Harriet Martineau's changing relationship to them has
not yet been drawn. A literary history that has traditionally privileged works
and authors more than genres and their dynamic interaction may have hidden one of Martineau's most striking gifts as a Victorian woman of letters—
aided in this by Martineau herself, whose genre ideology in 1855, as she wrote
the *Autobiography*, held that unique gifts or deliberate craft in the shaping of
discourse were just the attributes that a writer should most strenuously deny
having at all.

Harriet Martineau's *Autobiography* hardly contains a discussion of her
literary art that is not also a denial of conscious art, and the *Autobiography*
has exerted all the interpretive control over scholarly readings of Martineau's
career that the 1855 Martineau could have desired. But the book hoped for by
Deirdre David, the definitive account of the career of the Victorian woman

of letters and ideas who was "first, last, and always" a writer, will only be possible, I believe, when we have found a way out of that interpretive control, and learned to see Martineau's *Autobiography* not as a summative account, but as the document of one moment in a remarkable intellectual and discursive arc. Once we are able to read the *Autobiography* as the expression of one genre's ideals, chosen and articulated at a particular historical moment for excellent strategic reasons, we should be able to look more broadly across Martineau's oeuvre for further evidence of her evolving discursive history, which will almost certainly prove an invaluable index to the changing discourse of mid-Victorian Britain itself. When that happens, Harriet Martineau may become again for modern students of Victorian discourse what she always most wanted to be to all her readers: our best resource, our most powerful explainer, our indispensable guide and instructor.

3 | THE *Editor's* TALE

Anthony Trollope and the Historiography of the Mid-Victorian Press

All languages of heteroglossia, whatever the principle underlying
them nd making each unique, are specific points of view on the world,
forms for conceptualizing the world in words, specific world views,
each characterized by its own objects, meanings, and values. As
such they all may be juxtaposed to one another, mutually supplement
each other, contradict one another and be interrelated dialogically.
As such they encounter one another and co-exist in the consciousness
of real people—first and foremost, in the creative consciousness of
people who write novels.

MIKHAIL BAKHTIN, "Discourse in the Novel"

IN THE LAST CHAPTER I called attention to the desirability of a map of
Victorian genres, which would show their relative positions and competitive relationships at different points during the century. It is easy to foresee
the value this kind of "Galilean" map of genre interactions could have for
literary and historical scholarship, but less easy to see how data for such a
map could ever be collected and assembled into readable shape, whether
narrative, expository, or graphic.[1] Though no defeatist about the possibility
of ultimately achieving a usefully historicist genre criticism, Alastair Fowler
points out the limits any modern reader's own subject position imposes on
his or her ability to understand the state of any genre in a previous era. The
reader "cannot recover meanings that relate to the genre's earlier, 'innocent'
states," writes Fowler, and "scholarship can mitigate but hardly remove such
an obstacle. To have an earlier generic convention explained is to lose some

of its effect; to learn from annotation that a feature was once innovative is not the same as recognizing its first strangeness" (261). If our understanding of historical genres is necessarily limited even when we consider them one by one, it is reasonable to ask whether we could ever re-create something as complex as a guide to changing relationships of genres at previous historical moments, or whether the attempt might not inevitably bog down in problems of data identification, contamination, and observer bias.[2]

In passages such as the epigraph to this chapter, however, Mikhail Bakhtin suggests that useful records of genre relationships at previous moments should sometimes have been preserved by the creative consciousness of novelists, whose texts encode and preserve the relationships of power, cooperation, and competition among language forms that obtained when they were written, and who might therefore become our proxy observers. If this is true, most scholars interested in the mid-Victorian relationship between journalistic genres and literary ones in particular would surely assume that our best potential guides must be the era's two great acknowledged novelist-journalists, Charles Dickens and William Makepeace Thackeray. Contemporaries considered Dickens and Thackeray polymaths capable of any textual work, from lectures to serial novels, but especially as masters of the periodical press. It has always been part of Dickens's legend that his genius was shaped by reporting and sketch writing for the *Morning Chronicle,* and that he kept close ties to the press throughout his career as editor of *Bentley's Miscellany, Household Words, All the Year Round,* and (more briefly and less successfully) as founder and first editor of the London *Daily News.* Thackeray's early career gave him comparably deep and varied experience of journalism as a *Punch* humorist, Paris correspondent, and London periodicals contributor, and he became founding editor of the notably successful *Cornhill Magazine* while at the height of his artistic reputation. Thackeray's vivid portraits of London journalists and journalism in *Pendennis* (1848–50) did much to secure this reputation, with many British journalists later remembering a youthful encounter with *Pendennis* as a vocational moment.[3] Dickens and Thackeray have always been the novelists most closely associated with Victorian journalism, and much excellent scholarship has already been devoted to tracing their specifically journalistic careers.[4]

Anthony Trollope, who never commanded the same contemporary reputation for skill at Victorian periodical letters, initially seems far less qualified than either man to represent the Victorian press to modern readers. Trollope's association with the press began later in life, and his salaried editorial career was brief—only a few years at the helm of one shilling monthly. But I will argue that, surprising as it may seem, Trollope may become the modern scholar's best novelistic guide to the genre relationships between mid-Victorian literature and journalism, largely because of an artistic and conceptual breakthrough about journalistic discourse he seems to have made at more or less the same time that Harriet Martineau was becoming a convert to leader writing for the *Daily News*. In his novels of the mid-1850s, Trollope developed an interest in investigating and representing discourse functions and relationships that was to continue, increasing in sophistication and changing flexibly to reflect changes in press forms and relationships themselves, for most of the rest of his thirty-year career. While no single Trollope novel matches *Pendennis* for focused attention to the world of the Victorian press, his collected fiction and nonfiction are probably the most sustained thematic engagement of any British novelist, before or since, with the genres and functions of journalism. Still more valuable for modern readers, the questions about competing discourses that Trollope seems most interested in investigating in his novels are also the questions that have recently come to dominate the new scholarly subdiscipline of the history of the book.

So strong a claim—that Trollope created a substantive analysis of Victorian discourse, especially of its journalistic genres—may seem hard to justify. Trollope only began to acquire firsthand knowledge of the Victorian press when well into middle age, and his youthful apprenticeship was passed in the civil service, not in a printer's office or reporter's gallery as Dickens's was. The novels of the 1850s were written before Trollope even met real working Victorian journalists such as G. H. Lewes and Robert Bell, who later became his friends and colleagues.[5] Many scholars might also suggest that Trollope lacked not only the right credentials to accurately portray the Victorian press but also the right attitude toward it. Perhaps inspired by the traditional Sadleirian reading of Trollope as an instinctual rather than an intellectual artist,[6] modern observers who comment on Trollope's treatments of newspaper journalism in particular most often attribute attitudes to him rather than theories—and sometimes not even attitudes so much as grudges. Modern-day *Times* editor Simon Jenkins told the Trollope Society in 1992 that "Trollope could respect the church, politics, the law, medicine. But he could never resist a dig at the press. When in doubt, it seems, he could always sink his talons into a newspaper" (17).[7] Press Complaints Commission chairman John Wakeham told the same organization in 1997 that newspapers are usually "the bad guy" in Trollope's fiction, that he was "cynical about the press" and actually "disliked *The Times*" (12, 13). Trollope's first biographer, T. H. S. Escott, wrote that "Trollope loved newspaper writers even a little less than he did evangelicals" (263), and even such well-informed Trollope scholars as the authors of the *Penguin Companion to Trollope* echo this view, writing that "editors seldom received favourable treatment in Trollope's fiction in spite of his generally friendly relations with them in his literary career" (144).[8]

Even admitting that Trollope's editor-characters Tom Towers, the omnipotence behind the morning daily "Jupiter" in several Barchester novels, and Quintus Slide, an antagonist in three Palliser novels, are negative portraits of journalists, claims of how Trollope "always," "never," "usually," or "seldom" represented journalists are quantitative, and can be tested against the data of Trollope's large oeuvre. A look at those data (I offer a survey in appendix B) will hold some surprises for readers who think of Towers and Slide as Trollope's only journalists. Twenty-two separately conceived (not counting repeat appearances) editors *in addition to* Slide and Towers appear in Trollope's fiction, and they embody a wide range of attitudes, ethics, and degrees of professional skill. Trollope's fiction contains another nine separate newspaper writers, most of whom explicitly report to editors, and several more fiction writers who work under newspaper or periodical editors, including Charley Tudor of *The Three Clerks* and Julius Mackenzie of "The Spotted Dog." Trollope's nonfiction books and essays have thirteen more separate and substantial considerations of journalism and journalists in various contexts, with focused analysis of nine particular journalists, editors, and editorial situations, ranging from daily newspaper editing to the editing of American and other foreign newspapers, and including evaluations of the qualifications and performances of Trollope's editorial contemporaries Robert Bell, George Smith, G. H. Lewes, John Morley, W. M. Thackeray, Norman McLeod—plus self-reflexive analysis of Trollope's own work as an editor. Towers and Slide thus represent only a small fraction of nearly fifty formal representations or analyses of editors and periodical writers—a number that would seem to make journalists almost as indispensable a component of Trollope's lifetime body of work as modest young women, indecisive young men, MPs, and clergymen.[9]

To this published work can be added further evidence from Trollope's private letters, which make it clear that for him journalism, Editorship (a word he frequently capitalizes) and his own relations with periodicals and editors were subjects of deep interest and serious ethical and professional reflection. The letters show him indignantly turning down an offer of the nominal editorship of *Temple Bar* in 1861, for example, even though it would have been worth £1,000 a year to him, calling the offer a hollow "mock editorship." As a periodical contributor, Trollope also initiated searching exchanges about his relationships with editors with Lewes, his colleague and sometime editor at the *Fortnightly Review.*[10]

Trollope's engagement with the periodical press was clearly a significant intellectual axis of his work, and although some elements of his representations of the press over his career reflect personal changes in his own relationship to press work (over four phases I identify in the appendix, somewhat unsatisfactorily, as "reader," "contributor," "editor," and "editor emeritus"), his representations also seem to build an objectively valuable portrait of how press discourse functioned within Victorian society. The initial breakthrough upon which this larger portrait was built is deceptively simple, however, and had just two parts, both of which appear first in *The Warden:* the analytic insight that journalistic discourse and its relationship to other discourse forms were worth describing and studying, and the artistic insight that language forms and their relationships with other forms, with social institutions, and with their readers, could be represented in literary art using the focal and liminal figure of the editor.

The next section of this chapter will consider how Trollope deployed and developed these insights; a final section will try to justify my opening claim that the fictions of journalism Trollope created may, in the near term at least, offer as much or more value even than those of Dickens and Thackeray for helping scholars understand Victorian relationships between literary and periodical discourses, and for helping us begin to create a key to genre relations in Victorian discourse.

Portrait of a Discourse

When *The Warden* appeared in 1855, offering Trollope's first fictional portrayal of a modern newspaper and its editor, opinions about its success among those who knew the real world of Victorian editing and publishing were profoundly mixed. A publisher's reader for Longman praised Trollope's treatment of the editor "Tom Towers" and the London morning daily "Jupiter"[11] as accurate and clever, and a reviewer in the *Athenaeum* called them "excellent," adding that "no reader of newspapers will mistake the original of the 'Jupiter,'" which was of course the London *Times* (Smalley 34–35). But the reviewer for the *Times* itself, E. S. Dallas, singled out the same chapters for scorn, attacking "an account of newspaper management . . . by persons who know absolutely nothing about it" (13 Aug. 1857: 5). The disagreement is revealing, because the particular kind of realism Trollope was attempting in his portrait of a modern newspaper was indeed almost wholly new.

The *Times*'s Dallas was probably largely right that Tom Towers, a briefless barrister who controls the "Jupiter" invisibly from comfortable bachelor chambers at the Temple, hardly mentioning the paper even to his closest friends, was an unrealistic picture of the editor of a London morning daily.[12] But the Longman's reader and *Athenaeum* reviewer who applauded the portrait were right as well, because Trollope's use of Towers to personify the *Times* rang fully true to the *discursive* experience of a mid-1850s newspaper reader. Readers of the *Times* might not have known how editors really lived, but they knew very well how they wrote, and the persona projected daily in the 1,200–word leading articles of the *Times* had by the 1850s become a fully recognizable and consistent (discursively if not politically) public character, one who engaged and convinced—or depending on one's politics, manipulated and misled— the newspaper's many readers partly by its success in combining elements of discourse that should logically have been in contradiction. The editorial voice of the *Times* was educated, cultured, and class-marked as that of a gentleman, but with strong notes of populism; it was patriotic, but distanced from or disdainful of many traditional institutions. It was impudent to the point of arrogance, cynical about the motives of others, contemptuous and dismissive of opposing views, and yet repeatedly claimed the highest possible motives and ethical ground for itself and for the mission of the public press.[13] Most characteristically, it was serenely omniscient—on any given day it claimed to have weighed all available evidence and come to the only possible right answer: its mind was made up, for the right reasons, and not to be changed. This claim was usually implicit, but occasionally became explicit: the *Times* had itself declared, in a leading article published the same year Trollope began writing

The Warden, that its own mission was "to investigate truth and to apply it on fixed principles to the affairs of the world" (6 Feb. 1852: 4).

It was the voice and persona of this peculiar genre of journalism, the leading article, that Trollope undertook to depict realistically in *The Warden.* Whether *Times* writers such as Dallas chose to recognize the portrait or not, Trollope succeeded brilliantly, partly because he was able to show keen understanding of the discourse on so many levels. In *The Warden,* leading-article discourse is interpolated into the narrative itself (where two "Jupiter" leaders are re-created), and extensively commented on throughout the novel by the third-person narrator, who is keenly interested in the relative immunity newspaper discourse seems to have achieved relative to the traditionally powerful politicians, churchmen, and other figures it judges and attacks. "But to whom was he, Tom Towers, responsible?" muses the narrator. "No one could insult him; no one could inquire into him. He could speak out withering words, and no one could answer him: ministers courted him, though perhaps they knew not his name; bishops feared him; judges doubted their own verdicts unless he confirmed them; and generals, in their councils of war, did not consider more deeply what the enemy could do, than what the *Jupiter* would say" (124).

Still more effectively, however, Trollope weaves his study of leading-article discourse even into dialogue between characters, and he does this through the second great insight of the novel: the recognition that the role of editor could be used to bring a form of discourse into a novel as a living and speaking character. When Eleanor Harding's lover John Bold visits Tom Towers to ask him to drop the newspaper's interest in Hiram's Hospital—a subject Bold himself had suggested to Towers, but which now concerns his future father-in-law—Towers deftly frustrates and foils his reader/friend Bold's purpose by deploying leading-article discourse within their private conversation. (Trollope makes the generic trope unmistakable when he has Towers invoke the *Times*'s famous "anonymity," blandly denying the influence over the "Jupiter" that Bold is perfectly aware he has.) In a series of skillful moves fully characteristic of the *Times* at this era, Towers first deflects their discussion from Bold's original purpose to the supposed corruption of Mr. Harding ("the man who takes all the money and does nothing" [126]), then to the weakness and misjudgment of Bold himself ("it injures a man to commence a thing of this kind, and not carry it through" [127]), and finally to the great gravitas and supposedly unshakable ethics of the "Jupiter" itself. "Certain men are employed in writing for the public press," Towers tells Bold; "and if they are induced either to write or to abstain from writing by private motives, surely the public press would soon be of little value" (134). Towers thus manages to turn a potential conversation into a one-sided lecture, to win an argument without condescending to argue, to deny Bold's request without explicitly responding to it, and to adroitly recast the entire discussion to reflect only credit on his own judgment ("You've only to think of this, and you'll see that I am right" [134]) and discredit on the choices and motives of virtually everyone else involved. Trollope's narrator notes dryly that "the discretion of Tom Towers was boundless: there was no contradicting what he said, no arguing against such propositions," but Bold leaves the room "as quickly as he could, inwardly denouncing his friend Tom Towers as a prig and a humbug" (134).

The Warden deepens and strengthens its discursive portrait of modern journalism even beyond such passages, however, by following Towers's discourse in its effects and ramifications within the novel's world. Towers may be master in any direct discursive encounter, but other characters in the novel show themselves knowledgeable and critical readers of the leading-article form through their evaluations of and reactions to it. Bold's denunciation of Towers as he leaves the Temple is an attack on the founding assumptions of press discourse, cast in the same terms many readers are known to have applied to the *Times*. "Confound his arrogance!" Bold fulminates. "What is any public question but a conglomeration of private interests? What is any newspaper article but an expression of the views taken by one side? Truth! It takes an age to ascertain the truth of any question! The idea of Tom Towers talking of public motives and purity of purpose! Why it wouldn't give him a moment's uneasiness to change his politics tomorrow, if the paper required it" (134). In another scene, the bishop of Barchester and his son the archdeacon discuss how the success of leading-article discourse is partly a result of the competitive ruthlessness it has come to practice in its encounters with other discourses. When the bishop advises Mr. Harding to respond to the articles in the "Jupiter" with a letter, the archdeacon, "more worldly wise than his father," is able to foresee exactly how such a letter would fare against the "Jupiter" leading article that would answer it, and replies,

"yes, and be smothered with ridicule; tossed over and over again with scorn; shaken this way and that, as a rat in the mouth of a practiced terrier. You will leave out some word or letter in your answer, and the ignorance of the cathedral clergy will be harped upon; you will make some small mistake, which will be a falsehood, or some admission, which will be self-condemnation; you will find yourself to have been vulgar, ill-tempered, irreverent, and illiterate, and the chances are ten to one but that being a clergyman you will have been guilty of blasphemy! A man may have the best of causes, the best of talents, and the best of tempers; he may write as well as Addison, or as strongly as Junius; but even with all this he cannot successfully answer, when attacked by the *Jupiter*. In such matters it is omnipotent." (60)

Or not quite omnipotent, because, in a further insight that has unfortunately often been read as *The Warden's* chief artistic flaw, Trollope is also able to show that the "Jupiter," for all its undoubted power and immunity to direct attack, is constrained in its turn by its relationship to other powerful contemporary genres. When Bold pays his visit to Towers, a pamphlet "all but damp from the press" (127) is on Towers's table, and this turns out to be the work of Dr. Pessimist Anticant, a characteristically heavy-handed Trollopian character name that thinly disguises Thomas Carlyle. Towers has also been reading another popular writer, and refers in his conversation with Bold to the first shilling monthly number of a new serial novel, "The Almshouse," by Mr. Popular Sentiment, who is no disguise at all for Charles Dickens.[14] The reader learns, along with John Bold, that these powerful writers in other genres have also taken up the case of Septimus Harding and Hiram's Hospital, translating it into their own language forms and reconstructing it into a reflection of their own thematic interests and worldviews. The Carlylean discourse has employed the denunciatory language of the *Latter-Day Pamphlets* to present Septimus Harding to readers as an example of the modern breakdown of once-noble medieval social institutions and virtues, while the Dickensian one has painted Harding in "glaring colours" (137) as a case study in a self-absorbed tyrant's oppression of the virtuous and innocent.

Towers observes professionally of "The Almshouse" that it is "very well done, as you'll see: his first numbers always are" (132), and as he does, a further reason for Towers's refusal to drop the Hiram's Hospital issue becomes clear. Two powerful discourses—"two of the most popular authors of the day!" (132), as Bold notes ruefully—both of them reforming voices, have taken up the issue, and their discourses directly compete with the claims to a reforming ethos of Towers's leading-article journalism. For all the invulnerability of "The Jupiter" to any direct attack, Trollope shows, no single discourse—not even the *Times* at the height of its power—really has a discursive monopoly. Towers cannot drop his interest in Hiram's Hospital now at least partly because Dickens has taken it up as well, and both the narrator and Towers recognize Dickens as a formidable generic competitor: "Of all such reformers Mr. Sentiment is the most powerful" (135). The narrator notes, in an open reflection on the new genres that have subsumed the functions of scholarship and rhetoric, that in earlier periods "an age was occupied in proving a grievance, and philosophical researches were printed in folio pages, which it took a life to write, and an eternity to read. We get on now with a lighter step, and quicker: ridicule is found to be more convincing than argument, imaginary agonies touch more than true sorrows, and monthly novels convince, when learned quartos fail to do so. If the world is to be set right, the work will be done by shilling numbers" (135). With such competition for the discursive mantle of cultural critic and reformer, even the powerful editor of the nation's most powerful newspaper cannot afford to cede an interesting issue to be constructed, interpreted, and dominated by other generic voices.

The sophistication of this study of the genre forms and competitive situation of journalism in the mid-1850s is worth comparing to the work of other contemporary novelists who, as we saw briefly in chapter 1, were also responding to journalism's public success with their own fictional depictions of journalism. Most of these analyses undertake a much less analytical and less complex debunking of press discourse, and their major tactic is to represent newspaper writers and editors as conscious hypocrites, often by dramatizing conspiratorial private conversations between writers or publishers. In the Reverend W. J. Conybeare's *Perversion* (1856), which Dallas of the *Times* reviewed along with *The Warden*, the villain Archer, who writes for the leading London daily (here the "Vane"), coolly tells other journalists that his paper's Crimean War policy is purely a financial speculation, and that the wartime increase in sales will probably be worth £10,000 a year extra to his newspapers' owners. "Monstrous!" says one of his listeners; "and we are all under the despotism of men whose policy is dependent on their interests, and is liable to be biased by such enormous bribes as that!" (331). In J. M. Capes's serial novel "Compton Hall," the journalist-protagonist recalls overhearing his proprietor tell a group of owners, "I need not remind you, gentlemen, of the principle on which our journal is conducted. Our motto is, always be on the winning side" (33). Conybeare and Capes both draw on the conventions of an already-existing subgenre for these scenes, since private admissions of nefarious practices made by one journalist to another had been a regular formal trope of attacks on journalism in British pamphlets and periodicals since the later eighteenth century.[15]

In such scenes actual newspaper discourse is rarely represented or reproduced, for the obvious reason that such language is believed to contain only camouflage for the private agendas that will be revealed only in private conferences or unguarded moments. In "Compton Hall," only one leading article is read aloud to a group, and the purpose of the scene is to emphasize the (in this case literal) duplicity of its language: close to deadline, but unsure which of two positions on a major public question his publisher will choose as more profitable, the writer has formed his article so that it can strongly support either side if a few italicized words are retained or removed just before the plate of type goes to press.

Instead of dismissing press discourse as a tissue of hypocrisy, however, Trollope puts discursive form at the center of his analysis. Alone among the mid-1850s novelists who directly critique the press, at least of those I have found, Trollope does not treat its language forms merely as masks, comic or tragic, for true intentions, but sees that acquiring and using a professional discourse often requires the writer to consent, at least while using the discourse, to the values built into that discourse. This more Bakhtinian understanding of how genres function is already fully apparent in *The Warden*, as we have seen, but becomes clearer still in Trollope's subsequent treatments of journalism, including several published within the next few years. When the hobbledehoy Charley Tudor of *The Three Clerks* (1857) begins writing serial fiction for the "Daily Delight," he is delighted to work in a genre form that instantly renders him an all-purpose agent of social change, and he undertakes the charge in good faith. "The editor says that we must always have a slap at some of the iniquities of the times," Charley tells his friend Henry Norman. "He gave me three or four to choose from; there was the adulteration of food, and the want of education for the poor, and street music, and the miscellaneous sale of poisons" (218). Adds Charley, who even as a beginner at journalistic discourse can see that certain forms of language are peculiarly qualified to perform certain tasks: "The press is the only *censor morum* going now—and who so fit? Set a thief to catch a thief, you know" (219).

Trollope's consistent insight throughout these treatments is that journalistic discourse forms are meaningful in themselves, not merely a screen for their writers' real motives, but actually contributing to the formation of those motives. Genres are ways of seeing the world that genuinely and complexly, sometimes consciously and sometimes unconsciously, structure the belief systems of those who use them. Anyone in Trollope's mid-century novels who engages with press discourse, therefore, whether conscientious (Bold), manipulative (Towers), or naively reformist (Charley), seems to find himself agreeing on some level with the premise that the function of the press is social engagement, public oversight, and institutional reform. Simply engaging the genre at all seems to require a nod toward this ideological premise, to the point that Trollope's most Machiavellian writers and editors repeat it—even if only to themselves, even when their actions seem entirely self-interested. When Obadiah Slope of *Barchester Towers* takes advantage of friendship with Towers to ask for the dubious private favor of an endorsement, even the letter asking for special treatment invokes press ethics: "I am sure you will not suspect me of asking from you any support which the paper with which you are connected cannot conscientiously give me" (305). Later still, when Phineas Finn uses a legal maneuver to block Quintus Slide from printing Kennedy's letter about Lady Laura, the narrator observes that the editor Slide "did in truth believe that he had been hindered from doing good," while Slide's wrathful reflections employ language that could almost be printed in his next day's leading article: "If there be fault in high places, it is proper that it be exposed. If there be fraud, adulteries, gambling, and lasciviousness,—or even quarrels and indiscretions among those whose names are known, let every detail be laid open to the light, so that the people may have a warning" (238).

None of which is to say that Trollope's editors cannot also be dishonest. Quite the contrary: although Towers had refused Bold's request to ease up on Septimus Harding, he casually grants Slope's request for a "Jupiter" endorsement (*Barchester Towers* 418), while Charley's editor at the "Daily Delight," who had him attack the modern criminal code and the indiscriminate sale of poisons, defrauds Charley of payment for his stories by first telling him that newspapers don't pay until six months after publication, and later that it is "quite out of the question" (548) that Charley can be paid at all until the "Daily Delight" achieves a larger sale. But in all such exchanges, no privately conspiratorial language passes anyone's lips.

Trollope is invariably more interested in the public discourse of journalists than in guesses or deductions about their private discourse, perhaps partly so that he can show readers that they need not hide behind a novelistic arras to understand the workings of the press, since those workings are not actually hidden from anyone who understands the generic nature of journalism and can parse its published texts. Almost everything an intelligent reader needs to know about the real nature of the "Jupiter" or "Daily Delight" is already fully present in its printed texts, and the private world of the journalistic insider would only be what an astute reader could have gathered directly from that discourse itself, as Trollope himself had gathered it. Thus, not only Trollope's narrator, but intelligent characters throughout his fictions, such as the Barchester archdeacon, already know precisely how newspaper discourse functions and why, and have usually come to their knowledge without any need to meet an editor.

For the reader of a novel, however, "meeting" an editor can be a remarkably useful way to learn about a discourse form, its relation to readers, and its competitive relationships to other discourses. In his essay "Discourse in the Novel," Mikhail Bakhtin specifically discusses the value for the novelist of using a literary character as the personification of a discourse. "This process— experimenting by turning persuasive discourse into speaking persons— becomes especially important in those cases where a struggle against such images has already begun, where someone is striving to liberate himself from the influence of such an image and its discourse by means of objectification, or is striving to expose the limitations of both image and discourse" (*Dialogic* 348). Trollope's use of Tom Towers in *The Warden* seems devoted to just this task of exposing the true nature and limitations of leading-article discourse, but subsequent novels show Trollope making a still more artistically complex use of editor-characters. In his later works they are used not only to critique individual discourses but also to illustrate the pressures on and between multiple discourses.

Even with Towers, for example, Trollope had shown how the periodical discourse practiced in contemporary Britain seemed to make the editor a divided entity, with separate and partly incompatible existences in the material and discursive worlds. The mid-century novels *The Three Clerks* and *Barchester Towers* develop this idea further by making editors highly significant in the lives of major characters, but also keeping them mostly out of the reader's sight, so that they function mainly as foci for discourse even on the diagetic level of the novel's own world. Tom Towers is physically present, as we have seen, for a full chapter of *The Warden,* but he becomes a figure of discourse only in *Barchester Towers.* Charley Tudor's editor on the halfpenny "Daily Delight" in *The Three Clerks* is both more involved in the book's action and more elusive: he is Charley's "mentor" and "literary papa," closely controlling the content and technique of Charley's early stories, but is never named and appears physically in only one page of one chapter. He is present mainly as a discourse, appearing in the text when Charley invokes him by reporting his voice and opinions. So fully a creature of discourse is this editor that at the end of the novel even Charley's young wife, Katie, can summon him up convincingly when she writes—as a practical joke—an article supposedly from the "Daily Delight" damning Charley's new novel. When the "review" is read aloud to the family circle, Charley at first claims to be able to recognize the editor immediately as author of the anonymous piece. "How well I know the fellow's low attempts at wit!" Charley complains, squirming under the harshness of the review. "That's the editor himself—that's my literary papa. I know him as well as though I had seen him at it" (564).

As John Bold was the first of Trollope's characters to discover, the social and discursive lives of an editor can be difficult to integrate. Even Olympian editors such as Towers are human beings with families, friends, and professional colleagues, but when their social worlds touch their discursive ones, private motives can lead to poor editorial decisions, and correct editorial decisions cause hard personal feelings. The most professionally successful editors throughout Trollope's fictions—the best managers of discourse—are the ones who best avoid being seen as editors in the physical, or at least the social, world. The editors of the "Daily Record" in *He Knew He Was Right,* "Daily Delight" in *The Three Clerks,* and even "Jupiter" are broadly heard of and discussed, but usually absent from the novel's dramatized action, and rarely can such an editor be inveigled into taking a professional action for a nonprofessional reason. The 1855 version of Towers, who "scarcely ever named the paper even to the most intimate of his friends" (124–25), is almost surreally successful at separating the discursive from the personal.

The more conflicted editors of Trollope's "Editor's Tales" series of short stories in the 1860s, however, suffer all the awkwardness that can follow the collision of discursive and physical worlds. In these stories Trollope builds his original insight that editorship both requires and abhors the physical editor into a rich source of humor and pathos, using a variety of situations to force editors to confront their divided identities. The editors of these stories frequently find themselves treated by would-be contributors as human beings when they most want to be emanations of professional discourse, and as emanations when they particularly want to be just people. The most comic example is the first story in the series, "The Turkish Bath" of October 1869, in which a magazine editor who fancies himself as intangible as Tom Towers is confronted with his own dual nature literally with his pants down, when he is approached by a would-be contributor in a Turkish bath.[16]

Trollope's choice of the figure of the editor to represent discourse was by no means an obvious, or even promising, artistic move in the mid-1850s. It had been only relatively recently that British reading audiences began to understand the term "editor" as denoting the authoritative central intelligence of a periodical. Leslie Stephen, in "The Evolution of Editors" from *Studies of a Biographer,* considers the term anachronistic when applied to any periodical proprietor of the eighteenth century, noting that in Johnson's *Dictionary* of 1785 the "editor, that is as implying the commander of a periodical, is not yet recognized, and Johnson, if any one, would not have overlooked him" (35).[17] Neither previous fictions nor existing biographies had created any shared public understanding of what such a position entailed or what its duties were, and there seems to have been corresponding variance in editorship's actual practice, with different newspapers and magazines dividing editorship and subeditorship along quite different lines, and procuring the vital genre of the leading article in very different ways.[18] The epigraph to Robert Patten and David Finkelstein's recent essay "Editing Blackwood's; or, What Do Editors Do?" is the wry observation of Victorian journalist Henry Labouchere that "I have now been connected with newspapers over thirty years and I have never yet discovered what an editor is" (146)—and while this claim of confusion might have been partly tongue-in-cheek coming from an experienced working journalist (modern journalists are still known to joke that "managing editor" is an oxymoron), many mid-Victorian readers might have been genuinely puzzled to explain what editors were and did.

Trollope's own attempts at this time to describe and explain what editors did may also have helped shape his own attempt to construct a professional identity as an editor later in his career. Trollope's letters indicate that he was interested in an editorship almost as soon as he was introduced to the literary world, and as we have seen, he turned down an unsatisfactory "mock" editorship in 1861. In 1867, however, when the continuing success of Thackeray's *Cornhill, Temple Bar,* and *Macmillan's* seemed to show that magazines run by novelists were a good investment, Trollope negotiated an editorial command of his own, the shilling monthly *Saint Pauls,* bankrolled by James Virtue. From its first issue, *Saint Pauls* seems to have been Trollope's laboratory for experimentation with ideas for alternative ways to construct editorial voice and periodical discourse,[19] and the apparent failure of the experiments—and, after a few years, of the magazine itself—may be one reason Trollope's credentials as an authority on Victorian press have not subsequently shone more brightly. Trollope's opening essay in the magazine may not quite deserve the condemnation it routinely receives from modern critics, however. The introduction in the October 1867 *Saint Pauls* is rigorously, almost painfully, consistent with Trollope's by then well-developed beliefs about periodicals and editorship, and seems to be a remarkably good-faith attempt to avoid the manipulation and puffery he had portrayed in so many fictional editors. Compared to other instances of the mid-Victorian periodical prospectus, the essay is modest, wry, and free of exaggeration—Walter Houghton called it "anything but typical of such performances" (3: 359). Trollope openly discusses what he believes his new position honestly requires of him, and what the discourse of a new periodical might actually achieve. Read as a serious attempt at the highly conventionalized subgenre "prospectus," however, it struck contemporary reviewers in other periodicals, and probably many readers, as lacking energy and enthusiasm.[20]

Trollope continued his discursive thought-experiments with editorship in the series of "Editor's Tales" short stories that began to appear in *Saint Pauls* in October 1869. Trollope practically invents a new literary subgenre around the figure of the editor, creating a series of fictional editors as first-person-plural protagonists. (The narrating main characters refer to themselves throughout using the editorial plurals "we" and "us.") The stories study relationships between editors, publishers, and contributors or would-be contributors, and although they continue many of Trollope's other themes, for the first time the relationship between professional discourse and lived social experience is the major focus. Among the ideas explored in these stories is Trollope's realization that publication is not itself a single function, and that editorship and publishing have differing goals: one understanding the periodical as an entity of discourse, the other as an entity of economic and legal interests.[21] Although Tom Towers represents both capacities in *The Warden,* by the period of the "Editor's Tales," Trollope has clearly learned how distinct they are, and in short stories such as "Mrs. Brumby" and "The Panjandrum" he shows how editors can become caught between the contradictory demands of—or overcome by an unholy alliance between—publishers and contributors.[22]

Trollope's conceptual move in *The Warden* to study a discourse through fiction, and his choice to make an editor the narrative representative of the discourse, seems to have opened a vein that he was able to work for the rest of his career, using the (physical or discursive) figure of the newspaper and magazine editor to represent relationships, competitions, and points of conflict between different kinds and genres of discourses, between discourse interests and financial ones, between journalism and politics, between different conceptions of successful discourse, and between a discourse and its readers. By the 1870s the newspapers and editorships in his novels have become fully realized social as well as discursive entities. Their editors participate in others' plans as well as act on their own, sometimes back down under pressure from an angry reader, and in one case even marry. What is most striking about the editors of the later phase of Trollope's career is how well he seems to understand them, and their complexly interacting roles and functions within his fictional world. When the three newspaper editors of *The Way We Live Now* are each sent a manipulative private appeal by Lady Carbury for a good review for her book "Criminal Queens," they respond in three different ways, each shaped by the particular situation of that editor and the specific nature of his periodical, and Trollope gives lengthy consideration to exactly how and why each editorial decision is made.[23] In *The Prime Minister, Cousin Henry, The Way We Live Now, Dr. Wortle's School,* and *Mr. Scarborough's Family,* similarly, the simpler editorial mysteries of Trollope's earlier works are gone, and journalism and editorship have come to function as both workaday reality and an essential element in the discursive intercourse of local and national communities.

Dickens, Thackeray, and Trollope as Discourse Historians

If this discussion has given a sense of the scope and goals of Trollope's many representations of journalism, we may finally be ready to estimate Trollope's value for scholars, relative to the better-known Dickens and Thackeray, for solving the specific problem with which we began: our need for Victorian novelists to help interpret the dialogic relations between literary and journalistic genres in mid-Victorian discourse. Both Dickens and Thackeray obviously have a great deal of potential to contribute to such a project; one of Dickens's most celebrated gifts is his ability to use, invoke, contrast, and interweave a dizzying range of discourse registers from his culture, including parliamentary debate, advertising, journalism, Cockney dialect, and Blue Book officialese. As John M. L. Drew remarks, the young Dickens developed "a gymnastic voice: adept at assimilating all the different languages and forms—the different discourses—that were available for reporting this social and political flux, and developing a net metalanguage to comment archly upon it" (6). Dickens just as clearly knew the Victorian press from the inside in ways a civil servant such as Trollope never could. In the run-up to the launching of the *Daily News*, Dickens wrote to Lady Holland, without exaggeration, that he had been "as well acquainted with the management of [a newspaper], some years ago, as an Engineer is, with a Steam engine" (quoted in Drew 68).

While the voice and language of contemporary journalism is one of the discursive threads woven throughout Dickens's fiction, however, and often to striking effect,[24] the only major journalist-protagonist in his works is David Copperfield, and only a sprinkling of journalists in minor roles—such as the Eatanswill editors in *The Pickwick Papers,* and the newspaper illustrators and penny-a-liners in *Bleak House*—appear among the hundreds or thousands of characters in his famous oeuvre. Even the representation of this one major journalist's professional practices is strikingly brief, however, and almost extraneous to the thematic interests of the book. Copperfield's career progresses a few paragraphs at a time, never taking up anything like a full chapter: he struggles to learn shorthand to become a parliamentary reporter (chapter 38), and the next time his professional life is mentioned (chapter 43) is already making "a respectable income by it," is "in high repute for my accomplishment in all pertaining to the art" (692), and has begun writing and publishing magazine essays. When the subject comes up again (chapter 46), Copperfield is writing his first work of fiction, and the time after that (chapter 48) the novel is finished, published, and successful. That is all we know and all we apparently need to know of Copperfield's published writings, and the narrator says as much: "It is not my purpose, in this record, though in all other essentials it is my written memory, to pursue the history of my own fictions. They express themselves, and I leave them to themselves. When I refer to them, incidentally, it is only as a part of my progress" (758). Copperfield, at least, does not seem interested in having his creative consciousness mediate any Bakhtinian encounters between professional and autobiographical discourses.[25]

Perhaps partly because of Dickens's unwillingness to take too explicitly analytical a position toward the different cultural discourses he employs with such virtuosity, however, it seems to have sometimes been difficult for later readers to turn our recognition for Dickens's genius at periodical discourse into a clear understanding of what his purposes or achievements were in particular cases. Some of his most perceptive modern readers have come to contradictory conclusions about his relationship to the forms of journalism. John M. L. Drew in *Dickens the Journalist* (2003), for example, while he notes Dickens's remarkable sentence-level play with form, diagnoses a "general reluctance to experiment with graphic design where his journals were concerned" (155). Lorna Huett, however, comes to exactly the opposite conclusion in her 2005 VanArsdel Prize–winning essay in *Victorian Periodicals Review,* where she argues that Dickens deliberately played with readers' genre expectations for the appearance and form of *Household Words,* which "deliberately trod a fine line between genres" (79), blending design elements of highbrow reviews with some from penny periodicals.

If Dickens is more a subtle user of journalistic discourse than an explicit chronicler of journalists and journalism, however, Thackeray steps into this latter gap, putting journalists front and center in several fictions. Philip of *Adventures of Philip,* and Pendennis and Warrington of *Pendennis,* are fully developed major characters, and the large supporting cast of journalists in *Pendennis* includes publishers Bono and Bungay, leader writers Archer and Captain Shandon, and subeditor Jack Finucane. In Thackeray the thematic interests of Dickens with respect to journalism appear at first to be exactly reversed; journalistic careers are dwelt on, but the discourse genres of the press are kept at a relative distance. On closer inspection, however, representing journalism even as a career seems more peripheral than central to Thackeray's project as well. Arthur Pendennis is more the minor poet of gift books and the novelist-author of "Walter Lorraine" than a newspaper's staff writer; Warrington the political writer is really an MP manqué, only kept from pursuing his vocation by his marital troubles. Even the secondary characters among Thackeray's professional journalists generally draw the readers' attention to the presence of literary and professional absence, and to what most of these characters are *not* (gentlemanly, well-connected, responsible, professional, well-educated, intellectual, or sober) than to what they *are* as men of periodical letters. The narrator's direct summative dismissal of journalistic pretensions in chapter 34 of *Pendennis*—"there are no race of people who talk about books, or, perhaps, who read books, so little as literary men" (440)—was famously the cause of hard feelings among Thackeray's peers.

Though their explicit treatments of journalistic writers and writing take different formal shape, however, Dickens and Thackeray share an interest in written discourse as an expression or representation of the individual writer's personal situation, much more than as a larger phenomenon of social interaction or cultural influence. Both writers certainly represent the creative act of prose composition, and may even dramatize it—Dora sits by David Copperfield and holds his pens, David ponders his fictions as he walks, Aunt Betsey comments on his long working hours and the state of his desk, Pendennis "sports the oak" as he begins review writing for the "Pall Mall Gazette"—but only rarely do Dickens or Thackeray show the circulation of text, the reception of its content, and the repercussions of that content on individuals and communities. There are of course some references to these, such as the local newspaper article in *Great Expectations* that attributes Pip's good fortune to Pumblechook, and the Australian newspaper at the end of *David Copperfield* that seems to have been written largely by Micawber. But these are comic vignettes; no Dickens novel has any important part of a plot, or even of a subplot, turn on a journalistic text in the way so many Trollope novels do. In *Pendennis,* Arthur Pendennis writes book reviews magisterially and apparently successfully with help from the British Museum, but only a handful of people—his peers, his victims, and his mother, Helen—seem to read them. When Mrs. Pendennis wonders "where her boy could have acquired such a prodigious store of reading" (444), both her interest and ours is on Pen, not on the books or his reviews, which we hardly see at all. This focus on the writer as creative artist, rather than on the text created or the reader who reacts to it, is certainly an understandable—perhaps a nearly inescapable—perspective for a novelist to have. A writer's experience of writing is the intimate and solitary contact with manuscript pages; problems arising once the text leaves the writer might well seem far more abstract.

But the modern scholarly subfield of the history of the book has come into its own as an intellectual enterprise over recent decades partly as scholars have come to recognize, as Robert Darnton does famously in "What Is the History of Books?" (1962), that there is much more eventful history in and around books than is contained in the biographical experience of named authors. History of the book is both dynamic and integrative—it tries to see beyond the literary-historical focus on individual authors to the webs and circuits of relationship and filiation that condition the creation, relation, and reception of texts, and to see text as a complex site of cooperation and interaction rather than as a single artist's expression. A famous icon of this approach is Darnton's often-reproduced "Communications Circuit" (68), an attempt to graphically demonstrate how many historical actors participate in the creation of any book, how widely it circulates within a culture, and how many other elements of that culture—editorial, legal, commercial, and so on—have a role in that creation and circulation. Darnton describes the circuit, which he reprints and discusses in several places including *The Kiss of Lamourette* (1990), as running "from the author to the publisher (if the bookseller does not assume that role), the printer, the shipper, the bookseller, and the reader. The reader completes the circuit because he influences the author both before and after the act of composition. . . . A writer may respond in his writing to criticisms of his previous work or anticipate reactions that his text will elicit. He addresses implicit readers and hears from explicit reviewers. So the circuit runs full cycle" (111).

Whatever keen practical interest Dickens and Thackeray must have had as editors in how widely *Household Words*, the *Daily News*, the *Museum*, the *Cornhill*, or their serial fictions circulated within British society, however, neither novelist provides much direct data for the book historian within his fictions, because neither shows great interest in using his art to analyze how discourse circulates and ramifies within his culture. Their journalistic characters—and even their narrators—are, if anything, openly skeptical about how strongly periodical discourse influences the wider culture. Copperfield the young parliamentary reporter is coolly detached about the discourse he records and helps to publish to the nation; it is empty of real substance, and its publication has no significance or even noticeable consequences:

> Night after night, I record predictions that never come to pass, professions that are never fulfilled, explanations that are only meant to mystify. I wallow in words. Britannia, that unfortunate female, is always before me, like a trussed fowl: skewered through and through with office-pens, and bound hand and foot with red tape. I am sufficiently behind the scenes to know the worth of political life. I am quite an Infidel about it, and shall never be converted. (692)

Dickens, as well as Copperfield, certainly earned his right to hold this position. Both he and Thackeray had learned about Victorian newspaper journalism as young men via a strong course of disillusionment—in Thackeray's case, through hard financial times and the actual failure of his own periodical. Both had served eventful journalistic apprentices in the rowdy British press of the 1830s, the age of Maginn, and must have often seen the disconnect between many journalists' discursive self-representations and their true situations, of the sort captured by Thackeray in chapters 31 and 32 of *Pendennis* when Captain Shandon writes the prospectus for a newspaper representing itself as "written by gentlemen for gentlemen" (410) from a room in a debtor's prison.

It makes artistic sense, then, for Thackeray and Dickens to represent the journalism of characters such as these as a textual product empty of real content, produced mostly to fulfill an obligation or meet a financial need, and having little wider impact. Pen, Warrington, Shandon, and Archer all write, but most of *what* they write has no greater use or consequence in *Pendennis* than to be exchanged for dinner, drinks, a brief reputation, or a brief solvency. Neither Dickens nor Thackeray sees the texts of the periodical press as important enough to trace farther within their fictions, and for that reason, trying to map the press representations of either *David Copperfield* or *Pendennis* onto Darnton's communications circuit diagram would rarely require us to look farther than the box labeled "Author."

Before Anthony Trollope was far into his mature career, however, his structural interest in the functions of and competitive relationships between discourses had given him something to say about—and often an actual character to place in—almost every position on the circuit. He represents the professional world of books by creating publisher- and editor-characters literally by the dozen; he addresses warehousing and transportation when he counts and inventories newspaper publications (the 40,000 to 60,000 daily impressions of the "Jupiter," and still greater numbers of penny dreadfuls and penny dailies, are often remarked), follows them by rail, shows them being read on trains (*Last Chronicle of Barset*) and in reading rooms (*Barchester Towers*), and even tracks their trajectory overseas (*The Last Chronicle of Barset*). Individual articles are tracked around Darnton's entire loop from authorial composition to reader's reception, and sometimes over several laps, as Trollope shows how Victorian periodical texts could be solicited (*Phineas Finn, Barchester Towers*), drafted and rejected ("Frederick Pickering"), suppressed or nearly suppressed before publication (*The Warden, Phineas Redux*), litigated or threatened with litigation (*Cousin Henry, Dr. Wortle's School*), concealed from possible readers (*Framley Parsonage*), and passed between readers from hand to hand (*The Warden, The Last Chronicle of Barset*). Furthermore, characters in Trollope's books produce periodical articles not—or not only—for self-expression or financial gain, but to achieve a range of real-world political, economic, or professional goals, and these intentions may succeed, or fall short, or misfire entirely (as in *The Warden, Barchester Towers*, and *Framley Parsonage*, respectively). Trollope developed a similarly complex interest in the career of the working journalist, and he follows young male characters as they weigh literary careers (*Mr. Scarborough's Family, The Bertrams*), succeed as periodical writers (*He Knew He Was Right, Phineas Finn*), are diverted into other career paths (*The Bertrams, Orley Farm*), or fail utterly (poor "Frederick Pickering" again).

   Trollope further recognizes, and illustrates throughout his novels, that the publication of texts in his culture does not have effects only in the two-dimensional loop of the Darnton circuit, but that published articles also make contact with one another, begetting other articles that modify the original conversation, so that there can be no return "full circle" to an initial or near-initial state of discourse. Miss Mackenzie's love triangle with Mr. Maguire and her cousin is one sort of problem when it is still private, a different one after the Littlebath "Christian Examiner" starts printing Maguire's leaders about "The Lion and the Lamb," and a different one still when a metropolitan newspaper begins to comment on the matter, transforming it into a national conversation.

Finally, Trollope understands that genre is a key dimension and determinant of meaning in the world of discourse. He knows that different genres, for a variety of highly context-specific reasons, must interpret the same events differently, see different events as worthy of representation (and of different kinds of interpretation), and that these differences in worldview and the tensions between them are what actually produce the common reader's everyday experience of public discourse. Ferdinand Alf is a personal friend of Lady Carbury, but his professional knowledge tells him that "eulogy is invariably dull" and that a newspaper "that wishes to make its fortune should never waste its columns and weary its readers by praising anything" (12), and the result of this confluence of motives is his devastating treatment of "Criminal Queens." But Trollope also knows that Alf's paper is not the only one in existence, and two good reviews still make Lady Carbury's book a success. In *Barchester Towers,* Tom Towers's endorsement of Slope takes the shape it does partly because of their friendship, partly because of Slope's implied promise to support the "Jupiter" line on ecclesiastical matters, and partly also because Towers has relatively few topics on hand suitable for the omniscient treatment the leading-article genre requires, and he has a leader page to fill. Such complex intersections of situation with genre, Trollope knows, are simply how newspapers function.

Trollope is therefore a fully practical Bakhtinian theorist of periodical, literary, and public discourse. Coded into thirty years of his novels are a running series of observations and snapshots of the nature, relationships, and conflicts of the mid-Victorian world of letters, and these, read and analyzed today, may have nearly as much potential to contextualize our readings of generic interactions of mid-Victorian Britain as Darnton's original diagram had to expand author-focused literary history into a wider history of the book. Trollope may indeed be the first British book historian in the fully modern sense—the first to explore the ways a published text arises from, and takes part in, a sequence (or cascade, or chain reaction) of intersecting public conversations.

Trollope has no single portrait of a journalistic community as nuanced and multidimensional as the one in Thackeray's *Pendennis,* nor can he weave different discourse forms through free indirect discourse with the virtuosity of Dickens. These authors' achievements in journalism as well as literature fully deserve the attention and the full-length studies they have received. But their perspectives have a gap that Trollope does not have, and that perhaps only Trollope can help us fill. Though there are levels of characterization and discourse on which Dickens and Thackeray are the greater artists, and while their works may indeed ultimately reveal more of the nature of Victorian journalism, modern readers may not be able to comprehend those insights without the explicitly analytical reconstruction of the world of mid-Victorian letters that only Trollope seems interested in trying to provide.

Trollope's contemporaries were pretty sure they knew why *Saint Pauls* was a failure: there were levels on which the press outsider Trollope apparently just didn't know how to be a successful Victorian editor—though some of Trollope's apparent failure at *Saint Pauls* may not have resulted from his misunderstanding of the discourse, but rather from his refusal to adopt a discourse he understood all too well. But Trollope's disadvantage with respect to the real press insiders of his own time may turn out to be his crucial advantage for scholars today. Trollope may have the potential to become the twenty-first-century book historian's best proxy observer of Victorian journalism, precisely because he always seems to have seen periodicals with the perspective of a reader and consumer, and to always have remained interested in the way published discourse reaches and circulates within readers' lives. Trollope is less interested in how writers felt as they produced discourse than in the ways discourses make readers feel; less in the solitary act of writing than in the communal acts of publishing, distributing, sharing, and reacting to texts. Journalistic texts matter, in Trollope, less because of the writer's investment in them of time, experience, or creative power than because they will be read by hundreds or thousands (or forty to sixty thousand), bringing public matters into the ken of private lives, and exposing aspects of private lives to a public super-conversation that reaches nearly every member of the society. For the vast majority of the Victorian newspaper's tens and eventually hundreds of thousands of readers, it was Trollope's perspective—the circulating, omnipresent press as it appeared to its audience—that did the cultural work of journalism, and in that sense, an insider's view must always partly misrepresent how press discourse functioned in the lived experience of the real Victorian "common reader."

4 THE *Reviewer's* TALE

George Eliot and the End(s) of Journalistic Apprenticeship

Not an analysis of consciousness in the form of a sole and single *I*, but precisely an analysis of the interactions of many consciousnesses; not many people in the light of a single consciousness, but precisely an analysis of many equally privileged and fully valid consciousnesses.

MIKHAIL BAKHTIN, "Toward a Reworking of the Dostoevsky Book"

IF THE RELATIONSHIP BETWEEN JOURNALISTIC FORMS and the major works of Anthony Trollope and Harriet Martineau is only now and gradually being recognized, the same can certainly not be said for George Eliot. The first useful handlist of Trollope's journalism did not appear until 1983, and a selected edition of Martineau's *Daily News* articles first saw print in 1994, but an edition of the essays written by Marian Evans Lewes for the *Westminster Review* was proposed in 1860, and an authorized edition including a selection of them was already out in 1884, just a few years after her death. The scholarly edition still standard today, Thomas Pinney's *Essays of George Eliot,* was originally published in 1963. Furthermore, the journalistic essays of this great novelist have been taken seriously and studied closely by a full generation of George Eliot scholars, and two essays in particular seem to have joined the teaching canon of college undergraduate classroom texts.[1]

Scholars who use or comment on these essays seem to agree that Marian Evans Lewes's "apprenticeship" to mid-Victorian review journalism in the 1850s had a powerful formative effect on her later fiction, although they trace and interpret this effect quite differently. Some treat the journalistic essays as mature artistic productions of the novelist, as Barbara Hardy does when she includes them in her suggestion that the "tones of George Eliot's authorial voices are various, but there is enough unity and continuity for us to think of them as emanating from one source, and making up one coherent narrating character" (126). Others consider the journalism a course of training, a set of preparatory sketches, or a vital "proving ground" for the themes and voices of George Eliot the novelist, as G. Robert Stange does in "The Voices of the Essayist," a frequently cited article: "George Eliot's apprentice proving ground was the essay, and more noticeably than in the case of any other novelist, the interests and techniques of the essay writer shape her fiction" (312). It was as a review journalist, Stange continues, that George Eliot "came to master, as an essayist, the tonal range displayed by the narrators of her fictions" (315), and Alexis Easley has concurred that George Eliot's "work in periodical journalism played an important role in shaping her identity as a cultural critic" (118). All agree in finding the journalistic writings of the 1850s consistent both intellectually and artistically with the great fictions of George Eliot that followed them.

In the introduction to the 1963 edition of the essays, however, editor Thomas Pinney does acknowledge that Marian Evans the journalist conducts herself in some respects rather differently than George Eliot the novelist. "The reader familiar only with the wide tolerance of her novels will discover in her articles a surprising severity of judgment, and sometimes, as in her attacks on Cumming and Young, a fierce gusto in denunciation" (1), notes Pinney, who explains the difference in somewhat casual psychological terms: "George Eliot wrote most of her articles in the 1850s, after she had outgrown the self-conscious awkwardness of her provincial days and before she took on the new self-consciousness of her fame. They have in consequence the freedom and occasional raciness typical of her mind in those years" (1). But if the journalism was a product of her carefree youth, the author gave it up with surprising readiness, and if it served as a proving ground, she seems to have opted for some other way of testing ideas as soon as finances permitted. The great bulk of her journalism was produced in only two years of hard financial necessity, 1855 and 1856, and George Eliot left journalism with barely a backward glance from the moment John Blackwood paid her £50 for her first long fiction, *The Sad Fortunes of the Reverend Amos Barton.* "I have given up writing 'articles,'" she wrote Bessie Rayner Parkes soon after, and well before the breakthrough success of *Adam Bede,* "having discovered that my vocation lies in other paths" (*Letters* 2: 431). She wrote no more periodical contributions for many years, and only seven in the remainder of her life, none of them conventional review essays (*Essays* 455). Once she became an established novelist, in fact, George Eliot actually took steps to suppress her journalism. She flatly refused a request by John Chapman in 1860 to republish a collection of her work for the *Westminster*,[2] and though at the end of her life she did revise a few of the longer articles for an authorized edition, she left instructions that no others be republished (*Essays* vii).

Her decision to abjure, and then retroactively erase, her connection with periodical writing and journalism is in sharp contrast to the choices of other Victorian novelists at similar levels of reputation, who generally not only stayed close to the periodical marketplace but often took well-paid "star" editorships as one of the benefits of their success, among them Charles Dickens (variously editor of *Household Words, All the Year Round,* and the *Daily News*), Anthony Trollope (*Saint Pauls*), W. M. Thackeray (*Cornhill*), and M. E. Braddon (*Belgravia*).

It is hard not to suspect that, informed by Marian Evans Lewes's experience of the periodicals of the mid-1850s, George Eliot came into existence in 1857 with an aversion to journalism.[3] This aversion is actually attested in her letters, despite her loyalty to partner George Henry Lewes, who remained an active newspaper and magazine contributor, and her courtesy to many friends who also wrote for periodicals. "I am a wretchedly bad judge of what a newspaper should be," she confessed in a letter of September 1857 to Parkes (then editor of the *Waverly Journal* and soon to help found the *English Woman's Review*): "—a person who dislikes wine can never be a good 'taster' and I only read newspapers as a hard duty" (*Letters* 2: 379–80). So when scholars such as Stange write that "we read George Eliot's pieces because of the light they shed on the opinions and themes of a great novelist" (316), they are right in important ways they have yet to acknowledge. Before critics and literary historians can use the journalism of Marian Lewes to understand the novels of George Eliot, their first task must be to account for how and why the novelist's own ultimate response to those writings, and to much of the rest of Victorian journalism, was to reject them.

Reconstructing George Eliot's critique of her own journalism is a difficult maneuver, however, in the absence of any formal statement of it. The problem is especially difficult because the articles are undeniably *good* journalism—the reviews are well researched and written with craft, and the "slashing" satires of mid-Victorian "lady novelists" and Evangelical preachers remain wickedly witty even for a generation less familiar with their particular subjects. The author's "accurately informed, wide-ranging intelligence . . . gives her articles the weight and strength that has made them endure far better than the ordinary run of Victorian journalism," as Pinney remarks (1).

But perhaps the chief reason that George Eliot's rejection of journalism has been hard for critics to note and analyze is that scholarship on Victorian periodicals has rarely approached mid-Victorian journalism as a discourse that came preloaded with its own significant—and limited—worldview, rhetorical tools, and ideological assumptions. To modern readers unfamiliar with these specific conventions, the voice of teaching authority claimed by Marian Evans Lewes the reviewer sounds very much like the one used by George Eliot the novelist, and it has been easy for critics to overlook or minimize the differences between those voices in the search for a unified theory of the George Eliot oeuvre. In fact, however, the differences are profound, and of precisely the kind that George Eliot could tolerate the least. Only a clear understanding of how the genre conventions of Victorian review journalism constrained both what she could say and how she could say it will, I believe, enable us to understand why George Eliot disavowed journalism as soon as she found another way to make a living.

The dilemma apparently faced by Marian Evans the periodical editor and Marian Lewes the periodical writer in the 1850s was that her own beliefs about the ethics of authority and instruction conflicted with the major ideological assumptions and rhetorical practices of mid-Victorian review journalism. Believing in sympathetic connection between individuals, she found herself writing in a discursive model that constructed readers as passive and uncritical adopters of prepackaged opinions. Broadminded and tolerant on political, religious, and social issues, she had to write and edit articles that laid down dogmatic law on the intellectual and social questions of her day. This work went fundamentally against her grain, and the signs of discord and dissent are visible in her essays themselves, where the standard-issue authoritative voice of the anonymous Victorian "man of letters" is frequently undermined. I don't intend to argue here that Marian Evans Lewes's journalism was written in bad faith—the "gusto" in satire that Pinney identifies is also there—but even in the midst of her most severe "slashing" article, "The Poet Young," the author pauses for the self-reassurance of a short digression on the ways satire can be morally justified. More significant still, every target of one of her "slashing" reviews is ultimately convicted of the same fault: misusing—or improperly assuming—the voice of a public teacher.

In the first part of this chapter, I will consider the journalism of Marian Evans Lewes in its cultural context, showing some of the ways she used choices of topic, emphasis, image, and tone to modify and undermine the journalistic voice of authority she was using. In the second part, I hope to show that one of the projects of her earliest fiction was to critique the voice, methods, and assumptions of the review journalism she had just escaped— and in one striking case, to critique her own persona as a reviewer. In "Janet's Repentance" of 1857, George Eliot used authorial voice and narrative to study the real possibilities and fundamental problems of how to form a discourse meant to instruct or enlighten another human soul.

Editor and Reviewer

Quietly taking on the (unpaid) editorial management of the *Westminster Review* under publisher John Chapman from 1851 through 1853, Marian Evans entered review journalism when it was still at a high point in intellectual influence and authority within British culture. In the next decade reformers including Anthony Trollope, John Morley, Thomas Hughes, and Lewes himself (a cofounder of the signed *Fortnightly Review*) would experiment with less dogmatically authoritative forms for periodical writing, but throughout Marian Evans's stint in the periodical press, the persona of the periodical reviewer retained the form Francis Jeffrey and T. B. Macaulay had helped to give it earlier in the century: an impossibly knowledgeable authority who condescendingly did *"all the thinking"* for an intellectually passive reader.[4]

Chapman and Evans did try early in Evans's editorship to make the *Westminster* less intellectually monolithic than other reviews. They introduced an "Independent Section" in which articles could appear that the periodical did not necessarily endorse, and which could be an open forum and "an admirable device for admitting the most advanced opinions." The innovation was before its time, however; as George Eliot biographer Gordon Haight comments: "Contributors like James Martineau, who looked on the *Review* as an organ for advancing a definite program, did not want it to be open to differing opinions," and "after the second number the Section was abandoned" (*George Eliot and John Chapman* 44). The genre expectations of Victorian periodical read-ers and contributors thus defeated Marian Evans's first attempt to construct a public teaching voice of the kind she preferred. As articles began to come in to Evans and Chapman, in fact, it became clear that "advanced" as well as conser-vative thinkers expected to take the persona of an omniscient public oracle as soon as they became reviewers. Every Eliot biographer acknowledges the talent of Chapman's contributors; they included Herbert Spencer, J. S. Mill, Francis W. Newman, J. A. Froude, T. H. Huxley, and both James and Har-riet Martineau. But not even an intellectual "dream team" of this caliber could justify the claim anonymously made by W. R. Greg in the introduction to an article on labor relations, published early in Evans's editorship:

> It is a glorious achievement, and a rich reward for long years of toil and thought . . . [,] to have reached a standing point of mental height and dis-tance from which history can be seen as a connected whole; from which the long perspective of ages, so confused and perplexing when viewed from within, from below, or in detail, presents itself to the observer as a continu-ous stream. . . . Gazing from this focal elevation at that vast aggregate of facts, now glorious, now gloomy, which make up the sad story of humanity, it is sometimes given to us dimly to discern the meaning and the mystery which pervades its course. (61)

Not every *Westminster* article begins with such a remarkable assertion of the writer's own intellectual eminence, of course, but even articles that do not make claims of omniscience in such a brazen way often imply them. Through the popular subgenre of the "slashing article," a review writer could create an impression of intellectual and social superiority by loading an opponent with contempt and condescension. The *Westminster* inherited this tradition with the rest of the genre of the quarterly review. From its first issue in 1802, the *Edinburgh Review* had built much of its reputation and genre identity on the "aptitude for literary demolition" of founders Brougham and Jeffrey (Clive 37). This strategy remained just as effective in 1855, the year the new *Satur-day Review* began to earn its nickname of "Saturday Reviler." The *Westminster* published many articles in this popular mode, but Marian Evans was clearly uncomfortable with their weakness as intellectual discourse. Although she let the articles go into the review, she passed along to Chapman the complaint made by her friend Sara Sophia Hennell about one *Westminster* writer on contemporary English literature: "'In the theological it is mostly slash and scoff, without giving us any confidence that he has any opinions of his own'" (*Letters* 2: 50).

The essays the young Marian Evans had written before connecting herself with the *Westminster* were equally free of omniscience and "slashing." The short series "Poetry and Prose, from the Notebook of an Eccentric" in the *Coventry Herald and Observer* (1846–47) was a fanciful series of moral essays, each in a different genre, from "A Little Fable with a Great Moral," a parable on the lives of two hamadryads, to the dryly witty observations on social and literary interaction in "Hints on Snubbing," which already shows Evans aware of—and ethically opposed to—contemporary journalistic methods for constructing and wielding discursive authority:

> Editors of country newspapers, who feel themselves and their cause in a precarious condition, and who, therefore, as Paley said of himself, cannot afford to keep a conscience, may find a forlorn hope in snubbing. Let them choose for a victim any individual who presumes to avow an opinion in opposition to their own. . . . We assure the dullest poor fellow of an editor, that he may put down such an upstart, and utterly ruin him in the esteem of the majority, by keeping a stock of epithets, like so many little missiles, to be hurled at him on every favourable occasion. (*Essays* 24)

Even the first article she wrote at Chapman's request for the *Westminster,* before leaving Coventry for London, was a thoroughly positive review of Robert Mackay's *The Progress of the Intellect* (1850). The article keeps Mackay's own authority and ideas—not the reviewer's—constantly in the foreground, and Thomas Pinney reads this choice to stay "close to her text, relying heavily upon quotation, paraphrase, and summary" as a sign of intellectual immaturity. It is not until five years later, "the time of the article on Cumming," Pinney writes, that she "learned how to take advantage of the licence given the Victorian journalist to express himself with magisterial anonymity under pretext of noticing other men's books" (Pinney 2).

Little is known about precisely what Marian Evans wrote in the three years she was Chapman's subeditor, however, and what she learned during this "apprenticeship," and what she ultimately thought of the lesson, must be inferred from what she wrote later.[5] Her letters at the time are somewhat contradictory; usually she was frustrated and dissatisfied with each issue before it went to press, but more positive afterward. "I have been ready to tear my hair with disappointment about the next number," she wrote to Charles Bray on 18 March 1853. "We are actually obliged to pay for one paper and put it in the fire. The English Contemporary Literature is worse than ever and the article on Ruth and Villette is unsatisfactory. Then one of the articles is half as long again as it ought to be. In short I am a miserable Editor" (*Letters* 2: 93). Ten days later, after two straight days of "correcting proofs literally from morning till night," she wrote to Hennell: "The Review will be better than I once feared, but not so good as I once hoped" (2: 94). There were corrections of length or style to be made in every article, and although she was never paid for editorial corrections, much prose in every issue must be hers. Before one article could appear in the *Westminster,* she "had to reduce . . . ninety-six pages to thirty-six" but yet not alienate the author—"firmly convinced of his literary prowess"—who was one of Chapman's financial supporters (Haight, *George Eliot* 140). She wrote to Charles and Cara Bray in February 1853: "I am out of spirits about the W[estminster] R[eview]. The editorship is not satisfactory and I should be glad to run away from it altogether. But one thing is clear— that the Review would be a great deal worse if I were not here. This is the only thought that consoles me" (*Letters* 2: 88). Her professionalism did not prevent her from dropping hints to Chapman that her unpaid editorship could not go on indefinitely. Finally, she gave him notice and wrote to Hennell in November 1853: "I told Mr. Chapman yesterday that I wished to give up any connection with the editorship of the Westminster. . . . I shall be much more satisfied on many accounts to have done with that affair—but I shall find the question of supplies rather a difficult one this year (*Letters* 2: 127–28). She quit the *Westminster* after the January issue, and in July 1854 began her open relationship with Lewes by leaving with him for Germany.

When they returned they were effectively a married couple, but one in very straitened financial circumstances. If the question of supplies had been hard for Marian Evans alone, with her bare £100 per year inheritance, Lewes had additional financial responsibility for his legal wife, Agnes, and all the children Agnes had borne both to Lewes and to her lover, Thornton Hunt. Work for the *Westminster* paid better than any other periodical writing—£12.12.0 per issue for the Belles Lettres section alone[6]—and it was no coincidence that Marian Evans Lewes immediately became a prolific writer of review articles. Some of her topics were suggested by Chapman, some by Marian herself, but she wrote all of them quickly, and she clearly designed her articles to be accepted by her target market. The first priority was to sell copy, and she wryly told Charles Bray in January 1857 that she now measured her success as a writer in terms of income: "You needn't observe any secrecy about *articles* of mine. It is an advantage (pecuniarily) to me that I should be known as the writer of the articles in the Westminster. And I am a very calculating person now—valuing approbation as representing guineas" (*Letters* 2: 287).

The conditions of production of Marian Evans Lewes's review essays are thus that they were produced under the impetus of hard financial pressure for a periodical she had washed her hands of—with relief—just six months before. This incentive obviously does not make the work any less worthy of study ("No man but a blockhead ever wrote, except for money," said Dr. Johnson), nor does it follow from the pressures of this situation that Marian Evans wrote a single word she did not believe—her strong integrity would have forbidden that. But she had the strongest possible motive to write anything she did believe according to the generic rules and conventions that would guarantee a sale to Chapman's *Westminster*. This was no time for experiments and innovations that might, like the "Independent Section," fall flat.

Critics such as Pinney and Stange are no doubt correct, therefore, when they observe that the essays of 1855 and 1856 conform closely to Victorian conventions for essay journalism, and that "from the beginning George Eliot accepted, apparently not unhappily, the convention of the *male* reviewer. The voice she assumed in her anonymous articles is that of an experienced masculine commentator, wise, learned, balanced in judgment" (Stange 317). But they may go a step too far in assuming that her use of these conventions was a fully autonomous creative choice, which can therefore be read as a key to her later artistic practice—as when Stange argues that "the way the journalistic critic proposed to see and judge character is, we come to realize, a sketch of the procedure she will follow in her fiction. . . . The author assumes the functions of both social historian and analytic critic" (319). In fact, the argument I am pursuing here is that although the intellectual, social, and moral issues addressed in her essays are indeed frequently those George Eliot studies in her novels, the "procedure" it was necessary to follow to render these subjects into saleable copy in the genre of the quarterly review article is anti-thetical to her later practice as a novelist. Indications that she was troubled by the voice of the oracular and sometimes "slashing" Reviewer she has nec-essarily adopted appear both in the topics she chooses and in the rhetorical self-consciousness of her treatments of them. Marian Evans Lewes's earliest moves to critique her own journalism are thus embedded directly in the arti-cles themselves, as deliberate moves to distance herself ironically from the genre conventions of journalism.

Some of these moves are simple self-aware one-liners, as when she intro-duces a survey of new novels for the July 1855 *Westminster* with a reflection on childhood mushroom-hunting, and then explains, "We speak in parables, after the fashion of the wise, amongst whom Reviewers are always to be reckoned" (*Essays* 125). Some of them are rather subtler, as when the conclusion of her witty slashing article "Silly Novels by Lady Novelists" (October 1856) turns out to reflect as much on the voice of the Reviewer as on the silly novelist:

> A really cultured woman, like a really cultured man, is all the simpler and
> the less obtrusive for her knowledge. . . ; she does not make it a pedestal
> from which she flatters herself that she commands a complete view of men
> and things, but makes it a point of observation from which to form a right
> estimate of herself. . . . In conversation she is the least formidable of women,
> because she understands you, without wanting to make you aware that you
> *can't* understand her. She does not give you information, which is the raw
> material of culture,—she gives you sympathy, which is its subtlest essence.
> (*Essays* 317)

Notwithstanding such moments of reflexivity, the "Silly Novels" article, and others including "Evangelical Teaching: Dr. Cumming" (October 1855), "Worldliness and Other-Worldliness: The Poet Young" (January 1857), and the shorter *Leader* piece "Lord Brougham's Literature" (7 July 1855), are genu-ine "slashing articles" in the grand old style, and Marian Evans Lewes could slash with keen effectiveness. The first of these to appear in print is directed at Brougham, whose *Lives of Men of Letters and Science* (1845–46) is attacked as heavy and clumsy—"third-rate biographies in the style of a literary hack" (*Essays* 138)—but above all as hypocritical, since Brougham is notorious for the very faults he finds in others: "The first thing that strikes us in these *Lives* is the slovenliness of their style, which is thrown almost ludicrously into relief by the fact that many of Lord Brougham's pages are occupied with criticism of other men's style" (139).

Even here, however, there are hints that aggressive writing of this kind did not come naturally to Marian Lewes. She closes the Brougham article with a sudden self-consciousness, pointing out, interestingly, that there is a literary genre that is superior at the task she has been trying to perform through review-essay journalism: "We must remember that when indignation makes reviews instead of Juvenalian verses, the result is not equally enjoyed by the reader. So we restrain our noble rage" (142). And when a letter from Charles and Cara Bray objected to her treatment of Brougham, she wrote to justify herself: "The article on Lord Brougham was written conscientiously, and you seem to have misunderstood its purpose, in taking it for mere word quibbling. I consider it criminal in a man to prostitute Literature for the purposes of his own vanity and this is what Lord Brougham has done. . . . Literature is Fine Art, and the man who writes mere literature with insolvent slovenliness is as inexcusable as a man who gets up in a full drawing-room to sing Rossini's music in a cracked voice and out of tune" (*Letters* 2: 210). As this part of her letter closes, however, Evans moves once again to distinguish the ideas she believes in from the journalistic forms she does not: "I say thus much in vindication of my view of right, not at all in vindication of my article."

None of the slashing articles seems to have been undertaken for the fun of "literary demolition." Marian Evans Lewes had to feel strongly that a slashing was deserved, and only one transgression could provoke her to show that dangerous edge: an example of intellectual authority dishonestly invoked or improperly used. In the same month "Lord Brougham's Literature" appeared in the *Leader,* an otherwise positive review of Charles Kingsley's *Westward Ho!* finds fault only with Kingsley's awkward attempts to improve his swashbuckling historical romance with passages of moral instruction: "[Kingsley] sees, feels, and paints vividly, but he theorizes illogically and moralizes absurdly. If he would confine himself to his true sphere, he might be a teacher in the sense in which every great artist is a teacher—namely, by giving us his higher sensibility as a medium, a delicate acoustic or optical instrument, bringing home to our coarser senses what would otherwise be unperceived by us" (*Essays* 126). Faults of pedagogy are also the focus of a review of Geraldine Jewsbury's didactic *Constance Herbert.* The reviewer fully shares the novelist's "principle," but damns the "mode" Jewsbury uses to teach it: "The *mode* in which she enforces the principle [of duty], both theoretically in the *Envoi* and illustratively in the story of her novel, implies, we think, a false view of life, and virtually nullifies the very magnanimity she inculcates" (*Essays* 134). Jewsbury's novel had shown a heroine renouncing a lover on grounds of principle, then discovering that he had been unworthy of her all along. This method of illustration assures readers that they live in a universe that will make them happy as long as they are good. To the reviewer this teaching method is worse than overhopeful; it is actually harmful to true moral growth, since it tries to promote "morality" only on the basis of self-interest:

> It is not the fact that what duty calls on us to renounce, will invariably prove "not worth the keeping"; and if it *were* the fact, renunciation would cease to be moral heroism, and would be simply a calculation of prudence. . . . The notion that duty looks stern, but all the while has her hand full of sugar-plums, with which she will reward us by-and-by, is the favourite cant of optimists . . . but it really undermines all true moral development by perpetually substituting something extrinsic as a motive to action, instead of the immediate impulse of love or justice, which alone makes an action truly moral. (134–35)

Her next "slasher" is the famous castigation of the Evangelical preacher Dr. Cumming, and the first indication of her angle of attack is her title, which is not "Evangelical Belief" or even "Evangelical Doctrine," but "Evangelical Teaching." The second is her introduction, which dwells with heavy irony on Cumming's lack of qualifications to instruct anyone:

> Given, a man with moderate intellect, a moral standard not higher than the average, some rhetorical affluence and great glibness of speech, what is the career in which, without the aid of birth or money, he may most easily attain power and reputation in English society? Where is that Goshen of mediocrity in which a smattering of science and learning will pass for profound instruction, where platitudes will be accepted as wisdom, bigoted narrowness as holy zeal, unctuous egoism as God-given piety? Let such a man become an evangelical preacher; he will then find it possible to reconcile small ability with great ambition, superficial knowledge with the prestige

of erudition, a middling morale with a high reputation for sanctity. (*Essays* 159–60)

In this article, just as she had done in the review of *Constance Herbert*, Evans Lewes the reviewer reads the contradiction between the *message* of the public teacher Cumming and his *method*—or, in other terms, between the content of his language and its genre form—to argue that the pedagogical narrowness of Cumming is inherently harmful to his readers, even if some of his doctrines might be true. "We concern ourselves less with what he holds to be Christian truth than with his manner of enforcing that truth, less with the doctrines he teaches than with the moral spirit and tendencies of his teaching" (165). Even this seriously intended intervention in religious politics, however, contains a backhanded blow at the discourse and genre forms of actual journalism. After the tone of her critique has been established, one of her criticisms of Cumming is that he "is essentially a journalist, who writes sermons instead of leading articles, who, instead of venting diatribes against her Majesty's Ministers, directs his power of invective against Cardinal Wiseman and the Puseyites,—instead of declaiming on public spirit, perorates on the 'glory of God'" (*Essays* 164–65). (Could it have also occurred to Marian Lewes that a fair response to the rhetorical question that opened the essay, the one hypothesizing the best profession for someone who wishes to make a "smattering" of learning pass for profundity, would have been "a reviewer"?)

Serious moral energy is also behind the sharp satire in "Silly Novels by Lady Novelists," partly provoked by Lady Chatterton's *Compensation* (1856), even the title of which raised Evans Lewes's hackles. She wrote to John Chapman on 5 July 1856 that "I have long wanted to fire away at the doctrine of Compensation, which I detest, considered as a theory of life, "and two weeks later she wrote again to propose that "an article on 'Silly Women's Novels' might be made the vehicle of some wholesome truth as well as of some amusement" (*Letters* 2: 258).

The pose she adopts to write it is that of a literary naturalist. "Silly novels by Lady Novelists are a genus with many species," she begins, "determined by the particular quality of silliness that predominates in them—the frothy, the prosy, the pious, or the pedantic. But it is a mixture of all these—a composite order of feminine fatuity, that produces the largest class of such novels, which we shall distinguish as the *mind-and-millinery* species" (*Essays* 301). In these novels the heroines are credited with immense intellectual powers in addition to wealth and beauty, and part of the silly novelist's project seems to be to become a figure of intellectual authority herself by attributing wisdom and learning to her protagonist. The reviewer points out ironically that the effect achieved is exactly the reverse: "There can be no difficulty in conceiving the depth of the heroine's erudition, when that of the authoress is so evident" (305).

In the "*oracular* species" of novels, the lessons taught are generally High Church doctrine; in the "*white neck-cloth* species," they are Evangelical doctrine; and in "the least readable of silly women's novels ... [,] the *modern-antique* species" (320) of bad historical novels, they are a smattering of historical facts by which authors attribute "their rhetorical arguments to Jewish high-priests and Greek philosophers" (321). The chief fault with these subgenres is not so much their unlikely plotting and wish-fulfillment characterizations—though these are noted—as their clumsy attempts to "expound the writer's religious, philosophical, or moral theories. ... To judge from their writings, there are certain ladies who think that an amazing ignorance, both of science and of life, is the best possible qualification for forming an opinion on the knottiest moral and speculative questions" (310). At least one feminist critic has characterized this slashing article as "unsisterly" (McCormack 41), but the reviewer specifically acknowledges the "excellence" achieved by the non-silly novelists "Harriet Martineau, Currer Bell and Mrs. Gaskell," and makes it clear that the target of her satire is only the pretentious writers who assert intellectual credentials they have not earned, and who hurt the cause of education for women when they "volunteer themselves as representatives of the feminine intellect" (316).

The pose of the literary naturalist returns for the last time in "Worldliness and Other-Worldliness: The Poet Young," published just as the writer was making her transition to fiction. The longest—and, at £25.0.0, best-remunerated—article Marian Evans Lewes wrote for the *Westminster*, it is a tour de force of careful scholarship and keen aesthetic and moral textual analysis. Both the moral and the aesthetic points she argues are important and convincing, but the persona and stance she uses to make them are, oddly, an elevated omniscience comparable to that claimed by W. R. Greg:

> The study of men, as they have appeared in different ages, and under various social conditions, may be considered as the natural history of the race. Let us, then, for a moment imagine ourselves, as students of this natural history, "dredging" the first half of the eighteenth century in search of specimens. About the year 1730, we have hauled up a remarkable individual of the species *divine*—a surprising name, considering the nature of the animal before us, but we are used to unsuitable names in natural history. Let us examine this individual at our leisure. (337)

The pages that follow dissect Young the man sharply enough, as avaricious, fawning, and sycophantic to patrons and to the court. But the real point—and edge—of the argument appears when the reviewer turns to the moral teaching contained in Young's religious and satiric poetry. There are a limited number of moral and aesthetic justifications for using the genre tools of satire, this satirical reviewer argues, and as she enumerates them the passage becomes as much a justification of her own current rhetoric as an indictment of Young's: "His satire has neither the terrible vigour, the lacerating energy of genuine indignation, nor the humour which owns loving fellowship with the poor human nature it laughs at; nor yet the personal bitterness which, as in Pope's characters of Sporus and Atticus, ensures those living touches by virtue of which the individual and particular in Art becomes the universal and immortal" (362). "Genuine indignation" is clearly the warrant this reviewer intends to present, and her indignation is justified not merely because Young's poetry is superficial and mannered, but because the way he constructs religious belief is fundamentally false to lived experience and genuine morality. "If it were not for the prospect of immortality, [Young] considers, it would be wise and agreeable to be indecent, or to murder one's father; and, heaven apart, it would be extremely irrational in any man not to be a knave" (337–38). Her criticism of Young's reliance on moral abstractions, and on his argument that only religious belief can restrain human immorality, leads the reviewer to an eloquent defense of realism in art and simple sympathy in human relations. These passages are frequently cited by scholars as early statements of George Eliot's moral philosophy, and G. Robert Stange in particular observes that "in her analysis of Young's moral deficiencies George Eliot emphasizes just that set of vices and virtues which she was to treat again and again in her novels." Stange calls the essay "a prolegomenon to novel writing," and suggests that "if it were not for the unusually indignant tone of [the] last section, one could say that in these pages we were listening for the first time to the voice of the authoritative, learned narrator of the mature novels" (320–21).

Stange does acknowledge, however, that the tone of the Young piece is unlike the later George Eliot, that the writer's rhetorical pose as a "naturalist" is soon replaced by that of "a moralist and sensitive critic of art," and that her digression on the morality of satire seems significantly reflexive. But he does not put these observations together as signs that the *message* the ethical observer wishes to express in this essay is in fundamental conflict with the *genre* of the periodical review itself, and that the writer herself is struggling with that problem. The critique Marian Evans Lewes is trying to make about the shallow impersonality of Young's art seems close to hypocrisy (Brougham's damning fault, we remember) when it is spoken with the shallow impersonality of an anonymous periodical critic. Tellingly, near the end of the article the writer attempts to solve this problem by breaking out of the reviewer's monologic and authoritative voice to introduce a second and more intimate persona to her article who might make the moral critique more effectively. She summons up as a second narrator a religious skeptic with a conscience. "We can imagine the man who 'denies his soul immortal' replying," she begins, then switches to the hypothetical skeptic's first-person "I" to address the reader with direct earnestness: "It is a pang to me to witness the suffering of a fellow-being, and I feel his suffering more acutely because he is *mortal*—because his life is so short, and I would have it, if possible, filled with happiness and not misery. Through my union and fellowship with the men and women I *have* seen, I feel a like, though a fainter, sympathy with those I have *not* seen; and I am able so to live in imagination with the generations to come" (*Essays* 374). After a page in this voice, she returns to the original critical persona with a transitional "Thus far might answer the man," but she needs yet a third persona to buttress her reviewing voice before she can finish her critique. She chooses that of Young's eighteenth-century contemporary Cowper, and his contrasting artistic example is the note with which she is able to conclude. "In Young we have the type of that deficient human sympathy, that impiety towards the present and the visible, which flies for its motives, its sanctities, and its religion, to the remote, the vague and the unknown: in Cowper we have the type of that genuine love which cherishes things in proportion to their nearness, and feels its reverence grow in proportion to the intimacy of its knowledge" (385).

The textual history of the Young article bears out these many internal signs of discursive strain. Pinney notes that the article was begun "at some point before 5 April 1856," when Chapman agreed to her proposal to write on Young, but she deferred it twice for other projects, telling the publisher at one point, "I didn't think well of what I had written, and so was going to give it up, but when I read it to Mr. Lewes he said he thought it would be the best article I had written" (*Letters* 2: 258). She put the article aside again to write *Amos Barton*, and finally finished it only in early December 1856 (*Essays* 335–36). Even then she was not done with it—of the few articles George Eliot decided to revise late in life for what became the posthumous *Essays and Leaves from a Note-Book*, it is the one she altered most, and her changes seem largely meant to mute the journalistic brashness of the "slashing" voice.[7]

The writer's struggle in the Young piece is clearly not over the message itself, or the terms by which Young himself fell short; rather, the writer struggles to find a genre form and voice that can embody that critique appropriately. To borrow the terms she had herself applied to Geraldine Jewsbury, the writer needed to find a *"mode"* with which to "enforce" her ethical principles that would not itself tend to undermine or nullify them. As we have seen, Marian Lewes was keenly alive to the potential for tension and rupture between generic form and intellectual content, between teaching method and doctrine, and in her essays and letters as well as later novels she frequently records the conviction that the more important element by far is method. She can praise Thomas Carlyle and John Ruskin as great public teachers in the same passage in which she repudiates all the specific content of their arguments: Carlyle "does not, perhaps, convince you, but he strikes you, undeceives you, animates you," she wrote in an 1855 *Leader* essay. "It is not as a theorist, but as a great and beautiful human nature, that Carlyle influences us" (*Essays* 213–14). A few years later she wrote to Sara Hennell that she considered Ruskin "one of the great Teachers of the day—his absurdities on practical points do no harm, but the grand doctrines of truth and sincerity in art, and the nobleness and solemnity of our human life . . . must be stirring up young minds in a promising way" (*Letters* 2: 422). From great teachers she forgives even "absurdities," but the opposite case—where the doctrine seems right but the method is false—draws only scorn.

The method of truly moral teaching, for George Eliot, is to enlarge a listener or reader's worldview through discourse that calls forth a sympathetic emotional response, rather than merely winning intellectual assent to a set of views and opinions. "I have had heart-cutting experience that opinions are a poor cement between human souls," she wrote to Charles Bray in 1859; "the only effect I ardently long to produce by my writings, is that those who read them should be better able to *imagine* and to *feel* the pains and joys of those who differ from themselves in everything but the broad fact of being struggling erring human creatures" (*Letters* 3: 111). The journalistic review essay of 1856 had been proven to be an effective genre for conveying opinions and views, but it was not the vehicle to contain or express such a philosophy. She could not remain a journalist-reviewer and pursue this project—George Eliot the novelist needed a voice of her own.

The Voice of the Teacher

The narrating persona is intimate, personal, and earnest[8] in all three *Scenes of Clerical Life* George Eliot wrote in 1856–57 as her trial run as a novelist: "The Sad Fortunes of the Reverend Amos Barton," "Mr. Gilfil's Love-Story," and "Janet's Repentance." Eliot constructs her narrator for these stories as an older man reflecting with gentle sympathy on the events of his childhood and the history of his hometown. From time to time this narrator appears as a young boy at the fringe of the narratives, and George Eliot's use of this male persona was apparently so convincing that of her first readers, only Charles Dickens was certain that the unknown novelist was a woman.

"Janet's Repentance" is not often read today; it has been eclipsed for modern critics by the major novels that followed it, just as it was in George Eliot's lifetime.[9] A single, long direct address by the narrator of "Janet's Repentance" is one of the few parts of the story that scholars notice, and it is usually cited as yet another early statement of the philosophical program to be followed in George Eliot's fiction. Read in the context of the author's own journalism, however, the same passage is clearly also a look back at Marian Evans Lewes's journalistic practice, and an explicit renunciation of the voice and methods of the Reviewer. Pausing her narrative to consider the Evangelical curate Edgar Tryan, she invokes a disengaged and impersonal "critic" who should sound familiar:

Any one looking at [Tryan] with the bird's-eye glance of a critic might perhaps say that he made the mistake of identifying Christianity with a too narrow doctrinal system; that he saw God's work too exclusively in antagonism
to the world, the flesh, and the devil; that his intellectual culture was too
limited—and so on; making Mr. Tryan the text for a wise discourse on the
characteristics of the Evangelical school in his day. . . .

    "One of the Evangelical clergy, a disciple of Venn," says the critic from
his bird's-eye station. "Not a remarkable specimen; the anatomy and habits
of his species have been determined long ago." (229)

Marian Evans Lewes had recently treated two churchmen to the disdain of a
critical "bird's-eye glance," and twice she had herself taken the persona of the
critic-as-naturalist, first tallying up the species under the genus "Silly Novels," then dredging the eighteenth century to haul up the poet Young. But the
novelist-narrator explicitly positions herself differently:

> I am not poised at that lofty height. I am on the level and in the press with
> him, as he struggles his way along the stony road, through the crowd of
> unloving fellow-men. He is stumbling, perhaps; his heart now beats fast with
> dread, now heavily with anguish; his eyes are sometimes dim with tears,
> which he makes haste to dash away; he pushes manfully on, with fluctuating
> faith and courage, with a sensitive failing body. . . .
>
>   Surely the only true knowledge of our fellow-man is that which enables
> us to feel with him—which gives us a fine ear for the heart-pulses that are
> beating under the mere clothes of circumstance and opinion. Our subtlest
> analysis of schools and sects must miss the essential truth, unless it be lit up
> by the love that sees in all forms of human thought and work, the life and
> death struggles of separate human beings. (229)

In "Evangelical Teaching," the reviewer had tarred all of Evangelicalism with
the brush she used on Cumming, but in "Janet's Repentance," Tryan's doctrines are beside the point. His virtues are those shared by all effective moral
teachers, not a function of his sect.

    George Eliot explained this project in a letter to John Blackwood, who had
shown in a letter that he misunderstood the first part of her story. "The collision in the drama is not at all between 'bigotted churchmanship' and evangeli-

calism, but between *ir*religion and religion," she wrote to Blackwood on 11 June 1857. "Religion in this case happens to be represented by evangelicalism. . . . I thought I had made it apparent in my sketch of Milby feelings on the advent of Mr. Tryan that the conflict lay between immorality and morality—irreligion and religion. Mr. Tryan will carry the reader's sympathy. It is through him that Janet is brought to repentance" (*Letters* 2: 347).

"Janet's Repentance," set in a provincial English town in the 1820s, is carefully designed to reflect George Eliot's views of a better kind of engaged discourse between human beings on the level of plot, as well as to embody them within narrative voice. It does this partly by drawing conflicting examples of successful and unsuccessful discourses, almost irrespective of the actual content of each discourse, just as Eliot had promised Blackwood. The false teacher is the lawyer Dempster, husband of the protagonist, Janet Dempster. Though a leading figure in the town, Dempster is a brutal drunkard. He is given the first words in the story, and they characterize him immediately through his choice of a bullying, monologic discourse that figures and confronts its listeners in the abstract, rather than engaging anyone present in an actual conversation. "'No!' said lawyer Dempster, in a loud, rasping, oratorical tone, struggling against chronic huskiness, 'as long as my Maker grants me power of voice and power of intellect, I will take every legal means to resist the introduction of demoralizing, methodistical doctrine into this parish; I will not supinely suffer an insult to be inflicted on our venerable pastor, who has given us sound instruction for half a century'" (169). The reader soon learns that living with Dempster, who is physically as well as discursively a bully, has literally driven his wife to drink. Janet suffers keenly, numbs her pain with alcohol, and withdraws in self-pity from friends and family. But at the same time she remains under Dempster's intellectual domination, adopting his political and religious opinions as a matter of course. When he begins to persecute the new Evangelical curate, Edgar Tryan, who has proposed a series of evening lectures, she helps Dempster draw up a cruelly satirical playbill—the written genre form of his oral rhetorical abusiveness—and post it around town.

When she happens to overhear Tryan speaking compassionately and sympathetically to a dying woman, confessing his own fear of death, however, his voice of sympathy moves Janet deeply. When she reaches her own lowest point, having been thrown out of her own house late at night by Dempster, she agrees to talk to Tryan. In a single meeting he sets her on the path to recovery by reaching out to her in a wholly personal and nondoctrinal voice. Confessing his own sinful past and how he has tried to redeem it with a life of service, Tryan begins to draw Janet out of her self-absorption: "Ah, what a difference between our lives!" she tells him. "You have been choosing pain, and working, and denying yourself; and I have been thinking only of myself" (261). Under Tryan's guidance Janet finds relief from self-pity and isolation in service to his church, her family, and the community of Milby.

By poising Janet between Dempster and Tryan, George Eliot seems to have set up a discursive thought experiment, the terms of which have been made remarkably pure. Dempster's speech and writing are nearly the essence of what Bakhtin was (much) later to call monologic discourse—though it is heard by his audience, it is not directly or personally addressed to them, or to anyone in particular. Dempster does not converse with any individual listener; he prefers to orate to an audience or to post a handbill, constructing an audience for himself in both cases that is simultaneously everyone and no one. It is surely no accident that George Eliot makes Dempster, who represents the voice of the review-style "critic" in this short novel, a lawyer by profession; Fitzjames Stephen was to write a few years later in the *Cornhill* magazine that the "analogy between the speeches of counsel and [journalistic] leading articles is almost perfect, and is derived from the fact that the speaker and the writer are in essentially the same position" (54). Dempster does not seek to make contact *with* his listeners, much less to learn from them; he only tries to enforce his own point upon them.

By contrast, although he is a clergyman, Tryan never gives monologues, and in fact never even seems to give sermons. His actual, individual, and imperfect self is the basis of all his successful interpersonal encounters. To comfort the dying woman of Milby, Tryan speaks of his own fear of death, putting himself on a level with his listener as a sympathetic equal, rather than above her as a guide or instructor. To reach the alcoholic Janet, he confesses a much deeper past sin of his own. Janet's problems, Tryan realizes, stem less from any lack of moral information than from simple moral isolation. Following Marian Lewes's insight of a few years previously, then, he does not try to give her information or instruction, the raw material of human communication, but rather sympathy, its subtlest essence: "Mr. Tryan hesitated again. He saw that the first thing Janet needed was to be assured of sympathy. She must be made to feel that her anguish was not strange to him; that he entered into the only half-expressed secrets of her spiritual weakness, before any other message of consolation could find its way to her heart. The tale of the Divine Pity was never yet believed from lips that were not felt to be moved by human pity" (258). Just as George Eliot's narrator has already forsworn use of the "bird's-eye station" of the critic to analyze Tryan, Tryan himself here relinquishes all claim to an authoritative and morally superior voice, even when his task is to reclaim a sinful soul. He does this from sheer practical conviction that sympathetic discourse is not only the best way to communicate with and redeem Janet, but the only practicable way. The message he wants to convey cannot successfully be transmitted in any genre form but that of individual and engaged personal confession.

Dempster's rasping monologue that opens the novel, then, is actually the beginning of George Eliot's real project in "Janet's Repentance," and the key to her purpose in the story itself. Dempster values "sound instruction"—the doctrinal content of discourse—and conveys it through a bullying authoritative persona that handles responses or potential objections Reviewer-style, by slashing at them or beating them down. Tryan is Dempster's discursive mirror opposite; almost without specific religious doctrine, he is intimate and unrhetorical in his discursive approach, relinquishing personal authority in favor of moral equality with the person to whom he is speaking, and at least as interested in learning about his listener's experiences and thoughts as in conveying his own. The implicit contrast between the critical Reviewer (of Kingsley, of Jewsbury, of the silly novelists) that the writer had been, and the novelist-as-teacher that she had hypothesized in those articles, is here hypostatized into two personifications of discourse, whose damning or redemptive effects on a single human soul can be experimentally compared and observed within a fictional world.

Most critics have noted that "Janet's Repentance" is about sympathy and redemption. But it is also—and more crucially for this moment in George Eliot's early novelistic career—an exploration of the language forms that can either enable or foreclose sympathy and redemption. Sound views and unquestioned authority are the Reviewer's discourse, but no amount of this kind of authoritative holding forth, even of sound views, can communicate a lesson of sympathy, because the reviewer's authoritative discourse does not have the fundamental genre resources to communicate such a lesson. The greater flexibility and dialogic resources of novelistic discourse do provide this capability, however, at least potentially. This, perhaps, helps explain Marian Lewes's keen disappointment in Jewsbury, Kingsley, and the "silly novelists," each of whom had been using a discourse that gave them the potential power to achieve this kind of communication with readers, and who had all missed their opportunities. The genre resources of the novelist permit greater things, George Eliot here recognizes and shows, than any that can be done with the single authoritative voice. The medium of the novel can provide, to use the terms Bakhtin applied to the achievements of Dostoevsky in his own use of the novel, not only "an analysis of consciousness in the form of a sole and single *I*, but precisely an analysis of the interactions of many consciousnesses; not many people in the light of a single consciousness, but precisely an analysis of many equally privileged and fully valid consciousnesses" (*Problems* 289).

"Janet's Repentance" and the other Clerical Scenes were immediately followed—and thrown into shadow—by the critical and popular success of *Adam Bede* (1859), but George Eliot herself did not lose sight of them. In January 1860, having just finished *The Mill on the Floss*, she wrote to Blackwood asking him to keep her earliest stories before the public. "There are ideas presented in these stories about which I care a good deal, and am not sure that I can ever embody again" (*Letters* 3: 240). In February she pressed him again on this subject, specifically mentioning "Janet's Repentance": "I hope 'Clerical Scenes' are not being forgotten. I looked into them the other day, and felt that I had done nothing better than the writing in many parts of 'Janet.' All I want is that they should *not* drop out of memory" (*Letters* 3: 267).

For nearly ten years after "Janet's Repentance," as we have seen, George Eliot refused to write for the periodical press at all. In the spring of 1865, when her partner Lewes was attempting, despite ill health, two experimental new ventures in journalism, the newspaper *Pall Mall Gazette* and the all-signature, undogmatic *Fortnightly Review*, she relaxed her own prohibition on journalism so far as to write six journalistic pieces of varying lengths for his two periodicals. The *Fortnightly* and *Pall Mall Gazette* were already experiments in a less authoritative kind of review and newspaper, respectively, and George Eliot no doubt hoped that their successes might help create a better kind of public discourse than the newspaper article and review as currently practiced. Her six essays all avoid the standard genre forms of the review essay: none is anonymous, either implicitly or explicitly; all are signed and all are written using the well-developed and individual "I" of a fictional persona (Saccharissa, Felix Holt, George Eliot) rather than in the reviewer's lordly "we." In each case George Eliot gives her speaker real grounds for real knowledge, and conveys no information and argues no points that her persona would not be well qualified to hold and argue. For an analysis of "servants' logic," and other topics of modern social life, the persona chosen is a middle-class Beetonesque materfamilias, "Saccharissa."[10] For a topic about which she herself, George Eliot, would be the best guide, a review of Lecky's *Influence of Rationalism,* she wrote and signed herself George Eliot—but the review focuses on Leckie's own book and arguments. For the only other piece of journalism she wrote in her life, a contribution to *Blackwood's* two years later concerning the new Reform Bill, she again avoided the Reviewer's persona by resurrecting Felix Holt to have him give one of his trademark political talks as if speaking directly to fellow workmen.

This chapter has not argued that we need any major revision of our understanding of George Eliot's moral philosophy. There is no doubt that George Eliot believed strongly, as so many of her commentators have shown, that the great purpose of moral teaching should be to call individuals out of egoistic isolation into sympathetic relationship with other living souls. But scholars who try to see Marian Evans Lewes's journalism as an early and successful reflection of this philosophy have surely missed George Eliot's own pained conviction that her journalism had failed to achieve her goals at all. Hers was not a doctrine that could be inculcated as an "opinion" or in a set of "suitable views for sensible persons," and the journalistic forms of mid-Victorian Britain were incapable of communicating with readers in any other way. If George Eliot was ever an "apprentice" of journalism, the lesson journalism taught her seems to have been the same one it was teaching Elizabeth Barrett Browning's fictional Aurora Leigh at virtually the same historical moment—that an artist could hardly have too little to do with the genres of the mid-Victorian press. Hers was not, George Eliot seems to have decided after her brief stint as a journalist, a set of lessons that a distant critical voice—the kind required by the mid-Victorian genres of journalism—was capable of teaching at all.

5 THE *Clergyman's* TALE

Sensation Fiction and the Anatomy of a "Nine Days' Wonder"

> The prose artist elevates the social heteroglossia surrounding objects into an image that has finished contours, an image completely shot through with dialogized overtones; he creates artistically calculated nuances on all the fundamental voices and tones of this heteroglossia. But as we have already said, every extra-artistic prose discourse—in any of its forms, quotidian, rhetorical, scholarly—cannot fail to be oriented toward the "already uttered," the "already known," the "common opinion" and so forth.
>
> MIKHAIL BAKHTIN, "Discourse in the Novel"

THE THREE MAJOR GENRES OF WRITING called "sensational" in Great Britain in the 1860s—the sensation novel, the sensation drama, and sensational newspaper journalism—are now usually considered parallel and complementary projects, even as variations on the same cultural theme. Documenting a "direct relationship between the sensation novel and sensational journalism, from the extensive crime reporting in the *Times* and the *Daily Telegraph* to such early crime tabloids as the *Illustrated Police News*" (9), Patrick Brantlinger, for example, has shown how novelists including Charles Dickens, Wilkie Collins, and Charles Reade based characters, incidents, and whole plots on contemporary newspaper accounts (9–10). Two of the most frequently cited critical studies of mid-Victorian sensationalism go still further, arguing that periodicals contributed to sensation novels on the artistic levels of tone and theme as well as by providing raw materials of situation and plot. In *Deadly Encounters: Two Victorian Sensations*, Richard Altick presses a theory that newspaper coverage of two remarkable crimes in 1861 "set the tone, if not the stage, for the Victorian Age of Sensation" (158), while Thomas Boyle's *Black Swine in the Sewers of Hampstead* advances the thesis that "newspapers were indeed the source (or *a* source) of the troubled and subversive tone of the Sensation novels" (4).

In critical writing about the sensation novel, however, readings of a close artistic or thematic link between the journalistic and literary forms of "sensational" discourse in the 1860s have to coexist with knowledge that it was the hostile and offended journalists of this era, from *Times* reviewers to the higher journalists of the *Quarterly Review, North British Review,* and *Blackwood's,* who first identified and named the "sensation novel" genre—coining the term as a sneer—and that the most characteristic response of reviewers in the periodical press to the novels of Wilkie Collins, Mary Braddon, and Ellen Wood, considered as a genre, was to condemn them as a dangerous literary and cultural aberration.[1] For Victorian journalists to write "sensational" news stories even as they or their colleagues attacked sensation novels is not a logical contradiction, of course, but it has long been tempting—for some original sensation novelists and for modern scholars as well—to conclude that periodicals that printed highly colored crime coverage were guilty of either hypocrisy or a lamentable lack of self-awareness when they condemned sensation fiction.[2] This was certainly the position of Charles Reade, who answered a scathing *Times* indictment of one of his books in 1871 with a letter that told the *Times* it was itself a coauthor of the work, since Reade had taken his subjects, situations, and plots directly from its pages. "For 18 years, at least, the journal you conduct so ably has been my preceptor, and the main source of my works," Reade told the *Times.* It was "rabid egotism," he continued, for a journalist to claim that "he has any right to put into his leaded type and to amplify, discuss, and dwell upon any subject whatever, and that the poet or the novelist has not an equal right to deal with that subject in fiction" (31 Aug. 1871: 4).[3]

In this much-quoted letter, however, Reade glosses over important differences between the practices of novelists and those of the mid-Victorian journalists who "amplify, discuss, and dwell upon" crime news, and, like many other readers and critics who have accepted a simple equivalence between the Victorian discourses of news and the novel, overlooks the strong strain of anti-subversiveness, even anti-sensationalism, that characterized middle- and upper-class periodicals of the 1860s. Although Reade's letter to the *Times* is

quoted by both Altick and Brantlinger, neither scholar mentions the *Times*'s
response, which was first to deny Reade's credentials as its student ("we cannot help thinking that if he really had stood in that position he would not
only have written better novels but better letters") and then categorically to
deny Reade's premise that newspapers and novels stood in discursive equality.
Interestingly, while Reade's argument assumes that the "subject" is the important issue in discourse and that the genre within which a subject is treated
is relatively immaterial, the *Times* writer counters that difference in genres
powerfully affects which subjects are legitimate to address in which contexts.
While Reade the novelist argues the essential identity of his own novelistic
discourse and the *Times*'s journalistic discourse whenever their topics or con-
tents coincide, the *Times* journalist counters by asserting an essential difference based in genre. "Ours are public, his private, duties," the *Times* answered
Reade. "The columns of a newspaper necessarily contain 'facts' every day" that
a mother might forbid her daughter to read, but "they do not contain *fictions*
like Mr. Reade's" (31 Aug. 1871: 4). Even if the *Times* in this passage wields one
of its own discourse's less admirable tools to put down Reade—the "slash and
scoff" tone of contempt that had sat so ill with subeditor Marian Evans over
at the *Westminster*—the newspaper may also have had the sounder theoretical
understanding of genre on its side. There were indeed crucial differences in
the way Victorian news and novel writers treated "sensational" incidents and
characters, differences that do seem dictated largely by the conventions and
goals of their differing genres.

In what follows, I hope to use a particularly striking example of "sensational" journalism from early 1868 to show that even the most flamboyant
newspaper crime reports of the Age of Sensation may have been as generically
opposed to the projects of the 1860s sensation novel as many journalists, including Reade's *Times* reviewer, claimed. Newspaper coverage of the actual
six-week disappearance of the Reverend Benjamin Speke in January and February 1868 makes a good text for comparison of newspaper and novel sensations, I believe, because the near-absence of real factual information in the
case forced journalists to improvise their narratives and commentary, essentially creating a plot and characters to fit their own specifications. Unlike
more well-known coverage of the Road murder, Palmer poisonings, and deadly
Murray and Vidil encounters, the thousands of words of newspaper text produced during the Speke mystery are literally (though not intentionally) fic-

tions, texts formed almost solely from the materials of current genre resources, if only because there were no facts available to construct them out of any other materials. The unusual fact-free generic purity of the Speke case makes it important and even unique as a document of mid-Victorian newspaper journalism—and an ideal text to compare to the work of the sensation novelists.

"Missing, since Wednesday last, a GENTLEMAN"

Benjamin Speke was alive and well, to begin with. Like Jacob Marley's, his state of health must be clearly understood, or nothing wonderful can come of his strange story. No body, no bloodstain, no witness—no positive evidence at all—suggested that the Reverend Speke, MA, of the Church of St. Andrew, Dowlish Wake, Somerset, had come to harm after his arrival in London by train on 8 January 1868, and yet by early February the most respected daily and weekly newspapers were holding forth about his presumed murder in spine-tingling detail, speculating about the means and opportunities exploited by his killers, and weighing the implications of the crime for public safety and the state of British civilization. Newspaper interest and public alarm quickly reached such a pitch that the disappearance was compared to both the Road murder and the Waterloo Bridge mystery. The *Times* called it a "public alarm," the *Leader* wrote of a national "epidemic of fear," and even a year later, the compilers of the 1868 *Annual Register* recorded that the Reverend Speke's mysterious disappearance had "occasioned an almost universal panic among the public."

Considering that Speke's waylaying and murder occurred only in the imaginations of newspaper writers and readers, Richard Altick could hardly ask for a better illustration of his observation, in *Victorian Studies in Scarlet*, that "murder had a part in [Victorians'] imaginative lives that was far out of proportion to its actual incidence" (281).[4] The case unfolded over six weeks in January and February 1868, reaching a peak of public interest in ten frantic days of press coverage (it is almost literally a "nine days' wonder") between 5 and 15 February, during which the *Times* alone printed nineteen Speke items and the *Spectator* estimated that "twenty or thirty thousand minds . . . this week have been at work upon the case—minds including the whole body of police, the entire Bar, and the whole body of Clubmen—say, in brief, 5,000 of the quickest wits in Christendom" (8 Feb. 1868: 157).

Before I consider the plot and themes that newspapers chose for this story, its few facts may be briefly summarized. On Wednesday, 8 January 1868, the thirty-eight-year-old Speke arrived in London at Waterloo Station on the 4:33 PM train from Islington, near his parish in the southwest of England. He was to officiate the next morning at the wedding of a friend, and then return home on a mid-afternoon train. The youngest brother of the celebrated African explorer John Hanning Speke, who had died three years earlier in a much-publicized and mysterious hunting accident, Benjamin Speke had taken his MA in 1853 at Christ Church, Oxford. For the past eleven years he had been vicar of the Church of St. Andrew, Dowlish Wake, where (according to the 1861 *Kelly's Directory of Somerset*) he ministered to a rural flock of four hundred souls, and held a respectable living of £400 a year. Youthful-looking, with broad shoulders and an athletic build, he was dressed that evening in a black frock coat and overcoat, with a gray striped tie and high top hat with mourning band. He got into a four-wheeled cab at the train station, and was driven in twenty minutes, with his servant and a single piece of luggage, to the house of his brother-in-law at 79 Eccleston Square in west London.

Speke talked to the footman at the door of the house for about ten minutes without going in, and then at about 5:10 PM he left the house, this time alone. He told his servant he was going to buy a hat and do some business in Westminster, but would be back to Eccleston Square by 6:30 for an appointment, and would afterward dine in South Kensington. A hat shop in Warwick Street was just three minutes away, and Speke did buy a hat there, ordering it sent to his brother-in-law's house no later than 6:45 PM so that he would be there to pay for it. At 5:30 PM he left the hat shop, and at 7:30 PM a workman walking in Birdcage Walk, a promenade along the south of St. James's Park, half a mile to the north, found Speke's hat (the one he had been wearing, not the one he had bought) on the ground. When Speke did not return for his appointment or dinner engagement, his family became alarmed and called in the Metropolitan police. But no one was found to say they had seen the Reverend Speke after 5:30 PM. He had apparently vanished without a trace.

Within days the first public text about Speke's disappearance appeared in the *Times*, and with it signs of the emplotments that participants in the case had begun to consider. An advertisement in the agony column of the *Times* of 11 January offered a £3 reward "To Hotelkeepers, Tavernkeepers, and Proprietors of Lodging-houses—Missing, since Wednesday last, a GENTLEMAN, of about 36 years of age, height 5 ft. 9 in, gray eyes, black hair and whiskers, no moustache or beard." In addressing the advertisement to "Hotelkeepers, Tavernkeepers, and Proprietors of Lodging-houses," this writer implied that Speke was considered to be in voluntary hiding. The text soon changed, however, to suggest that the family was looking for a body rather than a black sheep: by 15 January the ad was no longer directed to hotel- and tavernkeepers, and one of the items of information was the initials on the missing man's linen. Meanwhile, the reward increased from £3 to £5, then to £100, and then on 27 January to £500. Shortly after this, Speke's brother-in-law Charles Murdoch (signing himself "C.T.M.") sent a letter to the *Times* telling the story of the disappearance, including the date Speke had arrived in London, the time he had disappeared, and the finding of the hat. He concluded on a note that made his own dark suspicions plain: "Any persons who noticed two or three people assembled [in Birdcage-walk] between 6 and half-past 7 o'clock . . . or in the parts of Westminster adjacent; any persons who observed two or more dragging or apparently helping another man; in fact, any who saw anything suspicious that evening . . . may possibly give the clue which will solve this distressing mystery" (3 Feb. 1868: 7).

Speke's own family thus gave the first hints of foul play to journalists and their readers, and a *London Review* writer was later to remark dryly that Speke's relatives "from the commencement . . . seem to have been inclined to grasp the difficulty of the situation in a dramatic style" (15 Feb. 1868: 143). But London's newspaper community was not slow to take up the hint, and Murdoch's letter drew a flood of responses from both readers and professional journalists. Although amateur correspondents and professionals shared many of the same concerns, differences in tone and purpose are immediately apparent between the letters from correspondents, signed with initials or pseudonyms, and the anonymous leading articles and news accounts of staff writers.

For most of the amateurs, Speke's disappearance served as a pretext for discussion either of their own missing friends and relatives, or of their own brushes with urban danger. Under title headings such as "Perils of the Streets / Another Mysterious Disappearance," *Times* readers learned of a young man who had vanished after arranging a passage for New Zealand, and of a twenty-year-old of "most exemplary character" who had disappeared from Regent Street at two o'clock in the afternoon in July 1863, while the *Western Morning Press* reprinted details of a Bristol disappearance case from

December 1866.[5] Although four cases in five years hardly seems to amount to an epidemic, the *Sunday Times,* among other papers, was ready to assume the worst: "Three or four cases [of disappearance] have been reported during the present week. Are these individuals murdered? Is there some secret associa- tion of assassins in London?" (9 Feb. 1868: 2).

While amateur newspaper correspondents spun out the Speke mystery with mysteries of their own, however, other amateur and more professional journalists became concerned with bringing it to a definite resolution. The most characteristic texts of the Speke mystery, in fact, are those of newspaper writers who attempted to analyze and synthesize the few bare facts related by Murdoch into a firm conclusion about the missing man's fate. A remarkable number of writers were willing to take this unpromising detective role, and their letters and leading articles make compelling reading. Almost all of them begin with a plea for clear-headed logic in the weighing of evidence, and reach their grim conclusions with all the satisfaction and finality of QED.

The first, "An Amateur Detective" (*Times* 6 Feb. 1868: 10), announces immediately that "the clue to the mystery must be sought in the character of the gentleman. . . . It may not be as perfect as 'C.T.M.' describes it, but domes- tic feelings had evidently a strong hold upon him." Assuming that Speke did not intend to disappear when he arrived in London, but genuinely meant to fulfill his engagements, "as it is almost impossible to disbelieve," it becomes obvious to the Amateur Detective that the case is one of murder in the course of robbery. Speke had paid the cabman at his brother-in-law's door in Eccleston Square, and "it is natural to suppose that some person lurking near that door in the dark may have caught sight of the gold, may have followed Mr. Speke to the hatter's . . . and may have tracked him in his further progress." Such a person might then have used a plea for help or charity to convince Speke to follow him into some "haunt" in Westminster, and killed him there. "A brave, athletic man, as the brother of Speke, the traveller, may be supposed to be, is not easily overcome—if attacked in the front; but in a narrow passage, in the dark, what avails strength against a treacherous blow from behind?" As for Speke's body, "is not a dead man's body easily disposed of *à la* Mannings, under the flags of the cellar?"

On 8 February, however, *Times* correspondent "M.T." refused to accept even the small amount of ambiguity involved in not knowing which cellar Speke might be buried in. "M.T." agrees with "Amateur Detective" in assuming that "this gentleman, "described by his friends as a man in perfect health, of evenly-balanced mind, high religious character, and of a cheerful and amiable disposition . . . had no intention of going on secret expeditions in Pimlico, or to get drunk, or, in fact, to do anything but what he had said that he was going to do." M.T. finds the rest of the Amateur Detective's scenario unlikely, however. Speke's train to London had arrived late, and he was pressed for time; the odds are that he would not have walked to Westminster, but hailed a cab just after leaving the hat shop. Speke had a married sister living in Queen Square who was out of town at the time of Speke's visit. This house was Speke's most likely destination, M.T. argues, and also the place where he was almost certainly robbed and murdered. "It is no uncommon thing at such a time for servants to leave a house unguarded. Somebody having temporary access to the place may have received him." Not satisfied, perhaps, at the official response to his deductions, M.T. wrote again to the *Times* two days later to ask rather grumpily whether "this house, including its cellars and the shrubbery and offices at the back, has been thoroughly searched not only by Mr. Speke's relatives, but by those who are accustomed to investigate cases of this kind" (10 Feb. 1868: 10).

Two even wilder theories surfaced that same week, the first when a writer in the *Pall Mall Gazette* suggested, no doubt on the basis of the photographs and woodcuts of Speke that had by this time become ubiquitous around London, that "Mr. Speke was very like Mr. Hardy, and might have been killed or kidnapped by Fenians in mistake for the Home Secretary. The likeness granted," commented the *Spectator*, "this seemed plausible; but Mr. Speke was twenty years younger than Mr. Hardy, and dressed in clerical costume" (15 Feb. 1868: 185). A second possibility, even more lurid than Fenian terrorism, was suggested with a touch of Sweeney Todd by the *Manchester Guardian*, which reported (falsely) that the police searching for Speke had found a chopping block attached to the floor in one of the Westminster slums. "By accident one of the police touched a spring, and the top (found to be a lid) flew open, and it was discovered that the sham block was not only hollow, but that it communicated with the main sewer." The *Times* immediately debunked this story, adding that "in the present state of public alarm occasioned by the disappearance, not only of Mr. Speke but of several other persons, such terrible inventions as chopping blocks communicating with main sewers might produce a panic" (13 Feb. 1868: 9).

A much more ingenious and widely noticed article in R. H. Hutton's *Spectator* of 8 February took all this speculation to a new height.[6] Although the "natural presumption when any one disappears suddenly is that he has disappeared voluntarily," the *Spectator* dismissed this presumption in Speke's case as "violently improbable," again on the basis of Murdoch's statement about the missing man's character. "His family hold,—and their evidence on such a point is practically eye testimony, quite as good as any testimony whatever,— he was totally incapable of any heartlessness of the kind." That meant, for the *Spectator,* "the only hypothesis admissable, the only theory, that is, which meets the facts, moral and physical, which have to be taken into the account, is murder, murder of a cool, deliberate kind, murder planned on system, carried out relentlessly, and dictated solely by the expectation of plunder." Speke must have been murdered by a well-organized gang that harvested its victims in the city (probably using a decoy hansom cab and chloroform) and drove the bodies to the countryside. These perpetrators were undoubtedly foreigners, since the crime was "too cool, too artistic, too complete, for the conception of the English criminal class" (8 Feb. 1868: 158).

This remarkable article, reprinted in its entirety by the *Times* on 11 February, was in its turn embroidered and developed by other correspondents. A writer signed "B" in the *Daily Telegraph* pointed out "that the trap-door on the roof of a hansom might assist such evil purpose, the head of the victim being immediately beneath it. The actual instrument or method employed, whether a life-preserver, air-gun, pistol, or other weapon, can only be guessed at, neither is it very material" (18 Feb. 1868: 5). The journalist William Hardman, in a letter to a friend in Australia that told the Speke story at length, commented, "This is a diabolical notion, and will assuredly have the effect of injuring the trade of the Hansom cabs after dark" (Hardman 314–15).[7]

While journalist-detectives were thus creating comprehensible and grimly complete narratives of Speke's death, leader writers in the *Times, Sunday Times, Illustrated London News, Saturday Review,* and other periodicals were just as assiduously extracting the lessons of the case, and translating them into either an indictment of modern law enforcement or a call for more sweeping social or administrative change. "If there were nothing in the papers but the advertisements for the discovery of the Rev. B. Speke . . . those announcements should be enough to set us all thinking, and to make us abstain from too much boast about our civilization," wrote the *Illustrated London News* on 6 February. "It is really a grave matter that a man can be thus 'spirited away' from the midst of us, and that all the skill of our officials cannot obtain the slightest clue" (143). While the *Sunday Times* called for active investigation of the possible London assassination ring, the *Saturday Review* of 8 February went higher up the ladder, calling for a thorough reform of the police system, while *Punch* began to demand the resignation of Sir Richard Mayne, head of the Metropolitan Police. The *Illustrated London News* of 15 February considered the case serious enough to warrant suspension of traditional British liberties and the granting of broad new powers for the police, including the power to force social undesirables to emigrate. Even the *London Review*, which ridiculed the amateur detectives of the Speke case in a generally satirical article, entered into the same spirit when it warned of "the unquestionable risk involved in reminding our predatory classes that such things [as Speke's murder] may be done with comparative impunity, and in defiance of every organization of law" (15 Feb. 1868: 143).

Enough threads of agreement run through these attempts at narrative and thematic closure to make the journalistic response to the Speke mystery quite coherent. There were clearly suspicions abroad (though few writers admitted to harboring them) that Speke had disappeared voluntarily, perhaps because of some sexual indiscretion—the *Illustrated London News* called these "the injurious surmises which occur to the cynical when a country gentleman is missed in London" (15 Feb. 1868).[8] Within little time, however, and on the basis of no additional information, these suspicions were disavowed almost everywhere, and something approaching a consensus had developed among professional journalists. The shared conclusions of the Speke commentators toward the end of the "nine days' wonder" may even be listed, giving the emplotment and themes chosen by newspaper journalists in a nutshell:

- Speke had not disappeared voluntarily.
- He was dead by violence in the course of a robbery.
- He was the victim of opportunistic professional criminals, who had probably never met or seen him before the crime.
- He had not courted his fate by seeking out a sexual liaison, or committing some other risky behavior.

- The chief lesson of Speke's case was that some element of the London criminal classes had become ingeniously and ruthlessly predatory, or was now moving to exploit the vulnerability of the upper classes.

It is worth repeating that there was no factual—or even reasonable inferential—basis for any of these conclusions. The "facts" marshaled by the amateur detectives were all vague negatives, most of which did not originate even with the detective police, but with the statements of Speke's brother-in-law that Speke had not been seen, had not left signs of a struggle, had not seemed to be planning any secret escapade, had no known bad habits, and had no family history of insanity. That journalists could use such general premises to draw such particular conclusions about foreigners, hansom cabs, and chloroform may seem to show primarily that all these writers' Occam's razors were badly in need of sharpening.

More important for my argument, however, the journalists' conclusions show clearly that the choices of plot and theme preferred by journalists were essentially different from those a Wilkie Collins or Elizabeth Braddon would have chosen for "sensational" effect. The random and predatory violence of the Speke "murder" as narrated in the *Times* and *Spectator* is certainly disturbing, but it is significant how tightly the issues the case is allowed to raise have been constrained, and how essentially conventional and conservative a plot has been chosen. Making the Speke case a robbery-murder, and Speke himself an unambiguously innocent victim, the newspapers deliberately excluded consideration of any emplotment that would have been genuinely "sensational" in sensation novel terms.

Making Sense of Sensation

As numerous critics have noted, the sensation novelists of the 1860s were dealing with much more challenging and vital issues than random urban violence.[9] It was these issues, in the form of a shared set of plots, themes, and character types, that seem to have made the sensation novel so noxious to so many Victorian periodical reviewers, and although they have been read and ranked by scholars in many different ways, a brief review of the most generally acknowledged characteristics of sensation fiction will show why the adjective most commonly applied to it is "subversive."

First, many sensation novels implied that both personal and class identity in contemporary Britain were fluid and unstable rather than secure, and thus potentially subject to manipulation, misrepresentation, and outright theft.[10] The plots of the most exciting and characteristic sensation novels of the 1860s turn on precisely this issue. Both of the great criminal secrets in Wilkie Collins's *The Woman in White* are manipulations of identity: Sir Percival Glyde has "stolen" his upper-class identity by concealing his illegitimate birth; partly to protect his secret, he and his partner Count Fosco steal another identity, that of Glyde's wife, Laura. In both Mary Braddon's *Lady Audley's Secret* and Ellen Wood's *East Lynne*, the main female characters deliberately disappear, changing their names and class identities in order to begin new lives. Braddon's Helen Talboys, shedding a husband along with her lower-class identity, eventually becomes Lady Audley, while Wood's Isabel Vane, moving in the other direction, steps down in rank to become the governess Madame Vine.

The second great preoccupation of 1860s sensation novels is the power of aberrant psychological states such as madness, addiction, or (especially) sexual desire to push personality and behavior outside socially accepted norms.[11] Her inherited tendency toward madness is the eponymous secret of Lady Audley, and stands as her own explanation for the arson and attempted murders she commits. The theft of Laura, Lady Glyde's identity in *The Woman in White* is more convincing because her sufferings have caused mental impairment, rendering her still more like the half sister whose identity she has been given. In the novel Collins was writing in 1868 as the Speke mystery unfolded, *The Moonstone*, the hero Franklin Blake ultimately discovers that he himself (in an opium-altered state of consciousness) committed the crime he has subsequently been working to solve. Meanwhile, the edgy depiction of women motivated by sexual desire, always a potential "third rail" for novelists throughout the century, drew down furious critical attacks on novels such as Braddon's *Aurora Floyd*, whose heroine marries a handsome groom.

The third provocative move of the 1860s sensation novelist was to locate these daring treatments of identity, madness, and sexuality squarely in the (implied) reader's own world, the respectable ranks of the middle and upper classes. Henry James said of Wilkie Collins that he had "introduced into fiction those most mysterious of mysteries, the mysteries which are at our own doors" (*Nation* 9 Nov. 1865), while H. L. Mansel saw the close identification of the novel's world with the reader's world as one of the most dangerously attractive moves of the sensation novelist: "A tale which aims at electrifying the nerves of the reader is never thoroughly effective unless the scene be laid in our own days and among the people we are in the habit of meeting. . . . The man who shook our hand with a hearty English grasp half an hour ago—the woman whose beauty and grace were the charm of last night . . . —how exciting to think that under these pleasing outsides may be concealed some demon in human shape, a Count Fosco or a Lady Audley!" (quoted in Skilton 77).

The final important thematic choice shared by many sensation novelists was to show the discontinuity and breakdown of established authority, both social and narrative. The contemporary writer and clergyman Francis Paget did not offer any specific examples to support his claim that sensation novels encouraged their readers to "set all authority, parental, social, and political, at defiance" (301), but Patrick Brantlinger has shown more convincingly how these novels, whether they employed Collins's technique of telling his story through several mystified participants in the plot, or Braddon's of using a coy "omniscient" narrator who withholds information from the reader, resulted in a general "undermining of the narrator's credibility" (15).

This group of shared characteristics seems to have made the sensation novel a remarkably offensive construct to periodical reviewers of the 1860s. Even many reviewers who were also working novelists, including Margaret Oliphant and G. H. Lewes, agreed that use of such themes and techniques produced not only bad and immoral art but also inferior social criticism and incorrect psychology. Human nature and lived experience, they argued, are simply not like this—indeed, two critics of sensation fiction asserted the fundamental psychological falseness of sensation fiction even while the Speke affair was in progress. On 15 February the *Saturday Review* described sensation novels as "narrations of highly improbable events brought about by the agency of utterly impossible characters," while Paget, in an afterword dated 15 January to his polemical (but oddly charming) anti-sensation novel *Lucretia* (1868), devoutly hoped "that no such women as many of the heroines of the true sensational novel have been represented to be, have ever existed,—so unprincipled, so degraded, so wicked" (309).

Charles Reade had accused the *Times* of inconsistency for reporting sensational fact while criticizing sensational fiction, but in fact the preferred assumptions about contemporary society and human psychology made by journalistic reviewers, and the assumptions driving the journalistic crime reports in the same pages, agree remarkably well. Far from sharing the sensation novelists' suspicions about class identity, for example, the journalists who covered the Speke case automatically endorsed the character of a man trebly class-marked as a beneficed clergyman, scion of an old county family, and brother of a heroic African explorer. A London Reviewer might complain that the average newspaper correspondent "has little hesitation in theorizing that Mr. Speke was a man of any character that will suit his hypothesis," but among professional journalists the spotlessness of Speke's escutcheon was earnestly defended, and his brother-in-law's vague encomium was accepted so completely that no one seems to have thought of asking why, if Speke were such a pattern of virtue, the first advertisements for him in the *Times* had been addressed to tavernkeepers.

In the newspaper writing about Speke, the more truly transgressive plots were sometimes mentioned, but they were raised only to be regulated, controlled, and then dismissed. Even the most far-fetched robbery and murder scenarios endorsed instead, as "sensational" as they may now seem, have much more in common with the anti-sensational writings of Paget and Mansel than with the projects of Collins, Braddon, and Wood. Where the sensation novel challenged easy assumptions about class identity and character, journalistic commentators and leader writers made Speke's character the primary and unassailable "fact" of the case. As the sensation novel pressed the boundaries of representation in matters of sexuality and morals, journalists asserted that sexual transgression on the part of a man like Speke was practically unthinkable. Where the sensation novel called narrative authority into question, the journalist-detectives who wrote about Speke almost desperately asserted their power to unravel and explain mysterious events. Finally, where the sensation novelists introduced readers to misdeeds "at their own doors," committed by members of their own class, journalists (when, as in this case, they were given a choice) firmly asserted that crime was naturally the province of either foreigners or the British "criminal classes."

One of the richest ironies of the Speke case, therefore, is that at the end of February the newspapers were proven wrong in a way that showed the whole case to be far more sensational—in the novelistic sense—than any journalist had publicly supposed. On 25 February, *Times* readers were stunned to discover that Speke had been arrested at Padstow, in Cornwall, dressed as a cattle drover, with £200 in cash and several disguises in his possession. He had been stopped on suspicion of being a man from Hull for whom the police were searching, and though he quickly proved he was not that man, his upper-class accent and cattle-drover dress were so clearly at odds that he was kept in custody—he had obviously done *something*—until someone thought of asking him if he were the Reverend Speke.[12] He reportedly told police that he had been making a walking tour of southern England, waiting for the search to slacken, at which point he planned to go abroad, work for his living, and preach the Gospel to fellow laborers. The *Western Morning News* immediately reported the new leading theories among Speke's friends to be "excessive Biblical study, leading to religious monomania," or "that Mr. Speke had a morbid dread of marriage . . . and he acted on the notion of flying from all inducement to commit so repugnant an act" (quoted in *Times* 28 Feb. 1868: 10). By 4 March the family's public relations line had been chosen, however, and select physicians reported in a letter to the *Times* a diagnosis of "hypochondriasis" aggravated by unsound advice from quack doctors. By mid-April the Reverend Speke was back at work at his vicarage. Commented the *Pall Mall Gazette*, "We hope that he previously had a satisfactory interview with his bishop" (16 Apr. 1868: 4).[13]

In the Speke case, then, the sensation novelists who had so often been accused of "improbable" and "impossible" plotting and characterization enjoyed an appropriate and thorough revenge on the journalists.[14] Not only had the journalists' own specific speculative plots all been proven wrong, but their assumptions about the range of possible and probable human nature on which the plots had been based—the underlying attitudes toward class, individual psychology, and modern life that had informed them—had all been shown to be wrong as well. The novelists' triumph was correspondingly complete: their themes of unstable class identity, secret lives in the middle and upper classes, and psychosexual transgression had driven a real-life drama, and the hero and victim of the Speke disappearance was revealed to be also its villain, in an appropriately *Moonstone*-ian twist. As for narrative authority, that of the newspapers, at least, was temporarily in tatters.

The way the newspaper writers handled the denouement of this strange story, however, remained consistent to their generic worldview, and consistently opposed to the way contemporary sensation novelists handled theirs. In Braddon and Collins, a sense of the deep mysteries of human nature, of human interconnection, and of the awesome workings of Providence pervade scenes of final revelation. "Who shall dare to try and order his own life after this?" muses Robert Audley, after learning (almost) the final pieces of the puzzle from Luke Marks. "Who can fail to recognize God's hand in this strange story?" (364). Walter Hartright believes that the "visitation of God ruled it that" he should meet Percival Glyde face-to-face only after Glyde's machinations had brought about his own death (541), and later shudders to think how divine justice has overruled his poor attempts at personal justice in the case of Fosco as well (643).

In the newspapers, by contrast, the revelation that more mysterious forces had been at work than those comprehended by newspaper writers was less the occasion for awestruck meditation than a reason to dismiss the entire matter as quickly as possible. The most common reaction to the news in the British press was not even gratitude for the life spared, but simply chagrin and disgust. The *Times,* whose fence-sitting approach had never quite ruled out a voluntary disappearance, could now afford to be at least a bit smug, but the *Sunday Times* (which had called for investigation of a secret assassination ring) quickly claimed to have dismissed the whole issue long before, and wrapped up its coverage with a short paragraph in which the words "contempt" and "fool" figure prominently. Hardman, who had told the story of Speke's disappearance at length to his Australian correspondent, gave a bare two sentences to his reappearance: "You will see that Mr. Speke has been found in Cornwall, and seems to be out of his mind. Confound him, he has upset his own relatives and everyone else." In its final leading articles on the case, the *Times* argued that Speke, as the "author" of "his own mystery," had committed "not only an offence against morality but against the public peace," and was guilty of criminal irresponsibility for "terrifying the more timid part of the population beyond measure" (25 Feb. 1868: 6). The *Leader* asserted that it had been the British public in general (not journalists) who had overreacted to the case, thus making the entire affair another vague symptom of national decline: "Amidst the history of national follies, surely the story of an eccentric clergyman who had chosen to hide himself, having alarmed a nation once mighty enough to win the battle of Waterloo, will stand pre-eminent and striking" (*Leader* 29 Feb. 1868: 378).

An honorable exception to this general offendedness and defensiveness was Hutton's *Spectator*, which both shared the laugh against itself and approved the erring clergyman's reported goal of leaving his wealthy family and class in order to work and preach as a laborer:

> We never heard of Mr. Speke in his life until Mr. Murdoch published his
> first letter, and shall be delighted never to hear of him again,—considering
> that he ought in common decency to have been murdered in a cab by
> foreigners,—but we would just ask Somersetshire to explain why, being
> Christian, and repeating litanies, and so on, it considers itself aggrieved?
> If Mr. Speke really thought, whether under the influence of mental disease
> or not, that he should be the better for not being Mr. Speke, why was it
> morally wrong for him to shake off his own identity? (29 Feb. 1868: 253)

So far from having learned any lessons about the dangers of drawing broad general conclusions from specific and unusual events, journalistic commentators post-Speke seemed just as eager to treat his safe return as a guarantee of the personal safety of the entire metropolis as they had been to treat his disappearance as proof of universal danger. "It is somewhat reassuring to Londoners, and dwellers in large towns generally, to learn that they do not, after all, live in hourly danger of being garroted, burked, carried off, buried, or in some other way got rid of," wrote the *Illustrated Police News* (29 Feb. 1868: 2), while at the top of the journalistic hierarchy the *Times* itself drew the same conclusion: "Great crimes are rare in this metropolis, considering its enormous extent and population, and it may be said confidently that in no great city of the world are the streets more safe to one who goes about his business steadily and soberly" (25 Feb. 1868: 6).[15] The weekly *Leader* was even willing to give credit for the suddenly and remarkably improved London public safety situation to newspapers themselves: "It is obvious that crime stands a far poorer chance of escape than before, in the fierce light which this modern ubiquity of information casts upon it" (25 Feb. 1868: 5). As for any wider conclusions than this, however, no journalist even tried to draw them, and indeed J. F. Stephen himself, in his *Cornhill* article on "Journalism" in 1862, had suggested that learning from the events they chronicled was precisely what journalists had the most trouble doing. A leading article writer, Stephen noted,

never, or hardly ever, gets the chance, even if he had the power, of taking a
comprehensive view of the whole subject, reducing the whole matter to
order and principle, and setting before his readers something like a real judgment upon it. The reader of a long series of leading articles in the same
paper on such a subject generally gets the impression that the writer of them
probably knows little more about the matter when he finishes than he did
when he began. Such articles never form a connected whole. They rarely
show traces of gradually increasing knowledge. (54)

Stephen's analysis here of the inability of journalists to see far into either the
past or the future interestingly precedes Mikhail Bakhtin's, who pointed out
in "From Notes Made in 1970–71" that "the journalist is above all a contemporary. He is obliged to be one. He lives in the sphere of questions that can
be resolved in the present day (or in any case in the near future). He participates in a dialogue that can be ended and even finalized, can be translated into
action, and can become an empirical force" (*Speech Genres* 152).

A Speke writer in the *Examiner* seems to be acting fully within the limits
of both Stephen's and Bakhtin's expectations, then, when he concludes that if
the strange case has a moral, it can't be a very important one, and that the case
has ultimately served the one practical purpose of having been an interesting
distraction at an otherwise slow time for news.[16] "The story, however, is not
without its moral, though it is not necessary that we should find it; and if Mr
Speke has been very severely handled for his conduct, some indulgence may
be extended to him in consideration of his having afforded a fruitful subject of
conversation at a very dull time of the year" (29 Feb. 1868: 130).

If the Speke case held out an opportunity to Victorian journalists—which
they universally and perhaps necessarily missed—to reexamine the nature
of their own discourse and the potential range of human nature, however, it
also offers modern students of mid-Victorian sensation fiction and the Victorian periodical press a lesson almost as challenging and as foreign to our
current assumptions. The newspapers that printed voluminous and colorful
crime coverage, yet criticized sensation novels and repudiated charges of "sensational" writing against themselves, were not either hypocritical or blind to
their own discursive practices. Mansel might coin the term "newspaper novels," and perceive the "true sensation cast" in newspaper leading articles, but

the similarity Charles Reade observed between the novelist's and journalist's subject matter only masks a far more crucial opposition of purposes. However charged its topics, the mid-Victorian periodical press was largely consistent in its mission—almost its generic imperative—to assert and defend traditional authority, minimize mystery, and dictate decisive action to those in power. Fitzjames Stephen had also remarked in 1862 the essential social conservatism of even the most politically liberal papers: "It is easy to trace in every [leading article] proof of the fact that its author has a strong interest in the maintenance of all the chief principles and institutions of society, and a general conviction that alterations in these are rash" (57). The *Times* might acknowledge that it reported the existence of immorality in modern society, and that "the wickedness of the age . . . is occasionally reflected in the columns of the press" (31 Aug. 1871: 4), but its intention in all this coverage was less to push the boundaries of acceptable representation than to guard them.

As it denied Charles Reade's imputation that it had been either "preceptor" or accessory to his novels, the *Times* argued that "in nothing does [Reade] more clearly show that he is not our pupil than in his impatience of well-merited reproof" (31 Aug. 1871: 4). By the same token, however, in nothing does mid-Victorian journalism show more clearly how far it was from sharing the projects and insights of the mid-Victorian sensation novelists than in the strange narratives it created for the blameless life, and many peculiar deaths, of the Reverend Benjamin Speke.

6 | THE *Scholars'* TALES

Theories of Journalism and the Practice of Literary History

Unfortunately, historians of literature usually reduce this struggle between the novel and other already completed genres ... to the actual real-life struggle among "schools" and "trends." ... They do not see beneath the superficial hustle and bustle of literary process the major and crucial fates of literature and language, whose great heroes turn out to be first and foremost genres, and whose "trends" and "schools" are but second- or third-rank protagonists.

MIKHAIL BAKHTIN, "Epic and Novel"

THIS BOOK HAS STUDIED SPECIFIC RELATIONSHIPS between Victorian writers and the forms of mid-Victorian journalism, but has also tried to suggest more broadly how book history and the study of print culture might benefit from Mikhail Bakhtin's insight that the dynamic interactions between genres are a powerful engine of literary history. It has tried to move this idea from a vague formulation that would probably be accepted by many (though not all[1]) scholars to a specific and useful critical praxis. To borrow a term from the social sciences, the secondary goal of this book has been to "operational-ize" this insight of Bakhtin.

The suggestion that genre can be a significant tool of historicist criticism does not quite come out of left field.[2] Although genre has not for many years been a fashionable interest within cultural studies,[3] scholars from several disciplines have been moving slowly over the last decade toward rediscovery of formalist critical tools including genre.[4] The American journalism scholar Michael Schudson has long argued that journalism's genre forms have powerfully and often invisibly influenced both its historical and its contemporary practice,[5] and renewed attention to genre in historicist literary studies at some point seems inevitable, if only because, as Thomas Pavel recently observed, "genre is a crucial interpretive tool because it is a crucial artistic tool in the first place. . . . Genre helps us figure out the nature of a literary work because the person who wrote it and the culture for which that person labored used genre as a guideline for literary creation" (202).[6]

But while methods to realize the potential of genre as an interpretive tool have remained relatively underdeveloped, many scholars of literature and journalism have been embracing a group of quite different theoretical approaches, originally developed in the social sciences, to understanding print culture and the periodical press. Three models in particular of how discourses function within cultures have become highly influential and are frequently invoked in periodicals studies, and this chapter will evaluate their potential usefulness as an alternative means of addressing the issues I have considered in this book. In the process it will try to explain (if anyone was wondering) why the concepts of "public sphere," "imagined community," and "literary field," which have recently become so popular in periodicals studies, have not been among my own theoretical tools.

The three theories invoked when scholars use these terms have come to do a large and increasing proportion of the work of theorizing the periodical press, and the terms themselves have entered the vocabulary of every book historian and periodicals-using scholar. "Public sphere" is, of course, the signature term of Jürgen Habermas, who first proposed in pathbreaking work done in the early 1960s that eighteenth-century European cultures, especially Britain, developed a qualitatively new kind of discourse that belonged neither to the private world of the family group nor to the official discourse of the state, and that served to monitor and check state power. In the briefly successful British "bourgeois public sphere" of the eighteenth and early nineteenth centuries, the periodical press fostered and sustained substantive debate on public issues in coffeehouses and other public spaces. This "public sphere" of discourse was characterized by several important innovations: it privileged "rational-critical public debate" conducted for purposes of reaching consensus, disregarded the social status of its participants,[7] opened topics for discussion that had formerly been monopolized by church or state, and at least potentially made its discussions broadly inclusive, rather than establishing or privileging an exclusive membership (*Structural Transformation* 28, 36–37). This original "public sphere" lasted only until the 1830s, however, when British periodical discourse began to degrade toward a more mass-market model that conceived of readers as passive observers and consumers of public conversation rather than as active and rational participants in it. Habermas has called this moment "the transformation from a journalism of conviction to one of commerce" ("Public Sphere" 53). Although modern industrial societies thus no longer have—and cannot re-create—the public sphere as it was originally constituted, Habermas's theory still treats its example as normative and searches for ways to reestablish the "rationalization of power through the medium of public discussion among private individuals" ("Public Sphere" 55). The two most substantial recent theoretical studies of the Victorian press are both directly inspired by Habermas: Jean Chalaby's *Invention of Journalism* (1998), which dates the replacement of politically valuable "publicity" by commercialist "journalism" in Britain somewhat later in the nineteenth century than in Habermas's original formulation, and Mark Hampton's *Visions of the Press in Victorian Britain* (2004), which closely parallels Habermas's original narrative of the replacement of a participatory public sphere by a more spectator-oriented press, positing that Victorians generally believed that an active "educational ideal" was the major function of the press at the mid-century, but had broadly turned to a more passive "representative ideal" by the 1880s.[8]

A second popular theoretical approach to journalistic discourse originates with the political scientist Benedict Anderson, whose short book on nationalism, *Imagined Communities* (1983, revised edition 2006), has inspired scholars in many fields. Anderson suggests that printed discourses, especially books and the newspaper (which Anderson calls the "extreme form" of book considered as commodity), act to create national identity by creating a shared "imagined" impression among their readers that national identity already exists. "Print-capitalism," writes Anderson, "made it possible for rapidly growing numbers of people to think about themselves, and to relate themselves to others, in profoundly new ways" (36). The reader of a newspaper is imaginatively conscious that the newspaper is being read simultaneously by "thousands (or millions) of others of whose existence he is confident, yet of whose identity he has not the slightest notion," an image that Anderson considers a particularly "vivid figure for the secular, historically clocked, imagined community" (35). For Anderson, this essential function of newspapers in constructing national identity explains much about newspapers themselves, including the apparent arbitrariness of selection and organization of any given newspaper's printed items, which have no real or logical relationships to one another, only "imagined" relationships.[9] A recent book-length application of Anderson's ideas to historical British journalism is Michelle Elizabeth Tusan, *Women Making News: Gender and Journalism in Modern Britain* (2005).

Finally, the French sociologist Pierre Bourdieu, in the most complex formulation, has suggested that our understanding of discourse can be scientifically transformed by one of the same intellectual tools that transformed understanding of the physical sciences in the nineteenth century: the concept of a "field." Instead of invisible fields of electromagnetic or gravitic forces, however, Bourdieu proposed that discourse itself within a society is organized into invisible but autonomous and structured fields of cultural force. The discourses of particular professions or interests organize themselves into fields and subfields, "journalistic" and "literary" among many others, which then act autonomously to create and distribute "symbolic capital" among the field's participants. Each field creates its own terms of value, which may well invert or oppose the values of other fields and of the wider culture. While acknowledging that fields (including the journalistic and literary fields) interact with each other to some degree, Bourdieu's model derives most of its explanatory power from the autonomous working of fields and subfields to set their own conventions and criteria of value for their own discourses.[10] Use of Bourdieu's ideas in literary and cultural studies has grown dramatically over the last decade, and the idea that discourse is organized by structured "fields" has been found persuasive even by many scholars who mainly use the terms of other models.[11]

A fourth approach that deserves to be mentioned is the use of concepts from two or more of these social science theorists serially or in combination. Such hybrid positions argue or at least assume that applying the approaches together can combine their persuasive power, and the position is hard to argue with, thus broadly framed. The title of Luisa Calé's recent "Periodical Personae: Pseudonyms, Authorship, and the Imagined Community of Joseph Priestly's *Theological Repository*" (2006) is Andersonian, but her argument is at least equally Habermasian, using both "public sphere" and "imagined community" as models. Jean Chalaby's *Invention of Journalism*, though fundamentally Habermasian, introduces a major Bourdieuian concept and Bourdieu's own terminology when it posits "a specialized and increasingly autonomous *field of discursive production,* the journalistic field" (1). In his work on Trollope and serialization in the 1860s, Mark Turner has explicitly argued that "it is useful to move freely from textual criticism to material criticism in what might be seen as theoretical eclecticism" ("Toward a Cultural Critique" 116), and Turner himself invokes not only Bakhtin and Bourdieu but also Barthes, Derrida, Foucault, Kristeva, and Raymond Williams.

It's tempting to say that an eclectic approach should not succeed in mixing and matching these three social scientists' ideas, however, because the theories of Habermas, Anderson, and Bourdieu are mutually incompatible in important ways. Not just their details but their major assumptions clash: Anderson's "imagined community" need not be democratic at all to succeed in creating a nationalism, for example, but for Habermas a bourgeois public sphere can exist at all only to the extent its society permits some level of democratic participation. Bourdieu's fields work only to the degree that they are exclusive (achieving autonomous action through in-group agreement among participants), but Habermas's and Anderson's models work only to the extent that they are inclusive, using broadly shared norms of discourse to open political participation despite significant heterogeneity in a population.[12]

But the three social science theoreticians do get used together notwithstanding, as we have seen, possibly because they share at least one common and crucial assumption: the unit of data for each theory is the individual human agent, seen specifically in relation to one or more social groups. Habermas, for example, defines his public sphere through the personal and rather culturally determined dichotomy individuals experience in the West between "public" (community-level) and "private" (family-level) spaces and discourses, already seen as distinct from governing (state-level) discourse. For Anderson, the important site of interaction between the human and the "imagined" national society is the imagination itself; for Bourdieu, again most complexly, fields of discourse are organized and structured by the interactions of their human participants, although in Bourdieu's full theory any given actor's relationship to the field is balanced and mediated by his or her individual "habitus," or set of developed, fixed, and "transposable dispositions" (Bourdieu, *Logic* 53), largely invisible to the individual who holds them, which determines much of that individual's beliefs and behavior.

It's not hard to understand why these theories would be based on a conception of the individual as contextualized social/political actor. They were
created by a political philosopher, a political scientist, and a sociologist, and
the purpose of all three disciplines is precisely to study the behaviors of individuals in groups. Theoretical modeling based in the relationship of individuals to groups is more problematic for the study of print culture or book
history, however, less because of what this dyad emphasizes than because of
a crucial factor that it ignores. Neither Bourdieu nor Habermas nor Anderson clearly conceptualizes what the researcher should do with data when they
come not in the sociological shape of a contextualized person or a contextu-
alizing group, but in the symbolic and encoded shape of *text*. Their theories
largely do not use—or, on some level, even permit—simple close reading,
because they were made to explain behavior, not to interpret words on pages.
Whatever considerable sophistication they bring to the study of societies and
politics, then, when it comes to reading a given issue or article in a periodical,
all three approaches seem to be of the nature that the intellectual historian Isaiah Berlin famously called "hedgehog" rather than "fox" theories. The strategy
of the fox, in Berlin's metaphor, is to survive by knowing many things, but the
hedgehog survives by knowing just one big thing it can apply in all cases.[13]
Social science–driven theories of cultural discourse, when applied to the periodical press, do not know many things about the interpretation and function
of texts in specific cultures at specific times, but just one big thing each about
what texts do. A periodical text for Habermas is a communicative action that
either does or does not aid normatively defined social interaction in the public sphere of a modern society; for Anderson, it is a medium to spread imaginative agreement about the nation and represent the group to the reader; for
Bourdieu, it is an attempt by a more or less rational and constrained actor
to win capital in the symbolic economy of a given field of discourse. Having
(like Dante Gabriel Rossetti in his sister Christina's sonnet) only just the one
meaning it is prepared to find and express, neither more nor less, each theory
tends to find just this one meaning in any text it encounters, without reference
to the text's own form and specific content, which all three theories, significantly, consider to some extent arbitrary.

Moreover, in each theory the real or operative meaning of *every* periodical
text is largely unsayable on the level of *any* periodical text's specific content.
For a text to articulate its function in these three theories would be, in most

cases, to cease to perform it. Anderson does not expect to find any Indonesian newspapers of the 1950s saying explicitly that they are spreading a certain conception of Indonesian national identity, and that they expect everyone to start reading them at 9 AM precisely; Habermas does not expect periodical texts before 1830 to call on their readers to put down the paper and gather in coffeehouses for discussions (nor, after 1830, to tell readers to keep reading and stay out of coffeehouses); nor does Pierre Bourdieu expect to read a French critic in the *Revue des Deux Mondes* declaring openly in his pages that he writes mainly to score points with other critics. These meta-statements and meta-motives, even if actually pervasive and omnipresent, are necessarily implicit. The social science theorists, realizing this, mostly don't expect confirmation from the primary texts of the periodical press itself, don't rely on it, and hardly bother to look for it.[14] All three theories rely for their persuasiveness and verification on elegant structure, consistent internal logic, and the reader's agreement with their normative positions, not on confirmation from primary sources, nor even on success at predicting or explaining any particular historical phenomena, since the theories are intended to apply across many cultures and historical periods.

The social science theories' inability to verify or corroborate themselves within the textual record might seem like a crippling limitation on their persuasiveness and usefulness, especially for scholars trained in literary and historical methods who are trying to solve specific problems in literary history such as those posed by the nineteenth-century British periodical press. The situation of modern periodical studies, however, may actually and oddly have rendered their apparent limitation a selling point. The fact that the theories of Habermas, Anderson, and Bourdieu do not require users to engage particular periodical texts *as* text may actually be a reason these disciplinary foreign imports have been able to compete so successfully against an alternative theoretical school that, in the later 1980s, was beginning to be constructed in literary and historically based periodicals studies itself.

Text has always been the great vexing problem, as well as the great central resource, of Victorian print culture and periodicals studies. The scholar who begins to use nineteenth-century British periodicals in her research immediately realizes she has far more text available than she can ever even look at, much less read closely. The textual corpus of the Victorian periodical press is hardly even scalable, probably uncountable, certainly unreadable by any one scholar. This was true long before the days of blurry-eyed on-screen reading of page images downloaded from Gale, ProQuest, or the Internet Library of Early Journals, even before the days of blurry-eyed reading of microfilm under fluorescent lights, and indeed all the way back to the days of blurry-eyed reading of bound journal files by candlelight. Michael Wolff published his first "back of the envelope" estimate of the size of the Victorian periodical textual base in "Charting the Golden Stream" in 1971, extrapolating from the 12,500 titles he knew to guess that a total of 25 to 50 million periodical articles had probably been published between 1824 and 1900. "Staggering as this figure may be," Wolff noted, "I should think that we are working with the right order of magnitude at least" (29). Subsequent research by John North for the *Waterloo Directory,* however, has shown that Wolff's staggering figure was an undercount by one full order of magnitude. North has estimated that some 125,000 journals were published in the Victorian era, and that their files comprise more than 100 times the text of all contemporary books combined.

To get a sense of the problems posed by trying to treat such a vast amount of text *as* text, we might compare the size of the textual base represented by the genre of the Victorian novel, and remind ourselves of how scholars have struggled to study that much smaller archive. John Sutherland estimates in the *Stanford Companion to Victorian Fiction* that there were some 7,000 "Victorians who could legitimately title themselves 'novelist,'" and "somewhere around 60,000 works of adult and juvenile fiction published 1837–1901." This impressive number is of course a far greater body of texts than any Victorian fiction specialist is expected to read, or even to know by title or author. (Sutherland specifically does not advise his readers to seek most of them out, adding that he "would not condemn anyone to the lower reaches of Victorian fiction" [1]). Familiarity with a hundred of the best-known authors and knowledge of a few hundred of their books—say 1 percent of the total—would qualify any current scholar as well read in Victorian fiction, although few scholars of the novel are perfectly happy with that state of affairs, and whole scholarly organizations and annual forums (such as the British Women Writers Conference) have been founded partly for the purpose of rescuing and recuperating worthwhile but obscure works and authors from the noncanonical 99 percent.

The situation for periodicals scholars who want to claim to understand their own field, however, is far worse. Sutherland's 7,000 novelists begin to look quite manageable when we consider that the *Wellesley Index* alone lists

12,000 separate contributors to the periodicals it indexes—close to double the total number of novelists—and that set of 12,000 writers contributed to only 43 Victorian periodicals out of North's 125,000, or just 0.05 percent. If North's estimate is correct, that the volume of text published in Victorian periodicals exceeds the volume of contemporary books (not just novels) by more than a factor of 100, the periodicals scholar who read whole bound volumes of periodicals by the tens of thousands rather than by hundreds would still, at the end of a long course of reading, have encountered a far smaller proportion of her field's text than even the fiction specialist's unsatisfactory 1 percent.

Clearly, the British periodical press had already by the nineteenth century achieved the condition that John Hartley in *Popular Reality* (1996) attributed to twentieth-century journalism: "far too big to observe, let alone render into a coherent object of study" (33). One of the few bodies of text comparable to the Victorian periodical press in size, heterogeneity, variety of contributors, and resistance to categorization is the modern World Wide Web. We can surely understand why the most common methodological observation made by scholars of the Victorian press is that no existing methodology can describe or explain it.[15]

That the relatively textless theoretical approaches of Habermas, Anderson, and Bourdieu have achieved the success they have is, in this light, much easier to understand. For an uncountable, unreadable, unknowable, overabundant mass of periodical text, each theorist has substituted a single plausible main issue and a single comprehensible abstraction. From the perspective of these theories, the vast and inchoate periodical press comes into focus as just one meaning: an instrument of national or community consciousness (Anderson), a system for the creation and distribution of professionally determined symbolic capital (Bourdieu), or a metric of the political health of a society (Habermas).

The difficulty for literary and historical scholars has only been avoided, however, not solved. The social science theorists escape the complications of dealing with specific texts and their individual meanings at the cost of rendering themselves unable to analyze any specific historical encounters between periodical texts and particular historical readers—that is to say, any specific acts of reading itself. Since, as we have seen, the social science theories have constructed themselves as studies specifically of the relation of individuals to groups, they are not predisposed to consider reading, the encounter between an individual and a text, as even occurring on their theoretical radar. Cultural capital in Bourdieu's literary and journalistic fields is mainly gained through *writing,* not reading, and for Anderson, the content of a given text read by a social actor is beside the point; what matters is that the text mediates contact between individual and group via imagination, the group in this case being the other people the reader imagines are also readers of the same text. Even Habermas's successful participatory public sphere only works, even in theory, when its participants *stop* reading and start talking to one another. For Habermas, the more reading-intensive later form of public sphere is actually a regrettable development, and reading itself, the passive consumption of text, one sign that the press of conviction has been replaced by one of commerce.[16]

This is where, although it too has taken different forms and involved divisions of its own, a theoretical approach to the periodical press that originated in the disciplines of history and literary studies, and that seemed to be developing in the late 1980s and early 1990s toward a full methodology of its own, still has an advantage over the social science theories. The literary and historical conversation about the periodical press, though it has sometimes wandered away from it, has on the whole framed its inquiry much more along the lines of the research question originally posed by Richard Altick in *The English Common Reader* (1957) concerning the dynamic contact between texts and their readers, and it has remained centrally interested in how that contact—reading itself—worked. In Jonathan Rose's paraphrase, the central question of Altick's book was "How do texts change the minds and lives of common (i.e., nonprofessional) readers?" (Rose 48). To ask the question in this way is to both propose and assume that the books and periodicals of nineteenth-century England and the English "mass reading public" were in a complex and interdependent relationship, the moments of which can be traced and reconstructed.

Altick himself apparently long found it frustrating that, for decades after *English Common Reader,* few scholars picked up on this central aspect of his project; he wrote to Rose in 1988 that "not much has been done to expand the scope of the ECR, which I constantly find cited in footnotes but with no indication that the author . . . is trying to fill in the map I outlined" (quoted in Rose 47). In 1989, however, periodicals scholars made major moves to reopen this central issue of how historical texts have interacted with their readers. Margaret Beetham, one of the writers who helped reopen the theoretical issues in periodicals studies in an important theory-themed issue of *Victorian Periodicals Review* edited by Laurel Brake and Anne Humpherys, noted that any given issue of a periodical is "not a window on the past or even a mirror of it" but rather "part of a complex process in which writers, editors, publishers, and readers engaged in trying to understand themselves and their society; that is, they struggled to make their world meaningful" (20). Beetham's essay drew on psychoanalytic theory to suggest a way of understanding the experience of reading periodicals as dynamically both "open" (the periodical itself, as an ongoing process, is fluid and resists closure) and "closed" (specific articles do close decisively into a fixed meaning). In the same issue of *VPR*, Lyn Pykett[17] agreed with Beetham in rejecting any simple view of periodicals "as a mirror reflecting Victorian culture, [or] as a means of *expressing* Victorian culture," but argued for a more Barthesian view of its texts in which periodicals were "a (or perhaps *the*) constitutive medium of a Victorian culture which is now seen as interactive" (7). Pykett seems to have seen the major methodological conflict as being waged between historians and literary scholars (the social scientists were not yet on the horizon), and to have been concerned with preventing historians from simply ignoring the press, while simultaneously preventing literary studies from colonizing "periodicals study by a purely literary or formal methodology." Both Beetham and Pykett remained resolutely committed to the close study of texts themselves, however: "I would want to argue the case for the importance to periodicals study of the close reading of text" and attention to "the formal properties of media discourse," Pykett wrote (16).

Historian or historicist, formalist and/or feminist, press theorists with disciplinary roots in literature or history seem to agree that the problem to be solved is the specific form of the relationship—Richard Altick's dynamic *how*—between the historical subject and the text, not that between the subject and the group. These approaches, culture-specific to Victorian literature and cognizant of the flexible roles of producers and consumers of Victorian print culture (with novelists working as journalists and journalists as novelists), seemed to hold the promise of giving scholars important keys to the nature of Victorian literary culture as a whole.

As we have seen, however, their manifestly better approach to the research problem has not led these scholars to a widely persuasive theoretical paradigm that has been able to inform and guide the research of others. Beetham's

"Open and Closed" model and Pykett's Barthesian reading of text as a cultural medium remain today at the level of prolegomenon and manifesto, while the social science models of Anderson, Bourdieu, and Habermas have become the substrate of a full Kuhnian "normal science" of research into periodicals. Literary scholars and historians may have framed the problem better, but the social scientists have offered the explanatory paradigms and models—field, sphere, imaginary—that have in the meantime gone into full scholarly production. The result, at this moment, is the success of a group of theories that, instead of succeeding in explaining textual data to researchers, succeed mainly in insulating those researchers from that data.

The current place of Mikhail Bakhtin in this theoretical conversation is complex. He is not a new name in the field; Bakhtin is identified with several concepts, including "carnivalesque," "dialogism," and "heteroglossia," that are already invoked in periodicals-centered research in a variety of contexts. In their 1989 theoretical issue of *Victorian Periodicals Review,* Brake and Humpherys were already recognizing potential for the study of periodicals in Bakhtin's ideas about the interaction of textual forms ("Critical Theory" 94). Scholars who use Bakhtin in their critical practice in periodicals studies today, however, most commonly try to suggest that the miscellaneous form of the periodical itself, always a compilation and to some degree a mixture of different textual forms and voices, can be considered a "heteroglossia" operating on its several discourses in ways comparable to those Bakhtin claims for the dialogic novel.[18]

This use of Bakhtinian terminology is not quite a fair extrapolation from Bakhtin's actual theory, however, and indeed contradicts some of the theorist's own observations about periodical discourse. Bakhtin specifically denies that journalistic and other "extra-artistic" texts can achieve real heteroglossia: he writes, "Every extra-artistic prose discourse—in any of its forms, quotidian, rhetorical, scholarly—cannot fail to be oriented toward the 'already uttered,' the 'already known,' the 'common opinion' and so forth." By contrast, "the prose artist elevates the social heteroglossia surrounding objects into an image that has finished contours, an image completely shot through with dialogized overtones; he creates artistically calculated nuances on all the fundamental voices and tones of this heteroglossia" (*Dialogic* 278–79).

The claim that Victorian periodicals could have always-already embodied real heteroglossia also has to work uphill against the historical observations that journalistic genre forms such as the review essay were notably, even determinedly, monologic, and that enforcing consistency of voice and opinion within a periodical was considered one of the duties of a mid-Victorian editor.[19] (We remember the fate of Marian Evans and John Chapman's attempt at an "Independent Section" for the *Westminster Review*.) Many separate monologic discourses collected in a single issue of a periodical cannot constitute Bakhtin's dialogized heteroglossia, but can only be a site where monologic discourse is multiplied. In the hands of a novelist such as Anthony Trollope, as we have seen, periodical discourses such as the leading articles of the *Times* could give true heteroglossia fine raw material, but only the creative consciousness of the novelist, for Bakhtin, could "dialogize" the diverse genres and languages of his or her culture by transforming them and bringing them into productive contact within and through the novelist's own discourse.

The mistake, perhaps, has been in trying to apply Bakhtin's ideas of heteroglossia and dialogism to periodical forms without previously grounding this kind of analysis the way Bakhtin himself grounds it—in an understanding of the universe of discourse as structured by the complex and competing language formations of genre and revealed in the works of individual historical writers who used, mediated, and influenced the development of these genres. Bakhtin's own critical practice begins by treating genres as what genres are—not via metaphors such as "field" or "sphere," but by actual function and almost by definition. Genres are historically contingent, situated, multiple, and competing tools—more precisely, technologies—of discourse, available in specific shapes to readers and writers at specific historical moments for use in solving particular discursive problems. Bakhtin thus anticipates Thomas Pavel's commonsense observation that genres must be of primary importance for the study of discourse because they are the tools most writers themselves chose among to express their worldviews and create their texts. Bakhtin also fully confirms, by a different theoretical path, Alastair Fowler's central insights that genres are in constant mutation, that recognizable sets of features originally formed within different generic kinds—Fowler's "modes"—retain their own content and communicative power, and that artistic and creative decisions made by writers can bring meanings and values from different genres into artistically productive contact within works of other generic kinds.

Applying this understanding of genres to periodicals studies may help scholars solve the overabundance-of-text problem in somewhat the same way that geology solves the overabundance-of-rocks problem and entomology the overabundance-of-bugs problem: by recognizing that most of what one needs to know to understand a given stratum, ecosystem, or moment in the history of discourse is the most specific and detailed qualitative understanding of each current *type*, much more than any catalog of instantiations or exemplars of the type. This is not a denial of the significant uniqueness of each individual text (or rock, or bug), but a recognition that variations in practice or in nature become meaningful and interesting only when the investigator knows the characteristics and distributions of the typical forms from which the individual instance varies. Some individual instances of text are of course particularly individual or powerfully influential on the genre itself, and these must be read closely—which Bakhtinian readings have tools to do (see, again, the fine essay on the chronotope). But not all or even most instances of text in a genre need to be read closely, because most uses of a genre—especially journalistic ones—only reproduce ready-made meanings already contained in the genre itself.[20] This is how, and why, genres work so well to enable and mediate communication. To decode most instances of most genres, readers need to understand only their genre-level meaning—what Bakhtin called their worldview.

What Bakhtin has done is to find a way to describe and conceptualize discourse within cultures as it actually acted on writers and readers. Readers and writers use genres to solve discursive problems; the worldview and assumptions built into genres have always helped writers determine what is worth saying and the ways it can be said, and thus have provided more than simply rhetorical tools, but full and multidimensional measures of value. Any genre provides its users with a more or less rich and complete way of seeing and describing the world. The fact that each genre already contains a specific, evolved, and historically contingent resource of meaning is (at least part of) what Bakhtin means when he points out that genres are not hollow forms into which writers pour meaning, but come preloaded with deep reserves of meaning of their own. And because genres offer writers specific bodies of meaning and specific tools to mediate how their users see the world, they necessarily compete with each other, both ideologically and economically, to win the widest possible acceptance for their specific worldviews.

For frustrated scholars of the Victorian periodical press, the crucial and fruitful change in methodology suggested by Bakhtinian theory is that we can be much less concerned either with tracking down every individually published periodical title or with trying to theorize the genre of "the periodical" as if it were a single discursive entity. The purposes of most scholarly investigations will be much better served by maximizing our knowledge of the historical discourse genres published *in* periodicals—the forms taken by articles themselves. Again, Bakhtin directs us toward the real practices and experiences of participants in the Victorian press. The individual article was the point of contact at which Victorians both wrote and read periodicals. Strictly speaking, of course, it was not even possible to "read" Thackeray's *Cornhill Magazine,* which was only a contractual agreement and a copyrighted title; readers sat down to and became engaged and absorbed in the specific articles and serials in any given issue, evaluating and responding to them according to contemporary genre expectations for those forms. The name *Cornhill* certainly did mediate the reader's expectations for the genres and subgenres to be encountered and the quality of the writers' performances to be expected, but the kinds of mental performance we call *reading* were engagements with texts on the article level. Similarly, readers did not approach new periodical publications expecting entirely new discourses, but expecting modifications and recombinations of the discourse forms with which they were already familiar. This insight of Bakhtin's potentially transforms the degree to which scholars can hope to understand Victorian press discourse, since while there may have been 125,000 separate periodicals and more hundreds of thousands of periodical writers, there was nothing like 125,000 genres for them to work in. As we have seen in previous chapters, and as Aurora Leigh learned early on, the Victorian repertoire of periodical genres was limited and easy for writers (and many nonwriters) to acquire throughout the century. Indeed, this had always been the case, as Fowler notes as well: "Each age has a fairly small repertoire of genres that its readers and critics can respond to with enthusiasm. And the repertoire easily available to its writers is smaller still: the temporary canon is fixed for all but the greatest or strongest or most arcane writers" (226–27).

It may seem that this view of genre simply introduces one more way to oversimplify periodicals, and—re-creating the central weakness in the theories of Habermas, Bourdieu, and Anderson—substitutes a single theoretical meta-meaning for the actual meaning of uncountable thousands of individual texts. I don't think this is the case, however, because the forms and discourses that a generically aware critical practice will direct us to read and try to place in relationship to one another at particular historical moments are not single but multiple, and determining their specific influences and mutual importance to each other is precisely the point of looking at the system through genres. Bakhtin also helps us another way, and offers another methodological advantage over the social science theories, to the extent that he clarifies that it is *genres* themselves that compete in any given culture and at any historical moment, more significantly than individual writers, groups of writers, "trends or schools." This makes him more responsive to observed discursive history than Habermas, Bourdieu, or Anderson, who—no doubt, again, because their disciplines are trying to explain human behavior—tend to pin the human actors in their theories down to single roles and purposes as participants in a sphere or imagined nationalism, or doubly determined fixities tied to both a habitus and a field. Bakhtin does not believe human agents can be fixed in this way. The worldview of a genre, as genre, may indeed—at any given moment, for some genres, and definitely in the case of journalism (*Speech Genres* 152)—be possible to fix, but the worldviews of men and women who employed genres at particular moments in history cannot be so clearly fixed into a final meaning.

To say this is not to attempt to smuggle an unreconstructed and unexamined humanism back into theoretical criticism through a side door, but simply to note a fully verifiable feature of the relationship of historical writers to their genre tools. The mid-century newspaper writer Henry Reeve wrote especially authoritative leaders ("Il Pomposo" was his nickname at the London *Times,* where arrogance had to be particularly pungent to attract attention at all) until he became editor of the *Edinburgh Review* in 1855, when in his first issue he cowrote, or at least approved, an article warning about the public danger posed by authoritative newspaper discourse. George Eliot was an effective writer of "slashing" reviews until she became the novelist whose early work reflected deep reservations about the slashing review. In his *Cornhill* review essay of 1862, James Fitzjames Stephen analyzed some of the inherent intellectual weaknesses and limitations of the newspaper leading article, but then went back to writing—with gusto, and apparently in good conscience—leaderlike essays for the *Saturday Review,* and, beginning in 1865, actual leading articles for the *Pall Mall Gazette.* W. M. Thackeray the novelist pressed against Mrs. Grundy's restrictions on the sayable until he became Mrs. Grundy's enforcer as editor of the *Cornhill,* and (as he has so often been posthumously reminded) would not publish Elizabeth Barrett Browning's "Lord Walter's Wife" because it contained the word "harlots."

Most writers who are not conscious hypocrites participate willingly—suspending possible objections, if not outright disbelief—in the worldview of their genre at the specific moments they use its discourse. But the genre's worldview operates in a determinative and permanent way only on the specific instance of writing produced in that process, not on the writer. Bakhtinian genre theory recognizes this, reifying and fixing what can and should be fixed—the status and interplay of genres at a given moment in history—and leaving "unfinalizable" what really must be unfinalizable—the genre-using human writer, who retains the potential at any moment to code-switch from one genre to another, to put on and take off different generic personae, choose and adapt different generic tools and modes, and echo different worldviews almost moment to moment. Because users of one genre are always also readers and analysts of other genres, their perceptual worlds are not confined to a single sphere or field, and they are able to repudiate, borrow, invoke, and reference the elements of other genres. Genres are therefore always in a mutual and dynamic interaction, between writers and within them, competing for the allegiance of more writers and of more talented writers, as well as for persuasive power over readers.

As the body chapters of this book should have helped to show, the mid-Victorian periodical marketplace was structured by relatively few discourse genres and the worldviews that inhered and evolved within them. The qualifications on a Victorian periodical writer's virtual resume were the demonstrated abilities to produce one or more of these existing genres.[21] Although periodicals present themselves to modern readers now in the form of published issues, the issue was not in fact the crucial organizing element of the periodical press as experienced by its original writers, since the composition of any given issue was opaque to everyone involved except the editor and subeditor(s), who were not (except in rare cases such as Dickens) also major creative composers of its discourse. The individual writer's real point of contact with his or her periodical was the contribution of discrete instances of specific genre types. To have mastered the forms of a genre in high demand (leader, middle), or to have achieved a flexible capability to produce a number of others, was to have the basis of a career as a periodical writer. The house variants on those genre forms favored by individual periodicals could be picked up almost unconsciously, as Walter Bagehot, G. H. Lewes, and Leslie Stephen all variously remark, by any writer who already knew the basic genres.

If facility with current genres was the necessary and sufficient qualification to succeed as a mid-Victorian periodical writer, however, it's probably fair to say that most Victorianists who write *about* the periodical press today or use its texts as sources have less specific working knowledge of its actual genres at any given moment in the nineteenth century than Anthony Trollope's poor hapless Frederick Pickering did. This is a problem not just for periodicals scholars but for all literary and book historians, since, as previous chapters have tried to show, the genre forms developed for and used in periodicals were the discursive competitors and companion forms of nearly all Victorian literature. Knowledge of these forms is surely as necessary a precondition of success—and failure to know them as certain a precursor of failure—in the case of our modern scholarly engagement with the Victorian literary marketplace as they were in the case of Pickering's practical one.

Theories of journalism that try to understand historically specific print cultures through mostly ahistorical theoretical tools—public spheres, imagined communities, journalistic fields—encourage the belief that through journalism's history its forms have naturally followed what the theorist sees as its social or political function, a function that is essentially transhistorical. This trap has been all too easy to fall into, given that modern readers who encounter historical journalism already tend to assume that we understand its basic forms—we've been reading newspapers all our lives—and that we need read only for content, not for generic form. Learning to read historical discourses as elements in a Galilean interaction of genres should prompt us not to focus away from the specifics of our data and toward some imagined ideal of journalistic discourse or print culture, but back toward the discrete features and specific phenomena we want to understand.

As we have seen, the approaches to periodicals studies developed outside of the social sciences have always been better conceived; the advantages of the theoretical approaches of Habermas, Anderson, and Bourdieu have been mostly their relative and somewhat misleading simplicity. They tame the confusion and seem to show the way to significant interpretive conclusions, while the methods being developed within history and literature seem to offer only the sweat, toil, and tears that come with any long period spent in front of a microfilm reader. With any luck, however, the body chapters of this book have done something to demonstrate that literary and historical theorists have always been on the better track, and that adding genre-conscious theoretical practices to periodical studies can indeed produce concrete and useful interpretive outcomes. A genre-based approach to historical discourse is both literary—focused on language and its forms—and historical—aware of the data of actual historical events. It may be able to help literary scholars and historians take full advantage of the specific strengths of their disciplines: the sensitive ear for form and voice, the rigorous insistence on documentation of historical fact.

Bakhtin's ideas about genre, considered as a guide for future critical practice in Victorian periodicals studies, have one more crucial implication. All three of the major social science theories tend to be synchronic in nature— they attempt to explain forces presumed to be stable as the scholar looks at them, or at least temporarily in balance. A "Galilean" system, however, can never be presumed to be a relatively unchanging field of reciprocal forces or recurring flows like a communication circuit, Andersonian imagined community, Bourdieuian field, or Habermasian sphere. Important relationships of relative power and influence between its elements must change as their orbits swing, and there can be no returns to a previous state. This last implication of Bakhtin's model of genres for periodicals studies—that you can never step into the same golden stream twice—will be the subject of my epilogue.

EPILOGUE

The Tale of the "Owls"

Literature, Journalism, and Genre after 1865

For any individual consciousness living in it, language is not an abstract
system of normative forms but rather a concrete heteroglot conception of the world. All words have the "taste" of a profession, a genre, a
tendency, a party, a particular work, a particular person, a generation,
an age group, the day and the hour. Each word tastes of the context
and contexts in which it has lived its socially charged life; all words and
forms are populated by intentions.

MIKHAIL BAKHTIN, "Discourse in the Novel"

THIS PROJECT HAS FOCUSED ON A DOZEN YEARS of British book history after 1855, studying relationships between journalistic and literary
discourses in just that era. I have kept within those bounds, though the rest of
the nineteenth century presents many equally significant interactions between
literature and the press, because (as I will discuss below) Bakhtin's formalist
ideas about genre also have strong historicist implications. In this short epilogue I want to look slightly beyond this mid-century period, however, and
sketch future directions I believe a Bakhtinian inquiry into Victorian book
history could take.

We have seen how change in the perceived influence of an important
nonliterary Victorian discourse genre had powerful and almost simultaneous
effects on many other genres and their writers. Within a few years at mid-
century, the success of review-essay journalism made outright converts of
some famous writers, such as Harriet Martineau, and attracted others to learn
and practice its forms even as they wrote in other genres, so that the other

genres were informed (or deformed) by journalistic language, tropes, and assumptions. During these years literary authors, including Elizabeth Barrett Browning, studied journalism closely; some of them, including George Eliot, ultimately rejected it, while others, including Anthony Trollope, integrated their discoveries about it into literary works. As novelists and poets reacted to journalism, however, journalism continued to act and react to the other genres, working to establish its own view of the world as normative, and competing with other forms, such as the sensation novel, that challenged important elements of its worldview.

If changes in a single genre can cascade so quickly into large simultaneous effects on and among other genres, then literary and nonliterary genres may always have been more closely interdependent, and more subject to rapid and wide-ranging change, than previous models of literary history have been able to acknowledge. If this is true, then discourse genres encountered in different time periods should be more difficult to compare, and sometimes almost incommensurable, and genres should function and interact in substantively different ways in different historical periods.[1] By focusing on the genre interactions of just over one decade, this book has tried to keep its lines of argument and causation relatively clear by limiting itself to what is in effect a single large case study of the short-term consequences to literary history of one change in the Galilean universe of mid-Victorian discourse. In what is probably a failure of nerve, I have deliberately avoided dealing with the complicated range of secondary effects and interactions that must have followed for both journalism and literature in later decades of the nineteenth century.

Scholars of British journalism who pursue these issues further than I have, however, may find there is significant explanatory power in a new appreciation of how rapidly and thoroughly Victorian journalism's everyday working genres were capable of changing. Although a few examples can only be suggestive, there are hints in the textual record to confirm that British press discourse was capable of changing so rapidly and thoroughly as to alter its basic generic nature, at least as that was perceived by contemporary observers. Nineteenth-century journalists often show a strange difficulty in appreciating—or even understanding—the journalism of the generation immediately previous to theirs. William Hazlitt, writing in the *Edinburgh Review* of 1823, challenged his readers to "look over a file of old newspapers (only thirty or forty years back) . . . and compare the poverty, the meanness, the want of style and matter in their original paragraphs, with the amplitude, the strength, the point and terseness which characterize the leading journals of the day" ("Periodical Press" 222). Forty years after Hazlitt's article on the periodical press was published, however, a journalist in *Chambers's Journal* in 1867 looked back at the leading newspapers of Hazlitt's own generation and found them anything but ample, strong, pointed, and terse.

> The man who takes up a volume of the *Times* or the *Morning Chronicle* for one of the early years of the present century, will be sadly disappointed if he expects to find in either anything resembling the articles which are now provided for him every day. A few bald lines of summary, and a stilted and ungrammatical sentence feebly echoing the gossip of the town, are all that he will find in the columns which are now filled with essays often of remarkable literary ability, and almost always written with force, clearness and elegance. ("Our Leading Columns" 449)

On the surface, both journalists seem to be applying the same criteria to both eras. Both see good journalism in their own times as intelligent ("the amplitude"; "remarkable literary ability"), forceful ("the strength"; "written with force"), and clear ("the point and terseness"; "clearness"), compared with newspapers of the previous era, which are characterized by intellectual barrenness ("the poverty, the meanness"; "feebly echoing the gossip of the town") and lack of literary skill ("want of style and matter"; "a few bald lines of summary, and a stilted and ungrammatical sentence"). But where Hazlitt looks at the journalism of his contemporaries and recognizes all the virtues, a later journalist who looks at the same texts sees only the weaknesses. Even the discourses of which a generation of journalists was most proud, it seems, can become nearly unrecognizable to their professional descendants, though the descendants would have said they were applying the same generic yardstick.

It is almost unnecessary to remark that this is rarely what happens to a given generation's first-ranked novels, poetry, or historical, critical, or even personal essays. The poems of Joanna Baillie and William Wordsworth, the novels of Sir Walter Scott and Jane Austen, and the familiar essays of Charles Lamb and even Hazlitt himself, although their individual reputations changed markedly, were admired—or at least consistently read—throughout the remainder of the century. Review-essay journalism at all levels, however, from an era's best daily newspapers to its best quarterly reviews, seems to have been subject to a kind of change so rapid and thorough that even the best of its texts came to seem antiquated or incompetent to readers within a few years. Older journalism was soon not only literally unread—yesterday's newspaper expects to be unread—but effectively unreadable to those with more current genre expectations, and greater elapsed time seemed to increase the effect. Another *Chambers's* article that looked back farther at the early London *Times* remarked that "a more melancholy specimen of journalism, as read by our present lights, it is not easy to imagine" ("'Tis Eighty Years Since" 689), while Leslie Stephen's attempt to look back from the 1890s at the brilliant early days of Sidney Smith and Francis Jeffrey's *Edinburgh Review* led him to the dejected conclusion that "every reader who is frank will admit his disappointment. . . . Few of the articles would have a chance of acceptance by the editor of a first-rate periodical to-day; and . . . the majority belong to an inferior variety of what is now called 'padding'" (244).

This effect on the status of journalistic texts seems worth closer study because it is not the familiar dynamic in which a later generation simply re-evaluates or reorders the texts that had been admired by the previous generation. It is a stranger case in which, as far as the later generation is concerned, the former generation produced *no* texts of even minimal competence. "We have indeed small reason to regret that we did not live three generations ago," wrote the *Chambers's* journalist. "At all events, if nothing else has improved, without doubt *Journalism* has" ("'Tis Eighty Years Since" [689]). A valuable project for someone interested in "charting the golden stream" of Britain's historical periodical press might be to find a way to use such texts to create a synchronic picture of the nature and timing of the changes in nineteenth-century journalists' genre practices and expectations.

Such studies may also test the hypothesis that journalism has changed more rapidly than other genres partly because change has always been more crucial to its competitive success. A genre developed to produce text in a few hours to specified lengths to meet the demands of nonspecialist audiences is surely less likely than other genres to give rise—at least on average—to textual performances that are accurate, wise, well-informed, or graceful on their own terms. Qualitative tradeoffs must be made for the emphasis journalists and editors necessarily place on speed of composition, contemporaneity, and wide accessibility to readers. Just as newspapers such as the *Times* notoriously succeeded partly by adapting themselves quickly to shifting political winds, British journalism as a whole throughout the nineteenth century may also have succeeded best when it adapted most quickly to the changing gravities and proximities of its Galilean discursive environment. A high degree of this kind of generic flexibility may turn out to always have been a key to journalism's modern discursive successes, equally important to, or even more important than, the communicative function that scholars of journalism sometimes claim all modern democratic societies need journalists to perform.[2]

A methodological approach to British journalism that assumes and expects a high degree of ongoing change in its discourse may also provide a new way to understand the specific history of nineteenth-century journalism. Current press historiography tends to focus on periods of obvious controversy and transformation (the "War of the Unstamped," the explosion of new publications after the repeal of the Stamp Taxes, the New Journalism) and give relatively little attention to periods of apparent stability. But learning to see change as normal and stasis as unusual may redirect our attention to some currently less-studied periods, such as the later-Victorian decades that immediately preceded the New Journalism. In most popular accounts of nineteenth-century British press history, the 1860s and 1870s saw only gradual changes in the discourse of the middle-class newspaper press, although more substantial change might well have been expected. The creation of the cheap popular press after the repeal of the Stamp Taxes meant that the ascendancy of traditional "quality" papers such as the *Times* had received a mortal wound, and the next important event to be chronicled by most press histories is the rise of the more sensational, more entertaining, more socially engaged, but intellectually lighter New Journalism.[3] But this did not actually happen for fully three decades. Not until 1887 was New Journalism inaugurated when Matthew Arnold famously named the genre (and characterized it as "feather-brained"). The 1860s and 1870s therefore seem to be a pause in the narrative—a time of stasis, or only gradual evolution, or of events preparatory to change, such as the 1870 Education Act, which helped create the future readers of the New Journalism.

A Bakhtinian view of discursive history may give us different eyes and expectations with which to view this period, however, and new tools to investigate what actually changes in discourses during the periods when little change seems to occur in the discourse itself. Periods of apparent stasis in journalism should be of especial interest, because Bakhtin's model of generic competition suggests that journalism in particular would suffer from continuing to use the successful forms of a previous era. The dynamic of novelization helps us see that as genres interact and change, any new or markedly changed genre becomes for some period and to some extent a discursive "black box" for other genres. Its full potential is unknown, and some contemporary observers will overestimate it, attributing powers to it that it does not really have, as the apparent power of leading articles in the *Times* in the mid-1850s provoked the *Saturday Review* and other observers to speculate that the *Times* had become the political ruler of the country. An older journalism, however, has almost by definition been around long enough for competing discourses (especially highly motivated official, clerical, and corporate ones) to take its measure and learn to avoid its strengths and exploit its weaknesses. If this is true, periods such as the 1860s when journalistic genres do not appear to change should not be times of stasis at all, but ones in which journalism is perceptibly *losing* influence and importance relative to other genres. Journalism that does not change should quickly become less effective relative to other discourses, and the longer it has been since its forms and norms changed, the greater should be its competitive disadvantage.[4] Studies of actual periods of stability in journalism's forms will give print historians an opportunity to test this implication of Bakhtin's ideas as well.

Observing and studying such complex discursive phenomena, however, will require us to rethink our assumptions about which primary sources are most valuable. Scholars of the Victorian periodical press since Walter Houghton have relied most heavily on texts written by journalists about journalism, or what we might call meta-journalism, to investigate and theorize Victorian periodicals. Houghton's helpful first list of meta-journalistic essays was given in his introduction to the first volume of the *Wellesley Index,* and includes such important essays as those of Walter Bagehot and James Fitzjames Stephen, all since drawn on many times by periodicals scholars (and in this book). If our objective must be not only to understand a genre's reflexive view of itself, however, but even more significantly to understand the relationship of genres to each other at a given historical moment, we will have to treat the claims made in meta-journalistic texts much more skeptically, and to take more careful note of their necessarily performative nature. A genre's account of itself, measured only with the yardstick of its own worldview, will often have the most to hide about its own limitations, and be the best at hiding it. As we have already seen, Walter Bagehot, Leslie and James Fitzjames Stephen, G. H. Lewes, and E. S. Dallas were far from neutral observers of the discourse forms they used, and not neutral commentators on other contemporary genres and subgenres.

Bakhtin's ideas should also teach us to read ordinary and non-self-referential instances of historical discourse genres more carefully. While we can learn to read the worldviews and conventions of these forms in the same way Anthony Trollope did, by patient and alert induction, it is dangerously easy to assume that historical forms will follow the conventions of their modern descendant genres (as when a modern reader expects nineteenth-century journalism to demonstrate "objectivity") or, still more insidiously, to assume that the conventions we have managed to reconstruct for a genre in one historical era will still operate in the same ways in a different era.[5] Here, again, our reading must be corrected against the perceptions of the genre's original "theorists"—its historical readers and competitors.

A more Bakhtinian approach to the study of historical journalism will therefore find many of its most useful sources not in the meta-journalism written by journalists themselves, but in what we might call the peri-journalism of poets, historians, and especially novelists who directly competed against journalism. These writers often had the greatest stake, as I tried to show in chapter 1, in assessing their rival discourses accurately. Elizabeth Barrett Browning, Anthony Trollope, Harriet Martineau, and George Eliot all became important theorists of journalism in the mid-1850s; for earlier in the nineteenth century, theorists of journalism from whose analyses we can benefit include John Galt, Edward Lytton Bulwer, and T. B. Macaulay; for later in the century, they include T. W. Robertson, George Gissing, and Grant Allen.

Another valuable source for a kind of book history that would build on Bakhtin's ideas will be texts generated at points of contact and translation between genres. If competition is built into the nature of genres themselves, genres should often reveal their natures most fully when competing actively for interpretive control, or when asserting their worldviews with respect to some particular event. Newspaper leader writers who attempted to explain the disappearance of Reverend Speke, and periodical critics who attacked the assumptions and psychology of the sensation novel, produced many such texts. Writers who transition into new genres, such as Martineau, or who renounce them, such as George Eliot, may also leave textual records, such as the *Autobiography* and "Janet's Repentance," that serve as generic contact points. Further research will turn up many texts that show attempts by genres or subgenres to analyze competing genres, and provide similar snapshots of moments of ideological conflict and negotiation. All these sources will be invaluable for book and periodical history, as long as we treat the genre that analyzes and the one that is analyzed as in a Galilean relationship, and avoid privileging one or the other. Texts of true heteroglossia—of different generic voices brought together in active dialogue as they existed at particular cultural moments—await close reading and study.

For the period that begins just as this book's mid-Victorian focus ends, one text I believe fits these criteria particularly well, and should particularly repay close reading, is T. W. "Tom" Robertson's hit play *Society* of 1865. Although now almost unknown to and unused by periodicals scholars, *Society* is a significant document of the history of British journalism, a journalism-themed play with a journalist-hero that was the hit of the 1865 London theater season.

Fictions of Journalism in 1865: The Owls and the "Earthquake"

Society opened on 11 November 1865 as the first production in Marie Wilton's refurbished Prince of Wales Theatre, formerly the Queen's Theatre— an unpromising property that had been known as "the Dusthole." Despite a triumphant first run of 150 nights (Savin 60), great popularity on the later-Victorian stage during several revivals, and its acknowledged importance to British theater history,[6] however, *Society* is infrequently performed today, and a summary of its plot and characters may be useful.

The hero, Sidney Daryl, is a baronet's younger son and a former Lancer. Before the action opens, Sidney has spent his mother's inheritance to redeem the family estate near the village of Springmead from his older brother Sir Percy's gambling debts. Sidney is now living in chambers in Lincoln's Inn, supporting himself in a precarious but genteel way (the stage directions read *"the room to present the appearance of belonging to a sporting literary barrister; books, pictures, whips"*) by writing for newspapers and periodicals. Sidney is in love with his distant relative Maud Hetherington, an orphan and the niece of Lord and Lady Ptarmigant; Maud returns his affection, but neither has money to marry. Lady Ptarmigant is trying to arrange a mercenary marriage for Maud with John Chodd Jr., a boorish social climber whose father, John Chodd Sr., has acquired a fortune through a brother's Australian gold mines and speculation. The ambitious Chodds hope to use their fortune to move John Jr. into high society and Parliament, and while they negotiate with Lady Ptarmigant for Johnny to marry the well-born Maud, they decide to advance their political prospects by starting a morning newspaper.[7] The Chodds engage middle-class journalist Tom Stylus to gather a staff of reporters and leader writers, and Stylus brings the Chodds to see his friend Sidney in the first scene of the play.

Stylus hopes only to enlist the well-connected Sidney to write social leaders, but Sidney gives him much more, extemporizing a name for the new paper—"The Earthquake"—and some of the prospectus on the spot. The two men then collaboratively imagine a prospectus that will claim the new paper has been called into existence to chronicle the social, economic, and political upheavals of modern times. (The ambitions of the Chodds are, of course, not mentioned.)

> SIDNEY: Don't you see? In place of the clock, a mass of houses, factories, and palaces tumbling one over the other; and then the prospectus! "At a time when thrones are tottering, dynasties dissolving—while the old world is displacing to make room for the new—"
>
> TOM: Bravo!
>
> CHODD SEN: (*enthusiastically*) Hurray!
>
> TOM: A second edition at four o'clock p.m., the *Evening Earthquake,* eh? Placard the walls. "The *Evening Earthquake*", one note of admiration; "The *Earthquake*", two notes of admiration; "The *Earthquake*", three notes of admiration. Posters: "The *Earthquake* delivered every morning with your hot rolls." "With coffee, toast, and eggs, enjoy your *Earthquake!*"

This passage, and indeed the entire scene, is dense with figured relationships between various kinds of press discourse, and with commentary on the contemporary value and uses of the press. In this exchange in particular, Sidney the leader writer and Tom the subeditor are surprisingly successful at dialogically integrating two forms of contemporary journalistic discourse, the commercial and the political. Tom the subeditor is as familiar with the tropes of 1860s-era newspaper advertising, which treat the newspaper as a consumer commodity, as Sidney the leader writer is with the inflated promises for its intellectual and political impact conventionally made in the prospectus. The juxtaposition of these two kinds of generic promotional language emphasizes their real similarity: Sidney's promises of a faithful journalistic chronicle of worldwide near-revolution, and Tom's of convenient breakfast-time delivery, turn out to complement each other nicely. (We can perhaps see, however, why Anthony Trollope, launching *Saint Pauls* two years later, might have wanted his own prospectus to take a different direction.)

A further irony developed in this scene is that although the newspaper's name, "The Earthquake," signifies extraordinary upheaval and permanent change, the new newspaper is intended by all concerned to be rigorously conventional, replicating existing journalistic forms in every way—except, of course, insofar as its politics will be pro-Chodd. Here, again, Robertson's text confirms and extends an analytical point about the press that Anthony Trollope was making at the same historical moment about the press—that while not all or most contemporary journalists were hypocrites, the discourse forms they used were strikingly not designed to fulfill their own explicit promises.

Tom and Sidney do not believe a word of the prospectus text they improvise in this scene, but neither man is in Robertson's treatment a rogue, a hypocrite, or a villain. The phrases they invoke are precisely those which, ten years earlier at the launching of many new inexpensive dailies after the repeal of the paper stamp tax, would have been taken seriously by both readers and writers. The language of the press in this scene would have been perfectly recognizable to that earlier audience, but the constellation of expectations around the language and for the language has changed significantly. Claims that would have been made ten years earlier in full seriousness—either honestly by a naïf like Charley Tudor, or quasi-deceptively by a more Machiavellian figure like Tom Towers—can by 1865 be created lightheartedly by two good fellows in full knowledge that the phrases have become only a form of words. The Galilean position of press discourse has therefore noticeably changed between 1855 and 1865, but its most important changes have been in what its language forms signify to writers and readers, rather than within the language forms and conventions themselves, which outwardly remain much the same. In

"Discourse in the Novel," Bakhtin notes the advantages of a dialogic view of discourse over more conventional interpretive close reading for recognizing precisely this sort of change in the status of text. "From the point of view of stylistics, the artistic work as a whole—whatever that whole might be—is a self-sufficient and closed authorial monologue," writes Bakhtin. "Should we imagine the work as a rejoinder in a given dialogue, whose style is determined by its interrelationship with other rejoinders in the same dialogue (in the totality of the conversation)—then traditional stylistics does not offer an adequate means for approaching such a dialogized style" (274).

How much the relationship of the existing generic tropes of newspaper writing to other kinds of discourse has in fact changed becomes still clearer in the next exchange, as Tom and Sidney improvise more potential text for the prospectus in the effortless way that highly conventionalized genres enable their writers to do.[8]

CHODD SEN: A cheap daily paper, that could—that will—What will a cheap daily paper do?

SIDNEY: Bring the "Court Circular" within the knowledge of the humblest.

TOM: Educate the masses—raise them morally, socially, politically, scientifically, geologically, and horizontally.

CHODD SEN: (*delighted*) That's it—that's it, only it looks better in print.

TOM: (*spouting*) Bring the glad and solemn tidings of the day to the labourer at his plough—the spinner at his wheel—the swart forger at his furnace—the sailor on the giddy mast—the lighthouse keeper as he trims his beacon lamp—the housewife at her pasteboard—the mother at her needle—the lowly lucifer seller, as he splashes his wet and weary way through the damp, dreary, steaming, stony streets, eh?—you know. (*Slapping* SIDNEY *on the knee—they both laugh.*)

CHODD SEN: (*to* CHODD JUNIOR) What are they a-laughing at?

The interpolated remarks of Chodd Sr. make it clear that he approves of this discourse; a reader of newspapers, but not a very sophisticated one, he recognizes what he hears as the forms of language a newspaper should contain, but cannot make the further recognition that the language he hears is by now utterly conventional and clichéd. (He does get part of the way there, however, when he notes that "it looks better in print.") But Chodd's failure to understand Sidney and Tom's laughter further suggests that by the time of *Society* in 1865, the discourse forms of journalism have become less the broadly inclusive and persuasive public discourse they were originally intended to be—a true "publicity"—than a professional, trade, or coterie discourse.

Robertson's thematic interest in exploring the intellectual and political staleness of 1860s journalistic forms continues in act 2, which introduces Johnny Chodd and the audience to the play's real locus of journalism, a public house called the Owl's Roost. The regulars at the Owl's Roost, referred to as the Owls, include only two avowed full-time journalists, Stylus and a "gentleman" who "does the evening parties on the *Belgravian Banner*," but all the other Owls are at least occasional journalists. Their other common denominator is being intellectual black sheep, men who have turned to journalism despite being mostly well-educated professionals capable of greater things.[9] In *Society*, the practice of journalism is therefore either a dead end—as it is for most of the Owls and even for Stylus, who has "started eighteen daily and weekly papers—all failures" (67), or a waypoint on the road to better things, as it is for Sidney. Its status as a career mirrors its status as a discourse, which is in Robertson's analysis negated or exhausted, consisting only of generic stock elements or misfired forms of other and better discourses. This point is made explicit in a set piece song in the "Owl's Roost," in which journalism is represented as one of four notoriously empty forms of speech (the others, each of which gets its own verse, are "commercial," "amatory," and "political"):

> When papers speak with puff and praise
> Of things and people nowadays
> Of kings, quack medicines, railways—plays—
> Old laws, inventions new
> Alliterative words and fuss
> Big adjectives, terms curious,
> Sounds fury—what's all this to us
>   But cock-a-doodle-doo
> Cock-a-doodle, cock-a-doodle, cock-a-doodle-doo.

The song is, interestingly, genre criticism: it identifies the most recognizable occasions, topics, and material forms (where applicable) of journalism, and then in the refrain equates all of them with empty crowing.[10]

In the last act Robertson shows the "Earthquake" opening up along the fault lines—both of situation and of discourse—of the discourse it contains. Stylus, though still working for the paper, has become disillusioned and angry at Chodd Sr. for not choosing him as the salaried subeditor. When he and Sidney discover that the Chodds have decided to try to put Johnny into Parliament as member for Springmead, the Daryl family's ancestral borough, Sidney impulsively decides to run for the seat himself. Tom chooses solidarity with Sidney over loyalty to the Chodds and rises in revolt against his own publisher, recruiting the Owls as Sidney's election workers. ("We can write for you," Tom tells Sidney—"And fight for you," adds one of the two Irish Owls.) The very first issue of the Chodds' own newspaper, therefore, delivered by train the next morning to Springmead, contains a surprise third leader that endorses Sidney's Springmead candidacy and ridicules Chodd, the paper's secret owner. This implicit resignation of the newspaper's entire staff, which ends the "Earthquake" with its inaugural issue, is communicated to the astonished Chodds only in the last act, after they proudly open their fresh copies to look at the leader page. By the end of the play, the Owls have helped Daryl win his family's seat in Parliament and Maud's promise to marry him, but the career of the "Earthquake" is over, as are Daryl's social leader writing, Tom's subeditorship, and presumably the Chodds' careers as newspaper proprietors.

The difference between the representation of the press in *Society* in 1865 and the fictional accounts of journalism created by Trollope, the Brownings, Conybeare, and other writers in the mid-1850s seems to merit close attention. The magisterial beginnings of the first two "Earthquake" leading articles read aloud by the unsuspecting Chodds indicate that Stylus's leader writers are still assuming the omniscient and arrogant persona Trollope personified in Tom Towers:

CHODD SEN: (*reading*) Look at the leader. "In the present aspect of European politics—"

CHODD JUN: "Some minds seem singularly obtuse to the perception of an idea."

These leader writers are clearly following well-established mid-century models: Both "In the present aspect of European politics" and "Some minds seem singularly obtuse to the perception of an idea" (even if the last is also a reflexive dig at the Chodds themselves) are classic authoritative openings in the mid-1850s *Times* tradition. By the mid-1860s, however, such phrases as these had been used by newspaper writers many more times, and even many readers who in the 1850s had been inclined to imagine that the successes of newspaper journalism had revealed some special powers inherent in such language forms might well have become disillusioned by 1865 about what they could achieve.[11] Robertson's analysis suggests that two decades before the acknowledged advent of New Journalism, such mid-century journalistic forms may already have lost much of their 1855 discursive authority.[12] Robertson's play may help us chart when and even how the British essay-review genre, so widely regarded as omnipotent in 1855, lost some of its former influence.

Historical events in this decade may of course also have had much to do with the timing of journalism's decline: the support of the *Times* and *Saturday Review* for the Confederacy, and their misreading of the U.S. strategic situation, meant that the U.S. Civil War did almost as much harm to the reputation of some major papers as the Crimean War had done good. Political contingency, bad editorial decisions, and even changing technology may not have been as harmful to journalism's authority, however, as the fact that their discourse had simply been around—in interaction with other discourses—for ten years longer, and as a result was understood quite a bit better by other discourses and their users than it had been before.[13] Harriet Martineau, who I noted in chapter 2 seems to have had a particularly sensitive ear for which genres had the most cultural authority at a given historical moment, seems to have noted a change in the wind at just this time, and ended her full-time leader writing for the *Daily News* in 1865. Though Martineau had proudly referred to the political power of "D. News" in letters written in 1858, and had told Florence Nightingale that year that she couldn't imagine writing fiction again after newspaper writing, Mary Elizabeth Leighton and Lisa Surridge have pointed out that she was trying her hand again at a few stories by the early 1860s.[14]

If any of my individual chapter studies of interactions between the press and literary forms have been successful, I hope they will encourage similar studies of interactions at other points in the century. The theories often used today to describe historical discourses such as journalism tend to assume that while writers and literatures have fraught and complex histories, genres of discourse have led a simpler background existence. A mature and well-developed history of the book, however, will be suspicious of any account of a nineteenth-century genre such as journalism that relies too much on any single narrative of decline (of a public sphere) or rise (of the popular press), or any simple binary structure (educative versus representative ideals, publicism versus journalism).[15] It will also be suspicious of any theory that represents journalism as a kind of discourse called into existence by a relatively unchanging human need for information.

Discourses too have densely eventful histories, and these histories can be traced much more closely than by large periods or epistemes. A full charting of the "golden stream" of public discourse in nineteenth-century Britain will not be intellectual history in the familiar sense—the history of thought itself—but rather the history of highly specific forms and tools of language that competed among and within British writers as they tried to express, encode, and frame responses to the world they lived in. Our successful recovery of more of this generic history—the story of the developing natures and theories of genres and their relationship to one other—is surely necessary for our understanding of both literature and the periodical press, and a precondition for any true history of the book.

Appendix A

Correspondence Sections of the *Monthly Repository*,
vol. 17, nos. 201–3, September–November 1822

Note: Discipulus is the pseudonym of the twenty-year-old Harriet Martineau.

September 1822:

CORRESPONDENCE.

Communications have been received from Messrs. Turner, of Newcastle; J. Marsom; G. Kenrick; D. Davis; D. A. Borrenstein; also from Christianus; R.C.; and C.

Vectis is respectfully informed that No. CXXI. for January 1816, may be had of the publishers. There must have been negligence (we cannot suspect artifice) in the book-sellers referred to.

When we have received another communication or two from *Discipulus,* we shall be better able to judge of his proposal; but our Correspondents are none of them of the description that he seems to suppose.

October 1822:

CORRESPONDENCE.

Communications have been received from Messrs. Kentish; Bransby; Bateman; James; T. C. Holland; Acton; H. Mace; and J. Cornish: from Captain Ross: and from Ben David; an Unitarian (Maidstone); Euelpis; F.B.; a Barrister (Harrowgate); and Edinburgensis.

The "Account respecting Coventry" is not yet received.

Had R.C. (whose communication was acknowledged last month) written as an inquirer, we should probably have inserted his letter; but he could not surely expect that we should publish common-place objections to Christianity which are completely refuted in the works of West, Ditton, Sherlock, and a hundred other writers, and which are repeated in as dogmatic a manner as if they were discoveries.

November 1822:

CORRESPONDENCE.

Communications have been received from Messrs. Theophilus Browne; T. C. Holland; Joseph Jevans; and J. W. Pigg: Also, from F.S.; I.B.; T.G.; S.C.; and I.B. (Sheerness).

The continuation of *Discipulus* has come to hand. His other proposed communications will probably be acceptable.

We design for an early Number the *Essay on the Principles of Criminal Law* from the author of "A New Version of some of the Epistles of Paul."

In our next we propose to insert Colonel Stanhope's further Letter on the subject of a Free Press in India.

X.'s Letter shall be sent to Mr. Wellbeloved.

The Letter on Bible Societies has, we fear, miscarried.

Mancuniensis is put into the hands of the Gentlemen referred to, as is also H.W.

By an accident, the continuation of the Review of the work on "Church Property and Church Reform" is deferred.

Letter II. from the late Rev. *James Nicol* was mislaid, but is recovered, and will be brought into the next Number.

Appendix B

Representations of the Periodical Press
in Anthony Trollope's Works

While I try to provide references to most significant treatments of journalism in Trollope, this tally is not intended to be exhaustive, and many readers might not agree with where I have drawn the line of significance. Very minor references to the press, such as the mentions of "Daily Jupiter" coverage in *The Bertrams* or the unnamed newspaper editors who attend parties in *The Way We Live Now* and *Sir Harry Hotspur of Humblethwaite*, are omitted if they do not engage other characters or the narrator. Trollope frequently creates and interpolates local periodicals into his action in passing, such as the "Leeds and Halifax Chronicle" in *Orley Farm* and the "Staines and Egham Gazette" in *The Duke's Children;* but when these are peripheral to plot, character, or theme, I have omitted them as well. Closer to the borderline, unspecific mentions of press coverage, such as the brief mention in *The American Senator* that the senator's actions "had been made matter of comment in the newspapers," with some elaboration of the comments, still seemed to me to fall just below the line.

TROLLOPE AS READER, 1848–60
Trollope had no direct knowledge of periodicals or journalists at this time, according to the Autobiography, *although he had sent articles and letters to the* Examiner.

The Warden (1855, wr. 1852–53)
The "Jupiter," a London morning daily modeled on the *Times*, appears throughout. Tom Towers is its personification and editor, manager, and/or chief leader writer. Anonymous and omnipotent, the "Jupiter" effectively rules the country; its leading articles (quoted in chs. 7 and 13) create the story's crisis. Towers lives at the Temple as a barrister, does not admit his newspaper connection, and refuses John Bold's personal appeal with, among other tactics, a defense of press independence (chs. 14–15).

"The New Zealander" (wr. 1855–56)
Daily newspaper discourse is studied in ch. 3, "The Press," where Trollope discusses the relationship between press discourse and public opinion, the newness of its discourse ("No one in fact knows what is the duty of the daily Press. That we have to arrange and fix among ourselves"), and the effective monopoly of the *Times*. He notes the way press discourse passes into society: "Men think, and speak, and act

the Times newspaper. Prominent social orators talk leading articles, while humble individuals content themselves with paragraphs." He calls newspapers' claimed ethical position "falsely high."

Barchester Towers (1856, wr. 1855–56)
The "Jupiter" and Towers reappear, though Towers stays physically offstage. He has genuine access to secret political information and grants a request from Obadiah Slope to endorse him for a deanship, but the resulting leading article (given in ch. 33) has no effect. Trollope adds more periodicals to his world: "British Grandmother," "Anglican Devotee," and "Eastern Hemisphere" (ch. 1).

The Three Clerks (1857, wr. 1857)
The "Daily Delight," a London "halfpenny" daily, employs Charley Tudor as a fiction writer. Its editor is Charley's "mentor" and "literary papa," but is not named and only briefly seen. Publicly, he sets an absurdly "moral" tone for the paper; privately, he avoids paying Charley and takes advantage of his naivete. In the last chapter Katie mimics this editor's written style.

Dr. Thorne (1858, wr. 1857–58)
Dr. Thorne airs a professional dispute with Dr. Fillgrave in a local newspaper (the "Barsetshire Conservative Standard"), from which it spreads to Bristol, Exeter, and Gloucester papers. Thorne then appeals to London medical periodicals, including the real *Lancet* and invented "Journal of Medical Science," "Weekly Chirurgeon," and "Scalping Knife." These press debates make Thorne a minor public figure (ch. 3).

Framley Parsonage (1861, wr. 1859–60)
Leaders for opposed daily newspapers are written by the novel's political aspirants: "Jupiter" leaders are written by Mr. Supplehouse, and leaders for the "Purist" are written or reviewed by Harold Smith. These leading articles are quoted or referenced in chs. 2, 18, 20, and 23. Tom Towers starts a dissolution rumor in ch. 29. A full "Jupiter" leader criticizing Mark Robarts is given in ch. 47, which causes Robarts much pain but has no effect on opinion in his circle.

Orley Farm (1861, wr. 1860)
Idealistic but briefless barrister Felix Graham writes poetry for periodicals, newspaper political articles, and at least one major article for a quarterly review: "He would sooner do this, he often boasted, than abandon his great ideas or descend into the arena with other weapons than those which he regarded as fitting for an honest man's hand."

TROLLOPE AS CONTRIBUTOR AND STAFF WRITER, 1860–67
Joined the Cornhill *and contributed serial fiction under Thackeray from 1860. Helped found* Fortnightly Review *with Lewes as editor, 1865. Joined the staff of* Pall Mall Gazette *with George Smith as his editor/proprietor.*

The Struggles of Brown, Jones and Robinson (1861, wr. 1857)
In a framing story, the *Cornhill* editor has solicited Robinson's first-person story and corrected its text. The frame with its references to periodicals is an 1861 addition to this 1857 novel.

North America (1862, wr. 1861–62)
Trollope hypothesizes the perfect newspaper, "a triumph of honesty and of art," which would have the specific virtues of British journalism (power, popularity, political focus, omniscience, critical ability, assurance) without the corresponding vices (pride, tyranny, lack of modesty). "Above all these things it should be readable, and above that again it should be true." American newspapers are by comparison unorganized, poorly written, and poorly informed: "They have made no approach to that omniscience which constitutes the great marvel of our own daily press" (ch. 15).

"Anonymity," *Fortnightly Review* (1865)
This article discusses the anonymity convention in English periodicals by analyzing how different types of periodicals are used by readers. It concludes that most periodicals should be signed, but that political newspapers should remain anonymous because of their special function as "an instructor and informant in politics" that is "accepted, not as the teaching of one man, but as an expression of concrete wisdom from a condensed mass of political information and experience."

Miss Mackenzie (1865, wr. 1864)
Miss Mackenzie's suitor Maguire is a contributor to the Littlebath "Christian Examiner," a religious weekly; its unnamed editor is also seen. Maguire's "The Lion and the Lamb" leading articles describing Miss Mackenzie's finances and personal situation are picked up and commented on by a "very influential" metropolitan newspaper, causing personal distress to both Miss Mackenzie and her other suitor, John Ball.

The Claverings (1866–67, wr. 1864)
The minor character Tom Jones is "editor, or sub-editor, or co-editor" of "some influential daily newspaper." Harry Clavering thinks editors are "influential people, who had the world very much under their feet,—being, as he conceived, afraid of no men, while other men are very much afraid of them." But Jones is "very quiet" and "almost submissive."

Last Chronicle of Barset (1867, wr. 1866)
Crawley contributes a Greek translation of "the very noble ballad of Lord Bateman" to a magazine. In a rare substantial use of real-world periodical titles within Trollope's fictional world, John Eames and Major Grantley read the *Times*, *Daily News*, *Spectator*, and *Saturday Review* on a train, and discuss the "merits and demerits" of that "enterprising periodical" the *Pall Mall Gazette* (ch. 27). News of developments in Barsetshire reaches English characters traveling in Europe via the English-language Paris newspaper *Galignani's Messenger* (ch. 70).

"Misfortunes of Frederic Pickering," *Argosy* (Sept. 1866)
The law clerk Pickering attempts a London literary career after publishing in a provincial paper, but fails because he does not know how to write any of the genre forms in which saleable copy can be produced, from London letter to magazine article to index. His journalistic contacts include Roderick Billings of the "Lady Bird" and unnamed editors of the penny "Daily Comet," the "International" ("a weekly gazette of mixed literature"), and "Salford Reformer," a provincial weekly.

Phineas Finn (1868, wr. 1866–67)
Finn briefly connects himself with a radical daily, the "People's Banner," and writes two leading articles. Quintus Slide is a staff leader writer who advises Finn that an ambitious MP should cultivate a newspaper connection to express his political views: "In public life there's nothing like having a horgan to back you" (ch. 26). Finn eventually objects to Slide's methods and cuts the connection (ch. 75).

"Mr. Robert Bell," *Pall Mall Gazette* (13 Apr. 1867): 11
This obituary of Bell praises him as "a contributor to periodical literature, working both as a writer and as an editor" who has "afforded one of the few instances we have that literature taken in early life as a profession, and as an only profession, may be made the means and the sole means of maintaining an honourable career."

TROLLOPE AS EDITOR, 1867–70
Founding editor of Saint Pauls. *Discontinued work for the* Fortnightly Review.

"Introduction," *Saint Pauls* 1 (Oct. 1867)
This prospectus article is a wry deflation of traditional prospectus language; Trollope writes that his magazine is "not established, on and from this present 1st of October, 1867, on any rooted and matured conviction that such a periodical is the great and pressing want of the age" (1). He notes the recent growth of periodical literature, and promises to be political, to avoid book reviews, and to mix the useful and the practical per the motto *Omne tulit punctum qui miscuit utile dulci.*

"Trade of Journalism," *Saint Pauls* 1 (Dec. 1867)
Trollope analyzes writing as a professional career for young men, defining journalism as "all writing, whether in magazines or reviews or newspapers, which is written for money, with the view, not so much of enhancing the individual writer's reputation, as of increasing the sale of the periodical in which it appears" (307–8). Journalists are not artists: "Professional journalistic writing belongs to a lower class of literature than histories, or poems, or works of fiction" (307–8). A hard-working journalist with ability should make "a couple of hundred pounds" his first year, and a successful journalist reach "eight to twelve hundred" a year (312–13). Other topics include the anonymity system, the professional writer's independence, and the career's relative ease of entry.

He Knew He Was Right (1869, wr. 1867–68)

Subplot protagonist Hugh Stanbury writes leaders for the radical penny newspaper "Daily Record," whose unnamed editor Stanbury calls "the tallow-chandler" because his father was a city grocer; and possibly also for the late hours he requires of Stanbury and other writers. Stanbury, honest and industrious, makes a major defense of the status of journalism in ch. 71, arguing that a major newspaper editorship is more important than the Lord Chancellorship. Louis Trevelyan's suspicions of his wife are inflamed by reading newspaper divorce cases.

The Eustace Diamonds (1873, wr. 1869–70)

The narrator reflects on the public effects of newspaper commentary as police search for Lady Eustace's diamonds. "Day after day, and almost every day, one meets censure which is felt to be unjust;—but the general result of all this injustice is increased efficiency. The coach does go the faster because of the whip in the coachman's hand, though the horses driven may never have deserved the thong" (ch. 49). Newspaper coverage of successive disclosures is mentioned in chs. 50, 63, 73, 78.

"The Turkish Bath," *Saint Pauls* 5 (Oct. 1869)

The editor-protagonist of the story believes his physical person should be separate from his editor function: "We think that as a rule editors should be impalpable." A charming Irishman engages him in private conversation in a Turkish bath, however, where his physical presence is inescapably present, and turns out to be a would-be contributor who offers a manuscript. The contributor is the editor's opposite: well spoken in person but incapable of written discourse.

"Mary Gresley," *Saint Pauls* 5 (Nov. 1869)

The narrator is the editor of an unnamed shilling monthly and acts as a literary mentor to Mary Gresley. Gresley publishes stories in periodicals, but ultimately renounces writing and burns the manuscript of her novel.

"Josephine de Montmorenci," *Saint Pauls* 5 (Dec. 1869)

In a thematic reversal, the palpable and named editor of the monthly "Olympus Magazine," Jonathan Brown, chases an impalpable and pseudonymous contributor.

"Panjandrum," *Saint Pauls* 5 (Jan./Feb. 1870)

"Panjandrum" is a projected periodical that is never published. The story's narrator is its nominal editor. "Mr. X," editor of the "Marble Arch," is to be the publisher. The utopian scheme of the periodical's intended founders does away with a single editor; decisions are to be made collaboratively, and the narrator is given no actual authority. Mr. X diagnoses the failure at the end: "You were very anxious to do something grand, but hadn't got this grand thing clear before your eye."

"The Spotted Dog," *Saint Pauls* 5/6 (Mar./Apr. 1870)

The "Penny Dreadful," a penny dreadful, employs tragic protagonist Julius Mackenzie for 45 shillings a week. Its editor is "a gentleman sitting in a dark cupboard." The narrator-editor's comments on the penny dreadfuls recall Wilkie Collins's in "The Unknown Public": "We had not even known of the existence of these papers;—and yet there they were, going forth into the hands of hundreds of thousands of readers, all of whom were being, more or less, instructed in their modes of life and manner of thinking by the stories which were thus brought before them."

TROLLOPE AS EDITOR EMERITUS, 1870–82
Maintained literary and journalistic friendships.

"Mrs. Brumby," *Saint Pauls* 6 (May 1870)
The narrator is "Mr. _____," the editor of "_____ Magazine," a shilling monthly. The narrator has a series of encounters with an untalented but highly manipulative contributor. He is ultimately forced by his publisher to pay for her unpublishable work, and his editorial authority is destroyed. His former clerk, who has become editor of the "West Barsetshire Gazette," a "red-hot Tory newspaper," is now "upon the whole the most arrogant personage we know."

Phineas Redux (1874, wr. 1870–71)
The "People's Banner" reappears (ch. 22), with Quintus Slide now editor. Slide changes the paper's politics from Radical to Conservative for personal reasons, but as an "experienced journalist" easily repels the jibes of other daily papers over this. Slide is "indefatigable, unscrupulous, and devoted to his paper. Perhaps his great value was shown most clearly in his distinct appreciation of the low line of public virtue with which his readers would be satisfied." His attempt to publish Kennedy's letter about Lady Laura is checkmated in ch. 27 ("An Editor's Wrath") by a legal injunction obtained by Phineas Finn. Slide's anger at Finn partly derives from his genuine belief in the powers and privileges of newspapers.

Australia (1873)
Trollope discusses newspapers as an aspect of national culture in ch. 9 in surprisingly positive terms. "With all the prejudice of a genuine Briton, I think that no country has ever yet produced newspapers equal to those of England. This fact—if it be a fact,—I attribute partly to her wealth, partly to her general energy, partly to her love of fair play, but chiefly to her determination that the press shall be free."

The Way We Live Now (1874–75, wr. 1873)
This novel introduces a trio of papers mentioned in subsequent novels: the "Breakfast Table," a morning daily, edited by Mr. Broune; the "Literary Chronicle," a weekly, edited by Mr. Booker; and the "Evening Pulpit," an evening daily, edited by Ferdinand Alf. Lady Carbury contacts each editor personally to solicit a positive review for her new book "Criminal Queens," with mixed success. She marries Broune in ch. 99. Trollope's notes identify the "Breakfast Table" with the actual *Pall Mall Gazette*, Broune with "Morrish" (?), and Booker with the journalist Alfred Shand.

The Prime Minister (1875–76, wr. 1874)
Quintus Slide is still editor of the "People's Banner," and his critical articles in opposition to Palliser's ministry and his inquiries about Lopez's election expenses torment the prime minister. Broune, Booker, and Alf and their journals reappear.

Is He Popenjoy? (1877–78, wr. 1874–75)
Mr. Grease, the public and "nominal editor" of the "Brotherton Church," a provincial religious weekly, has tried and failed to receive holy orders. Mr. Groschut, who has actual control of the paper, uses it to pursue a private anti-Ritualist, anti-Dean agenda.

Autobiography (1883, wr. 1875–76)
Trollope discusses his acquaintance via George Smith with the journalists Robert Bell, W. H. Russell, G. H. Lewes, "Jacob Omnium," E. S. Dallas, G. A. Sala, and Fitzjames Stephen in ch. 8. He discusses the *Fortnightly Review* under Lewes and Morley, the problems that led to editor Norman Macleod's rejection of *Rachel Ray* for *Good Words*, and the debate over anonymous journalism in ch. 10; the *Pall Mall Gazette* under George Smith, including its "Amateur Casual" stories and Trollope's own varied work for the paper, is in ch. 11. *Saint Pauls* under Trollope himself is discussed in ch. 15.

Cousin Henry (1879, wr. 1878)
Mr. Evans is editor of the "Carmarthen Herald," a provincial weekly. Evans risks a libel suit to accuse Henry of wrongdoing, and his articles faithfully reflect current public opinion. Mr. Brodrick considers him "a man specially noble and brave in his calling" (ch. 16).

Thackeray (1879, wr. 1879)
Thackeray's performance as editor of the *Cornhill Magazine* is critically analyzed. "Of a magazine editor it is required that he should be patient, scrupulous, judicious, but above all things hard-hearted. . . . A man so susceptible, so prone to work by fits and starts, so unmethodical, could not have been a good editor" (ch. 1).

Dr. Wortle's School (1880, wr. 1879)
When the "Broughton Gazette" editorializes on Dr. Wortle's behavior with the wife of his teacher, the story is picked up by "Everybody's Business," a local gossip weekly: "It was the purpose of the periodical to amuse its readers, as its name declared, with the private affairs of their neighbors." Wortle threatens a libel action, and his lawyer meets offstage with an unnamed editor who is willing to publish any retraction that doesn't "make him eat too much crow."

Mr. Scarborough's Family (1882–83, wr. 1881)
Henry Annesley's school friend Quaverdale writes and does editorial work for a paper called "The Coming Hour"; his editor is mentioned but not seen. Annesley

briefly considers a journalistic profession, but Quaverdale's no-nonsense description of the career deters him.

A Note on Sources: For aid in tracking down Trollope's journalists and editors, I have turned to Trollopians much more knowledgeable than I am in reference sources including, especially valuably, Richard Mullen and James Munson's *Penguin Companion to Trollope.* For the errors of omission and commission that must have occurred as I reviewed and assessed so large an oeuvre, I am obviously solely responsible.

Notes

Prologue

1. John Hartley notes in *Popular Reality* that most academic courses on journalism remain preprofessional in focus rather than analytical or scholarly. "Rarely do journalism courses ask their students to consider the conditions for journalism's existence: where it comes from, what it is for, and how it works, in the context of modernity. Students are simply asked to *do* it without understanding it" (35). Michael Schudson's diagnosis of the research climate in academic journalism is bleaker still: "Journalism schools have not to this day nurtured a substantial research tradition; near the bottom of the academic pecking order at most institutions (Missouri and Northwestern are notable exceptions), their university colleagues do not expect or demand much from them" ("News, Public, Nation" 481).

2. The little rigorous scholarship done on the genres used in earlier periodicals has been produced mostly in the last decade. In his 2002 review article in *American Historical Review*, Schudson praises Jean Chalaby for the innovative "genuine contribution" his *Invention of Journalism* (1998) makes in simply "locating media history at the level of genres, texts and literary forms" (488). Schudson's own pioneering study on the history of the news "interview" genre is in *Power of News* (1995). I made a first attempt to trace the origins of the British newspaper editorial in "Who Invented the 'Leading Article'?" *Media History* 5.1 (1999): 5–18. One index of the amount of work remaining in this area, however, is that even modern journalism's most-used genre form, the "inverted pyramid," has only recently begun to have its generic history traced by scholars. For a debunking of the long-standing myth of the U.S. Civil War genesis of the genre, see Errico. For a tracing of its modern appearance in journalism pedagogy, see Vos.

3. Major review essays on periodicals studies have recently appeared in the two most significant journals for Victorianists. Kay Boardman's "'Charting the Golden Stream': Recent Work on Victorian Periodicals" appeared in the Spring 2006 *Victorian Studies,* and Sean Latham and Robert Scholes's "The Rise of Periodical Studies" in the March 2006 *PMLA.*

4. Successful recent examples include Marysa Demoor's *Their Fair Share* (2000), a survey of the writing careers of female contributors to the later *Athenaeum,* and Alexis Easley's *First-Person Anonymous* (2004), which studies the periodical writing of Harriet

Martineau, Christian Isobel Johnstone, Elizabeth Gaskell, George Eliot, and Christina Rossetti.

5. Beetham's essay "Towards a Theory of the Periodical as a Publishing Genre" and Pykett's "Reading the Periodical Press: Text and Context" have been handily reprinted in Brake, Jones, and Madden's *Investigating Victorian Journalism*.

6. B. E. Maidment noted his "overwhelming sense . . . that there is almost no attention paid to Victorian periodicals in themselves, though many articles and essays depend on evidence drawn from periodicals to substantiate, illustrate, or reinforce arguments constructed out of other kinds of scholarly evidence" (143).

7. One of the few points of agreement in periodicals studies is that this scholarly subfield has as yet no agreed-upon methodology. Laurel Brake astutely observes that the problem stems partly from the difficulty of the material itself, but also partly from the historical effects of so many diverse disciplines trying to use periodical texts as primary sources: "Methodology is the problem that haunts study of the press: it is a practical problem that never goes away because the form is so ungainly—single units that are infinitely continuous, but the text of the press is also the site where the multidisciplinary origins of those in the field are most visible and in struggle" ("Production of Meaning" 166). Lyn Pykett has written similarly that "students of the Victorian periodical press have persistently confronted the double problem of defining the object of study, and devising an appropriate methodological framework within which to conduct that study" (3–4), and Ann Parry has observed that "study of the periodical press is, and has been bedeviled, by the lack of generally accepted investigative procedures that satisfactorily connect institutional studies with social and political structures" (18).

8. The claim that Victorian periodicals can provide modern scholars transparent access to their original writers' thoughts may have reached its zenith in a recent advertisement for a microfilm collection of major Victorian magazines and reviews. The ad, which ran in several scholarly journals, was illustrated with a phrenological skull and promised that purchasers would "read the minds of those who lived IN THE NINE-TEENTH CENTURY."

9. After John Holloway made the first (and still almost sole) successful attempt to reconstruct the worldview and conventions of a specific Victorian discourse genre through close readings of its actual texts in his landmark *The Victorian Sage* (1853), the scholar A. Dwight Culler expressed doubts that Holloway's project had been worth doing at all. Culler wrote, "One does not need by indirections to find directions out when he has those directions plainly before him . . . [,] methods devised to translate the symbolistic and suggestive language of poetry into the abstract and explicit language of criticism are less useful in the case of a literature which is already written in that language" (2).

10. Other genre theorists have reached, sometimes by other paths, the same conclusion about this function of genre. Alastair Fowler's classic study *Kinds of Literature*, though it begins from a different set of assumptions, similarly concludes that "there is

no doubt that genre primarily has to do with communication. It is an instrument not of classification or prescription, but of meaning" (22).

11. In her classic *Reading the Romance,* for example, Janice Radway convincingly abstracts a single cluster of themes and messages that seem to operate in all successful texts of the modern American mass-market romance novel genre.

12. Bakhtin writes, "This stratification is accomplished first of all by the specific organisms called *genres.* Certain features of language (lexicological, semantic, syntactic) will knit together with the intentional aim, and with the overall accentual system inherent in one or another genre: oratorical, publicistic, newspaper and journalistic genres, the genres of low literature (penny dreadfuls, for instance) or, finally, the various genres of high literature. Certain features of language take on the specific flavor of a given genre: they knit together with specific points of view, specific approaches, forms of thinking, nuances and accents characteristic of the given genre" (*Dialogic* 288–89).

13. In this context it is interesting to revisit, as a comment on genre function, George Orwell's ironic observation in his essay "Politics and the English Language" that writers can avoid much of the hard work of creative composition "by simply throwing your mind open and letting the ready-made phrases come crowding in. They will construct your sentences for you—even think your thoughts for you, to a certain extent—and at need they will perform the important service of partially concealing your meaning even from yourself" (135).

14. Alastair Fowler's remarks about the differing ways writers of different abilities use genre parallels Bakhtin's closely: "Great writers have found a challenge in genre rules," writes Fowler, "while minor invertebrate talents have been positively supported by them, as by armatures" (29). Fowler's impressive study, which goes beyond the sifting and evaluation of historical approaches promised in its title to make valuable contributions of its own, is *Kinds of Literature: An Introduction to the Theory of Genres and Modes* (1982). John Frow's recent introduction to genre theory, *Genre* (2006), is so thoroughly informed by Bakhtin that its own central argument is the straightforwardly Bakhtinian one that "far from being merely 'stylistic' devices, genres create effects of reality and truth which are central to the different ways the world is understood in the writing of history or philosophy or science, or in painting, or in everyday talk. . . . Genre, like formal structures generally, works at a level of semiosis—that is, of meaning-making—which is deeper and more forceful than that of the explicit 'content' of a text" (19).

15. As recently as 1982, in *Kinds of Literature,* Fowler was skeptical both that nonliterary genres had a useful structural relationship to nonliterary ones (a proposition he thought denied "the integrity of literature" [18]) and that it could be useful to think of literary genres as being in dynamic contention with each other. Fowler considered the latter idea interesting, but, at least in the form developed by Jurij Tynjanov, too preoccupied with the idea of conflict. "In short, Tynjanov's theory of generic evolution is too Darwinian" (250).

16. While we "may not yet have the perspective to be sure whether the nineteenth

century is the most prolific of all literary periods in experimentation with genre," Fowler observes, "it certainly offers an embarrassment of riches" (206).

1. The Poet's Tale

1. Quoted text is from the revised second edition of 1859, by way of Margaret Reynolds's 1992 Ohio University Press edition. Variant lines, of which there are several interesting examples in this passage, are helpfully given at the bottom of the page in Reynolds's edition.

2. Barrett Browning seems to have considered replacing "that" with "which" for the 1859 revised edition of *Aurora Leigh*. The change would have made the line clearly refer to the artistic deficiencies of saleable poetry ("No one lives by verse which lives") rather than possibly also to the starvation of professional poets ("No one lives by verse that lives").

3. This passage contains Jesus's instructions that his disciples' good works be done secretly rather than ostentatiously: "But when thou doest alms, let not thy left hand know what thy right hand doeth."

4. The harm periodicals are doing to England's national literature and international reputation is the organizing idea of this part of Bulwer's discussion. "This is a great literary epoch with your nation," said a German to me the other day. "You have magnificent *writers* amongst you at this day, their names are known all over Europe; but (putting the poets out of the question) where, to ask a simple question, are their writings?" (256). At the end of this section, Bulwer can answer the German's question: "We must seek them not in detached and avowed and standard publications, but in periodical miscellanies" (261).

5. For another, later example of the same arguments, see "Periodical Literature at Home and Abroad," *Month* 3 (Dec. 1865): 551–60: "Many minds and many pens, that might in former centuries have laboured in the composition and setting forth of ponderous folios or goodly quartos ... [,] are now devoted to supplying the ephemeral demands of an insatiable public" (551–52). An earlier and somewhat more light-hearted one is William Hazlitt's 1823 essay "The Periodical Press" in the *Edinburgh Review*.

6. At this historical moment, with anonymity almost universal for periodical texts but out of fashion for literary ones, anonymous writing would have been effectively synonymous with periodical writing.

7. Stephen's prediction has so far been fulfilled by only a single literary historian. George Saintsbury's *History of Nineteenth Century Literature* devotes two chapters out of twelve to periodicals, and Saintsbury declares, "Perhaps there is no single feature of the English literary history of the nineteenth century, not even the enormous popularization and multiplication of the novel, which is so distinctive and characteristic as the development in it of periodical literature" (166).

8. John M. L. Drew remarks in *Dickens's Journalism* that "it has, of course, long been a topic of debate whether the writings of an in individual 'in the public journals' (*OED*),

or journalism in general, can be said to constitute a distinct genre, or whether journalism is simply a form of printing and distribution which can transmit texts conforming to any of the established 'literary' kinds" (2).

9. Alistair Fowler also makes this point when considering another theoretical model for genres as systemically related—that, for example, "when epic declined (the argument might run) its functions passed to the georgic and novelistic genres, which correspondingly rose in status and grew in scope to occupy some of its fictive space." But he concludes that this "hydrostatic" model for generic change is hard to support. "We do better to treat the movements of genres simply in terms of aesthetic choice" (226) by writers of a given era.

10. For a particularly valuable discussion of the role and duties of the Victorian periodical editor, which they analyze usefully in terms of seven specific functions, see Patten and Finkelstein.

11. James Mill's argument ties the periodical form so closely to a range of intellectual vices, in fact, that he has an awkward time explaining how his own new quarterly review will avoid them. "What! Are we, it may be asked, superior to seducements to which all other men succumb? If periodical writing is by its nature so imbued with evil, why is it that we propose to add to the supply of a noxious commodity? . . . We have no claim to be trusted, any more than any one among our contemporaries: but we have a claim to be tried" (222).

12. Lee Erickson asserts in chapter 3 of *Economy of Literary Form* that "a hard-working" Victorian magazine writer "could reasonably expect to make a middle-class income of £300 a year" (71), citing contemporary evidence from journalist G. H. Lewes, among others. But this level of income seems to have been difficult to achieve and precarious to maintain in practice, however theoretically possible market rates of pay made it. Lewes's friend Anthony Trollope explores some of the problems with relying on literature as primary income in "The Trade of Journalism," and refers to them implicitly in the obituary he wrote in April 1867 for his friend Robert Bell, who, Trollope wrote, "afforded one of the few instances we have that literature taken in early life as a profession, and as an only profession, may be made the means and the sole means of maintaining an honourable career" ("Mr. Robert Bell" 11). Some formidable nonfinancial obstacles to periodical writing's becoming a profession are explored in contemporary articles including James Fitzjames Stephen, "The Profession of Journalism," *Saturday Review* 1 Jan. 1859: 9–10, and James Payn, "The Literary Calling and Its Future," *Nineteenth Century* 6 (1879): 985–88.

13. John Morley, G. H. Lewes, and Leslie Stephen all also remark this assimilative function of contemporary journalism. Leslie Stephen, for example, later rereading an old file of the *Saturday Review,* couldn't tell his own contributions from those of other contributors, and concluded that his younger self "had unconsciously adopted the tone of my colleagues, and, like some inferior organisms, taken the colouring of my 'environment'" (*Some Early Impressions* 130.) This influence of the periodical environment on the writer was frequently cited by opponents of the anonymity system as a reason

to encourage signed publication. I discuss the debate over anonymity in this period in "Salesman, Sportsmen, Mentors: Anonymity and Mid-Victorian Theories of Journalism," *Victorian Studies* 41 (1997): 31–68.

14. In his memoir *My Life's Pilgrimage,* the *Lloyds Weekly Newspaper* editor Thomas Catling recounts how he started working in the paper's composing room in 1845(–46); hard work and enterprise enabled his rise from composing to subediting (65). This career trajectory is reflected in the fictional Quintus Slide of Anthony Trollope's Palliser novels, who is lower-class by origin but writes and schemes his way to the editorship of a London daily newspaper.

15. There is also the problem that using Bakhtin's ideas in the service of a more expansive or abstract "theoretism" seems to risk betraying the entire Bakhtinian project. In her preface to the 1984 English edition of *Problems of Dostoevsky's Poetics,* editor and translator Caryl Emerson remarks that "theory, in the quantitative sense of a 'technology,' is not to be found in [Bakhtin's] work" (xxxi). I have tried to theorize in moderation.

16. Bakhtin specifies a few historical moments of generic change provoked by the novel's success: "Several times in the Hellenic period, again during the late Middle Ages and the Renaissance, but with special force and clarity beginning in the second half of the eighteenth century" ("Epic and Novel," in *Dialogic* 5).

17. I consider the different manifestations of the Victorian review essay form, from newspaper leader to quarterly review article (but as opposed to, among others, the personal or familiar essays), as members of a closely and modally related family of genres, drawing on the analogy between genres and families offered by Fowler, who wrote that "representatives of a genre may then be regarded as making up a family whose septs and individual members are related in various ways, without necessarily having any single feature shared in common by all. The analogy proves extraordinarily suggestive. . . . Genres appear to be much more like families than classes" (41). More justification for this position should appear in the course of my argument; for a further exposition and a conjecture as to how this family relationship might have begun, see "Who Invented the 'Leading Article'?" *Media History* 5.1 (July 1999): 5–18.

18. Greg is cited in the *Wellesley Index* as the author of this anonymously published article, but it seems likely that the *Edinburgh Review*'s new editor Henry Reeve, who had just in 1855 taken up that post after a long period as one of Delane's chief leader writers at the London *Times,* contributed to the arguments and text—especially since the article shows traces of Reeve's distinctive bombastic style. Some (friendly?) sniping between the current *Times* leader writers and their former colleague might also be detectable in the *Times*'s rejoinder to the *Edinburgh Review* article, in which the *Times* puckishly characterizes the "great trimestrial critic" as "a calm being whom we imagine sitting at a study table with a blue-book, a glass of water, and a paperknife" (15 Oct. 1855: 6b).

19. For example, Angus Hawkins reads the political history of this period as almost entirely a matter of internal parliamentary issues and alliances, with journalism's influence marginal and peripheral. By contrast, James Vernon pointedly rejects any reading of

the major mid-century parliamentary reforms as a result of "high political manoeuvring" rather than of "pressure from outside Westminster" (2). Further, although it seems to have long been the conventional wisdom among press historians that the *Times*'s great reputation and power at this time "enabled it to destroy the Aberdeen administration in the Crimean War" (Innis 45), and that the government immediately responded by punishing the *Times* through new stamp tax legislation, this line of causation seems not to be shared by parliamentary historians. For a recent articulation of the press historians' position, see Conboy.

20. This memorable formulation of Bagehot's has been explicated at length by Walter Houghton in a major essay, "Periodical Literature and the Articulate Classes." Houghton expands on Bagehot to distinguish between the two forms. In the "essay-like review," Houghton wrote, "the focus was first shifted, partially or entirely, from the book itself to what the book suggested. In place of critical examination, the 'review' might become a series of observations woven into an essay that is illustrated, here and there, by reference to the text, or that combines currents of thought drawn from one passage or another. In either case, there is a movement out and in, away from the book and back to it." In the other form of essay, such as the one in which Bagehot actually coined these terms, Houghton writes, "The books are not so much as mentioned. This is the review-like essay" (6). I am not sure my own reading of Bagehot authorizes so straightforward an interpretation of what seems intended as a fluid and nuanced genre distinction.

21. I will explore this decision and its possible sources at much greater length in chapter 4.

22. Bakhtin notes in "Discourse in the Novel" that "for any individual consciousness living in it, language is not an abstract system of normative forms but rather a concrete heteroglot conception of the world. All words have the 'taste' of a profession, a genre, a tendency, a party, a particular work, a particular person, a generation, an age group, the day and hour. Each word tastes of the context and contexts in which it has lived its socially charged life; all words and forms are populated by intentions" (*Dialogic* 293).

23. The journalism scholar Michael Schudson has made observations about twentieth-century American journalism that closely parallel Bakhtin's insights into the content of genres and their influence over writers. Schudson notes that the forms and genres of today's journalism encode important content, and can control the writers who use them. Journalism's forms of discourse, "which [journalists] must control if they are to be respected professionals—have an extraordinary power to control the journalists themselves and, through them, their readers," Schudson writes, and he calls for citizens as well as journalists to "recognize the substantive message and substantial authority of narrative form" ("Politics of Narrative Form" 111). Schudson discusses "the institutionalization of interviewing in journalism as "both a social practice and a literary form" (73) in his chapter "Question Authority: A History of the News Interview" in *The Power of News*.

24. There were mid-Victorian novelists who did "journalize" in a more literal sense,

experimenting with forms of fiction that would be directly imitative of journalistic discourse. The journalist George Augustus Sala wrote novels that were a deliberate conflation of fictional narrative and journalistic style, while the more popular Charles Reade went so far as to formulate and publicly defend a fact-based theory of fiction modeled on newspaper journalism. See Poovey for an interesting recent reading of Reade's project, in which it is seen as a possible alternative direction that British fiction as a whole could have taken at this point in literary history.

2. The Authoress's Tale

1. All page references to the *Autobiography* in this chapter are to Linda Peterson's handsome new edition (2007).

2. As a graduate student in the 1990s preparing manuscripts to go into the mail, I was so moved by Martineau's description of her first professional triumph that, although I had no research to do at that time that involved it, I sought out the microfilm of the *Monthly Repository* in the library of the University of Iowa simply to read the same words she had, the editorial "request to hear more from V. of Norwich," and to vicariously share the joy of first professional success. My surprise at what I found instead was the germ of this chapter.

3. Martineau writes in the first volume: "I do not mean that any amount of literary connexion would necessarily have been of any service to me; for I do not believe that 'patronage,' 'introductions' and the like are of any avail, in a general way" (129).

4. "On five occasions in my life I have found myself obliged to write and publish what I entirely believed would be ruinous to my reputation and prosperity," Martineau writes in period 4, section 1. "In no one of the five cases has the result been what I anticipated" (163). Caroline Roberts's recent *The Woman and the Hour: Harriet Martineau and Victorian Ideologies* (Toronto: U of Toronto P, 2002) is organized around those five occasions and works, which Roberts identifies as the *Illustrations of Political Economy* (1832–34), *Society in America* (1837), *Letters on Mesmerism* (1844), *Eastern Life, Present and Past* (1848), and *Letters on the Laws of Man's Nature and Development* (1851).

5. The later part of the *Autobiography* has two anecdotes to this effect. In the first, Martineau tells of strongly repelling even well-meant suggestions about a text in progress. A friend who advises her to soft-pedal observations about the treatment of women in a book on American society receives this crushing reply: "It is one of the most sacred acts of conscience to settle with one's own intellect what is really and solemnly believed, and is therefore to be simply and courageously spoken. You ought to be aware that no second mind can come into the council at all. . . . You may think I am making too serious a matter of this. I can only say that I think it a very serious one. The encroachment of mind upon mind should be checked in its smallest beginning, for the sake of the young and timid who shrink from asserting their own liberty" (445–46). In the very next story, Martineau tells of another friend who had asked to "see and criticize" the first chapter of her *Retrospect of Western Travel*. Finding that he had penciled numerous word and

sentence edits onto her manuscript, Martineau "put it to him what would become of my book if I submitted the MS. to other friendly critics, equally anxious to deal with it. He could not answer the question, of course; so he called me conceited and obstinate, and I rubbed out his pencil marks." Concludes Martineau: "It is to be hoped that, some time or other, literary works of art,—to say nothing of literary utterance being a work of conscience,—will be left to the artist to work out, according to his own conception and conviction" (447).

6. Gaby Weiner's introduction to the 1983 Virago edition of the *Autobiography*, for example, notes that the book "is highly selective in its inclusion of reviewers' comments, inclining towards the favourable rather than the hostile," but adds: "One suspects that this apparent distortion of the truth was the unintentional consequence of a highly selective memory rather than a deliberate manipulation of reality" (xvii).

7. Martineau's first major biographer is also the first exception. In *Harriet Martineau*, Florence Fenwick Miller writes that Martineau's "little errors about these facts must be corrected, because the truth of the matter is at once suggestive and amusing. . . . The youthful authoress had presented herself to her editor in a manly guise, . . . [and] Harriet Martineau adds another to the group of the most eminent women writers of this century who thought it necessary to assume the masculine sex in order to obtain a fair hearing and an impartial judgment for their earliest work" (39). John Nevill's *Harriet Martineau* also accuses Martineau of designedly concealing her sex from her first editor, but neither book points out the other counterfactual statements in the *Autobiography*'s vocation story.

8. Vera Wheatley's *Life and Work of Harriet Martineau* (1957) and R. K. Webb's *Harriet Martineau: A Radical Victorian* (1960) ignore the minor errors entirely, going so far as to restate Martineau's incorrect date of 1821 for her publication. It seems to have been Valerie Kossew Pichanick, in *Harriet Martineau: The Woman and her Work* (1980), who inaugurated the subsequent practice among Martineau scholars of using paraphrase to silently amend Martineau's details and dates, avoiding the necessity of comment or the awkward interpolated "[*sic*]" by avoiding quotations that contain factual inaccuracy.

9. The concluding paragraph reads: "I propose in my next article to offer some remarks on the productions of other authors of the same class. DISCIPULUS" (596).

10. Martineau noted its power with pride in an 1858 letter to Florence Nightingale, in which she praises "D. News" as "powerful, & increasingly so" (quoted in Frawley 437).

11. Trollope's self-reported average output was 40 pages a week, roughly half of Martineau's, though his peak of productivity, 112 pages a week, is better than hers. He also seems to have shared Martineau's views on single drafts, advising post office colleagues to write their reports in a single unrevised draft.

12. Since Collins's protagonist Hartright has been supporting himself at this point in the novel as a newspaper illustrator, this climactic encounter in *The Woman in White* is a confrontation between journalists.

13. In a 1986 article comparing the autobiographies of Martineau, Margaret Oliphant,

Fanny Kemble, and Elizabeth Missing Sewell, Valerie Sanders suggests that Martineau's denial of personal volition represents, "in its purest form, the denial of personal choice, which becomes the central theme of a woman autobiographer's professional life" (58).

14. Amanda Anderson's *Powers of Distance* does not discuss Martineau at great length, but notes the self-awareness with which *How to Observe Morals and Manners* engages its own strategies of discourse (15). George Levine's *Dying to Know* reads Martineau's self-effacing language as strategically similar to that of other Victorian women scientists and intellectuals including social scientist Beatrice Webb and mathematician Mary Somerville, whom Levine sees as using suppression of self as an energizing and liberating means of pursuing intellectual inquiry (129). Levine's specific discussion of Martineau is on 131–42.

15. In *Barchester Towers*, Trollope writes of the difficulty Obadiah Slope has had as a sometime writer for the newspaper press, learning the hard way that writers for the daily "Jupiter" must "surrender all individuality" (296–97). This is a bit of an oversimplification, however—even as a characterization of the massively impersonal *Times*. According to contemporary press ideology, as Dallas had pointed out, periodical writers need surrender only their private motives; they could retain public ones, along with all their own powers of judgment. "Certain men are employed in writing for the public press," Tom Towers tells John Bold in *The Warden;* "and if they induced either to write or to abstain from writing by private motives, surely the public press would soon be of little value" (134). Trollope's narrator notes, "The discretion of Tom Towers was boundless: there was no contradicting what he said, no arguing against such propositions," but John Bold nonetheless is not satisfied, and leaves the room "as quickly as he could, inwardly denouncing his friend Tom Towers as a prig and a humbug" (134).

16. Deirdre David does this herself in *Intellectual Women and Victorian Patriarchy* when she writes that "Martineau's career is primarily devoted to a kind of safe elaboration, repeating in its fully developed form the repetition of received text that she performed as a child when she recited Milton's poetry" (35).

17. Alastair Fowler makes a similar observation about the surprising ease with which some readers acquire some genres, a phenomenon that puzzles him more than it does Bakhtin, perhaps because he is less inclined to see genres as having a consistent internal logic linking language to worldview: "Sometimes readers can grasp a genre with mysterious celerity, on the basis of seemingly quite inadequate samples, almost as if they were forming a hologram from scattered traces. This ease of acquisition remains problematic. . . . The problem admits of no immediate solution, but is mentioned as a promising subject for future research" (45).

18. Linda Peterson anticipates my own point here when she argues that "Martineau studied long and hard the maps other authors had left her, even as she forged into the territory beyond" ("Reinventing Authorship" 348).

3. The Editor's Tale

1. In *Kinds of Literature* (1982), Fowler specifically assesses some existing attempts at the cartography of literary genre, and concludes that "the whole enterprise of constructing genre maps is theoretically unsound. In mimicry of scientific procedure, it invents a spurious objectivity and permanence for entities that in reality are institutional and mutable" (249).

2. Some of the calls other scholars have made for more attention to genre in literary studies highlight this apparent feasibility problem. Romanticist Judith Thompson, working from Ralph Cohen and Frederick Jameson's theoretical writings on genre, argues that "the object of the critic thus becomes to trace the dynamics of this generic interaction, to reveal the earlier ideological messages encoded in the present usage, and to account for the author's manipulations or translations of these messages" (122–23). While Thompson cites Alan Liu's *Wordsworth: The Sense of History* as a successful example of such a critical practice, the daunting size of Liu's volume is for her a "testament to the difficulty of a fully historicized and dialogic genre theory" (123).

3. See, for example, George Saintsbury's "Journalism Fifty Years Ago": "Not a few men of letters have actually confessed that the famous chapters of *Pendennis* which tell how Warrington taught his pupil to supplement his last five-pound note were their own incitement to Press work; and a great many more than have ever confessed it might, I think, have done so on the actual banks of Isis and Cam in those days" (430).

4. Most recently, a fine multivolume edition of *Dickens' Journalism* has been published by Dent and Ohio State University Press, and useful recent studies include John M. L. Drew's *Dickens the Journalist* (2003) and Richard Pearson's *Thackeray and the Mediated Press* (2000).

5. Trollope notes in the *Autobiography* that at the time he wrote *The Warden*, "I had not even heard the name of any gentleman connected with the *Times* newspaper, and could not have intended to represent any individual by Tom Towers. As I had created an archdeacon, so had I created a journalist. . . . If Tom Towers was at all like any gentleman then connected with the *Times,* my moral consciousness must again have been very powerful" (99–100).

6. A major document of this approach to Trollope is John Hagan's "The Divided Mind of Anthony Trollope," which proposes that the historical value of the novels lies "in what they may unwittingly reveal to us about the mind of their author," and that "the unconscious, unarticulated perplexities of that mind are often as much an index to the deeper currents of the age in which the novels appeared as are their overt record of customs and manners" (1).

7. To do him justice, however, Jenkins did see more clearly than many Trollope critics how significant a place the newspaper press had in Trollope's project: "I take comfort from the centrality of newspapers to Trollope's stories. *The Jupiter* offered a fulcrum on which the great Barchester saga first turned. The press's pomposity and arrogance; its waywardness; its salaciousness; were woven into the Palliser novels. Like Adam Smith's

'unseen hand' of the free market, the unseen hand of the press acts as a Mercury to each Trollopian actor. News of a Gresham appointment, a Finn speech, a Eustace theft, a Bonteen murder, a Melmotte crash, moves down the telegraphs and into the newspapers" (22).

8. Not every modern Trollope reader makes this mistake—Laurel Brake has correctly observed that Trollope actually liked the *Times* very much.

9. This claim is not meant hyperbolically. To realize the significance of twenty-four editors, nine contributors, and so on, to Trollope's other recurring interests and topoi, we can remember that the novels contain only some fifteen foxhunting scenes.

10. In 1864, for example, he wrote to G. H. Lewes, who was planning to withdraw as editor of the *Fortnightly Review*, saying that he felt "more strongly perhaps than I can explain to you" the need to work only with and for an editor with whom he could share sympathies. Lewes reconsidered and edited the *Fortnightly* until late 1866, but when he did resign in that year for health reasons, Trollope wrote him yet another agonized letter, worrying that he barely knew the qualities of the new editor, John Morley, at all. "When you want a new pair of boots it is pretty nearly enough for you to know that you are going to a good bootmaker," Trollope wrote to Lewes, "But this going to an Editor is a very different thing. A man may be a most accomplished Editor,—able at all periodical-editing work,—and yet to you or to me so antipathetic as to make it impossible that the two should work together. You will understand what I mean when I say that should I find I dont like the nose on our new Editors face, I must simply drop the Review; and that therefore I cannot but be very anxious" (*Letters* 354).

11. This chapter and the corresponding appendix B indicate *fictional* periodicals with quotation marks, reserving italics for actual historical periodicals and books. This seems a vital stay against confusion, especially since I mention both Thackeray's fictional "Pall Mall Gazette" and George Smith's real *Pall Mall Gazette.*

12. Somewhat coincidentally, however, the *Times*'s real editor at this time, J. T. Delane, *was* a young man and *did* live in chambers—though family and friends of course knew what he did. Perhaps the most unlikely element in the encounter with Tom Towers in *The Warden* was that a visitor such as Bold would find the editor of a morning paper awake early in the day, considering the hours the position imposed. All working journalists knew that editors of morning papers had to turn night into day, and E. E. Kellett speculated that Delane in particular had seen "more sunrises than any man in England." When Trollope later learned the true working hours of newspaper editors and leader writers, he put subsequent journalist characters including Quintus Slide and Hugh Stanbury on a more realistic work schedule.

13. The *Times* was happy to talk about itself in more or less these terms in its own leading articles. For two fairly typical examples, both in style and in argument, of the mid-Victorian meta-journalism of the *Times* when discoursing on itself, see the leader pages of 6 Feb. 1852 and 15 Oct. 1855.

14. Trollope makes the identity of Sentiment explicit when the narrator comments

that "Mr Sentiment's great attraction is in his second-rate characters," who will live "till the names of their callings shall be forgotten in their own, and Bucket and Mrs. Gamp will be the only words left to use to signify a detective police officer or a monthly nurse" (135–36).

15. A well-known example is Edward Copleston's *Advice to a Young Reviewer,* whose narrator lays down "a fundamental position, which you must never lose sight of, and which must be the main spring of all your criticisms—*Write what will sell*" (2). Newspaper variations on the theme include Caleb Whitefoord's *Advice to Editors of Newspapers,* which points out that editors "may even go so far as to forge an entire Paris Paper" (7), as well as "Rules for the Conduct of Newspaper Editors with Respect to Politics and News" in the *Examiner* of 1808, and in 1850 W. E. Aytoun's "A Lecture on Journalism: By an Old Stager" in *Blackwood's.*

16. Mark Turner offers a very different reading of Trollope's use of the physical editor-narrator in "The Turkish Bath," and other stories in the series, in *Trollope and the Magazines.* Turner proposes that the series is marked by "intensely sexual language and the editor's role as a sexual predator," and that for Trollope the editing process, "based upon an uneven power relationship, is conceived of in terms of hetero- and homosexual male fantasy" (183).

17. Stephen uses a Murray dictionary to date its first use in this sense to 1802, and considers Thackeray's reference to an "editor" in *Henry Esmond* an error: "The scene is otherwise quite accurate, but Esmond, in his anxiety to be smart upon Swift, makes an anachronism" (35, 36).

18. "Our Leading Columns" is a contemporary article in *Chambers's Journal* explaining how leader writing is done at a newspaper using a council system, in which writers confer as a body with the editor to work out policy. In the "cellular" system used by the *Times,* by contrast, each writer met the editor individually, and leader writers were prohibited even to speak if they met accidentally. Patten and Finkelstein identify three major editorial strategies at mid-century: "big name" editors such as Thackeray who capitalized on "literary connections" but left "most of the day-to-day details to subordinates" (150); "hands-on" managers such as Dickens who might take part in every aspect of copy, makeup, and production; and "the publisher-proprietor model" (151) followed by the Blackwoods, who always saw their periodical as one piece of a larger commercial publishing operation.

19. John Sutherland has suggested that Trollope's true motive for taking a magazine editorship at this time was political and parliamentary rather than discursive: "part of his preparation for a career (as he fondly hoped) in Parliament as a Liberal MP" (Introduction vii). Trollope biographer Victoria Glendenning makes the same assumption that "by involving himself in these periodicals he was regrouping his energies for one last throw in that [parliamentary] direction" (347).

20. Contemporary reactions to the piece, some of which were positive, are discussed at greater length in Srebrnik (456). Houghton's discussion of *Saint Pauls* in the *Wellesley*

Index notes that "far from trying to sell his periodical by great and vague promises, he was remarkably candid and straightforward" (3: 359). Houghton describes Trollope's "excessive modesty" in the article as offering "a few examples of what an editor should not say to prospective readers" (361). N. John Hall calls the essay "an odd performance. One wonders what [James] Virtue thought of it" (310).

21. See, in this context, Patten and Finkelstein's recent analysis of Victorian editorship as a locus of what they call "the principle of mediation," which seems to them to "apply to editing in nineteenth-century Britain particularly well. It was a time when, on the whole, editors were more directly connected to publishers, writers, copytexts, and production" (171).

22. I should not oversimplify Trollope's complex position on this issue; although he sees the discursive and financial aspects of publication as separate, Trollope also notes in the *Autobiography* that men who can perform both might be ideal editors: "Publishers themselves have been the best editors of magazines, when they have been able to give time and intelligence to the work. . . . The proprietor, at any rate, knows what he wants and what he can afford" (288). In *The Way We Live Now,* the successful Ferdinand Alf is both his newspaper's editor and its owner.

23. Ferdinand Alf of the "Evening Pulpit," who has discovered that eulogy doesn't sell well, ignores Lady Carbury's letter and has a staff writer named Jones pull the book to pieces "with an almost rabid malignity" (83), but Alfred Booker of the "Literary Chronicle" gives it a good review, bribed by Lady Carbury's implicit promise of a positive review for one of his own books. It is Nicolas Broune of the "Morning Breakfast Table," however, motivated by sexual attraction to Lady Carbury, who gives the book the two columns of fulsome praise that make it a success. The literary and journalistic subplot of *The Way We Live Now* seems to have particularly interested a writer in the *Saturday Review,* who devotes the last third of his review to Trollope's editors and their relationship to Lady Carbury, and remarks that "Mr. Trollope implies for himself a very exact and intimate knowledge of the editorial status and its chances" (88).

24. In the immensely document-laden and document-themed *Bleak House,* for example, the first long paragraph of chapter 33, "Interlopers," is a free indirect pastiche of penny-a-liner newswriting as practiced by "two gentlemen not very neat about the cuffs and buttons," who report "in as many words as possible" (512) the spontaneous combustion of Krook using the full range of contemporary journalistic clichés and periphrastic constructions.

25. Drew, for one, is not convinced, seeing Copperfield's account of the discovery and development of his own vocation as a writer "bald and unconvincing in ratio to its lack of corroborative details" (188).

4. The Reviewer's Tale

1. The two essays are "Silly Novels by Lady Novelists," originally from the *Westminster Review,* and "Margaret Fuller and Mary Wollstonecraft," originally from the *Leader.* It is

unfortunate that they now represent her to so many American undergraduates, since neither essay was chosen for *Essays and Leaves from a Note-Book,* indicating that the novelist did not wish them reprinted. The current edition of *Longman Anthology of British Literature* prints "Margaret Fuller and Mary Wollstonecraft" plus "Brother Jacob"; the *Broadview Anthology of British Literature* prints "Silly Novels" only. The *Norton Anthology of English Literature,* to its shame, prints both essays at length, a total of fourteen pages, while offering only two pages from *The Mill on the Floss* to represent the actual fiction. Herbert Tucker and Dorothy Mermin in *Victorian Literature, 1830–1900,* to their credit, represent George Eliot through a text she would have been more proud to own, the famous chapter 17 of *Adam Bede.*

2. The motive for the refusal was no doubt at least partly personal—neither G. H. Lewes nor Marian Lewes had been on good terms with Chapman since his clumsy and insensitive attempts to find out if she was the author of *Adam Bede.* Gordon Haight records that Marian did not reply to Chapman at all, but gave his letter to Lewes, "who records the 'cool request' in his Diary with the laconic comment: 'Squashed that idea'" (*George Eliot and John Chapman* 102).

3. I refer to my subject in this chapter at the various stages of her career by the names she actually used at each period, names that match her shifts between discrete writing genres. The subeditor of John Chapman's *Westminster Review* from 1851 to 1853 called herself Marian Evans (although she was effectively anonymous to readers and many contributors). After her elopement to Germany with G. H. Lewes in 1854, the independent contributor to the *Westminster* insisted on being called Marian Evans *Lewes,* and I therefore use that name to refer to the author of the 1855–56 articles. "George Eliot" came into existence just as the journalism ended in January 1857, with virtually no overlap. For thoughtful remarks on the problem of how a critic should refer to a novelist with so many public and private names, see Rosemarie Bodenheimer, *The Real Life of Mary Ann Evans* (Ithaca: Cornell UP, 1994).

4. This expectation for the mid-Victorian press, in this case specifically for newspapers, is summarized in these terms by W. R. Greg in the *Edinburgh Review* of October 1855: "Not only does [the press] supply the nation with nearly all the information on public topics which it possesses, but it supplies it with its notions and opinions in addition. . . . It inquires, reflects, decides for us. For five pence or a penny (as the case may be) it *does all the thinking* of the nation" (477).

5. Good biographical and critical accounts of these years of editing and reviewing are available, however; see Uglow (especially 44–81), and both Haight's *George Eliot: A Biography* (96–210) and his *George Eliot and John Chapman.*

6. Gordon Haight lists the *Westminster* contributions for 1855–56 and their proceeds in *George Eliot and John Chapman* (86, n. 39). Chapman's payments, about 12 guineas per "sheet" of sixteen typeset pages, ranged from £12 for "Silly Novels by Lady Novelists" to £25 for "Worldliness and Other-Worldliness: The Poet Young." In all, the six major articles and seven Belles Lettres collections were worth just over £207, while the writer's

yearly income from her inheritance was only £100. Other journalistic writing was less profitable: articles written for the weekly *Leader* could be much shorter, but paid only a guinea each (177).

7. The deleted passages are indicated in Pinney's edition of the *Essays;* see particularly pp. 338, 339, 353, and 375–76.

8. A different opinion is held by Alexis Easley, who reads the "we" Eliot uses in *Amos Barton* as the conventionally editorial one rather than an earnest invocation of community between the narrator and the reader (123). For an insightful discussion of the voice of earnest engagement sometimes used by Victorian women novelists, see Robyn Warhol, "Toward a Theory of the Engaging Narrator: Earnest Interventions in Gaskell, Stowe, and Eliot," *PMLA* 101 (October 1986): 811–18.

9. Modern critical writing on "Janet's Repentance" is sparse and fairly eclectic. One index of this is that one of the best single sources of critical articles on the story is a special issue of the interdisciplinary journal *Literature and Medicine,* and one of the better articles in this issue begins with the words "I am a fungal geneticist." Both J. W. Bennett's "The Apprenticeship of George Eliot: Characterization as Case Study in 'Janet's Repentance'" and J. Clinton McCann Jr.'s "Disease and Cure in 'Janet's Repentance': George Eliot's Change of Mind" (*Literature and Medicine* 9 [1990]: 50–68; 69–78) are thoughtful explorations of the way George Eliot uses physical pathology to suggest spiritual illness. Nonmedical readings of the piece have also, of course, been proposed. Thomas Noble's monograph *George Eliot's "Scenes of Clerical Life"* (1965) discusses the story entirely in terms of Eliot's sympathy ideal; but Derek and Sybil Oldfield, in "'Scenes of Clerical Life': The Diagram and the Picture" (in Barbara Hardy, *Critical Essays on George Eliot,* New York: Barnes and Noble, 1970: 1–18), consider it a straightforward illustration of the humanist religion of Feuerbach. Peter Fenves, in "Exiling the Encyclopedia: The Individual in 'Janet's Repentance'" (*Nineteenth-Century Literature* 41 [1987]: 419–44), reads the story as an allegory of the Passion, with Tryan as Christ and Dempster as Satan. Jennifer Uglow, however, working to link the three Clerical Scenes thematically, suggests that they share a motif of "fruitful sacrifice" of women for men, and that it is not Tryan who is sacrificed for Janet, but Janet who is sacrificed for Tryan: "The women in *Scenes of Clerical Life* are holy sacrifices through whom men's lives are given spiritual meaning" (89).

10. Two of the "Saccharissa" essays are printed in Pinney's *Essays;* the other two are helpfully given as part of Kathleen McCormack's discussion of the entire series, "The Saccharissa Essays: George Eliot's Only Woman Persona." McCormack also notes that artistic experimentation with modern as opposed to early-century settings seems one goal of these pieces, and that "there is scarcely a material detail from 'Futile Falsehoods' and 'Modern Housekeeping' that does not recur in *Deronda* and/or *Theophrastus Such*" (46).

5. The Clergyman's Tale

1. The virulence of anti-sensation novel reviewers has been remarked by many critics, and quoting the more outraged and outrageous passages is a favorite pastime among scholars who study the sensation novel. Commentaries on the Victorian critical furor over the sensation novel, with extended excerpts, are provided by Winifred Hughes (passim), Leckie (112–53), and Altick (*Deadly Encounters* 145–58).

2. For example, Christopher Kent has pointed out how fully the Victorian newspapers of this era reported details of court cases including "murders, indecent assaults, breaches of promise, 'criminal conversations,' bankruptcies, or libels," and correctly observed that "to read these stories, particularly in respectable journals such as *The Times,* is to get a sense that some sort of double standard was at work. The society that was so prudish, as Thackeray and others maintained, about what was proper to the novel could read the fullest accounts of the coarser aspects of life every morning and especially on Sundays" (107).

3. In what follows, I will generally provide reference information to daily and weekly newspaper articles in the text, rather than referring the reader to a bibliography entry or endnote. Since virtually all of the newspaper articles about Speke were anonymous or pseudonymous, and many of them shared similar titles ("The Rev. B. Speke" was particularly popular), this seems the best way to avoid confusion.

4. Altick does not notice the case, however, in any of his major works on sensationalism. Speke's disappearance has become extremely obscure; the only secondary source I have found (outside the *Annual Register*) to discuss it is a popular collection called *Strange Disappearances,* by Elliott O'Donnell (New York: Dodd, Mead, 1928), which recounts the story of the disappearance and reappearance, with imperfect accuracy, from the original London newspaper accounts.

5. "W.D.," "The Rev. B. Speke," *Times* 7 Feb. 1868: 5; "H.," "The Rev. B. Speke," *Times* 13 Feb. 1868: 7; "Perils of the Streets / Another Mysterious Disappearance," *Western Morning Press,* reprinted in the *Times* 11 Feb. 1868: 4.

6. The *London Review* said that the *Spectator* had done its detective work "cleverly and gracefully," and the *Times,* in addition to the compliment of reprinting the story, later noted that it accounted for the facts "very prettily." The *Pall Mall Gazette,* on the other hand, was critical of the piece.

7. I am indebted to Patrick Leary for discovering the passages about Speke in the Hardman papers, and generously sending me their entire text by e-mail.

8. One of the relatively less injurious of these surmises, championed in two articles in the *Illustrated Times* of 8 and 15 February, was that the Reverend Speke might have gotten a black eye "in a nocturnal broil" and was waiting for it to heal: "We can scarcely imagine a stronger reason for a clerical gentleman's keeping out of the way—from a wedding party especially" (15 Feb. 1858: 111).

9. Jonathan Loesberg points out that very little happens randomly in true sensa-

tion novels, and that their plots follow an almost deterministic "principle of inevitable sequence depicted alternatively as either a chain made of links or as a providential unfolding" ("The Ideology of Narrative Form in Sensation Fiction" 117).

10. A thorough and provocative discussion of the sensation novels' treatment of class fear and class identity is provided by Loesberg (ibid.), who reads it in the context of the contemporary debate over the 1867 Reform Bill. Another angle is explored by Ronald Thomas, who discusses identity in the sensation novel in terms of the increasingly powerful Victorian professional discourses of law and medicine. Winifred Hughes (20–21) approaches the question of identity by pointing out consistent patterns of doubling among the main characters of sensation novels. In her reading of *Lady Audley's Secret,* Katherine Montweiler provocatively suggests that the book served almost as an instruction manual for women wishing to transgress class boundaries.

11. For a consideration of the significance of altered mental states in sensation fiction, see Brantlinger. For a thorough consideration of the metaphor of drug addiction both within sensation novels and as it was applied by critics to the culture of novel reading, see Leckie 112–53.

12. If the Reverend Speke had gathered from sensation novels such as *The Woman in White* that a lower class rank was easy for members of the upper classes to assume as a disguise, he underestimated the British police of his era. "On the way [to Bodmin] the officers seem to have become convinced that the man was no drover, but one who had been accustomed to the refinements of life. His gentlemanly demeanor and conversation showed that the prisoner was of a much higher grade in society than he assumed to be" (*Daily Telegraph* 26 Feb. 1868: 5).

13. The further traces of the Reverend Speke's life as seen by the *Times* are few, but still appropriately charged with both sexuality and mystery. A year later, the newspaper printed a small item noting a *Bristol Times* announcement of Speke's engagement to "a daughter of a Wiltshire squire" (24 Apr. 1869: 9). In 1881 the *Times* announced Speke's death by drowning thirteen years to the day after it had announced his rediscovery. Speke apparently committed suicide the day after his wife died. The couple left eight children (25 Feb. 1881: 10).

14. Unfortunately, the timing of the Speke case prevented some novelists from appreciating this "sensation" and its outcome as they might otherwise have done. Charles Dickens was overseas on his last American tour during the whole of the Speke affair, though he must certainly have learned about it, from newspapers or friends, upon his return. It is at least interesting that the book he began immediately afterward was *The Mystery of Edwin Drood.* Wilkie Collins, though ordinarily a close reader of newspaper sensations, seems to have been fully concerned during this time with writing *The Moonstone,* and with his mother's final illness; his diary entries and published letters in January and February 1868 take no notice of Speke's disappearance.

15. Speke's case was not, however, to be the last mid-Victorian crime scare to be mediated through the newspapers. A fascinating account of "'perceived' outbreaks of street

robberies" (1) and how newspaper accounts shaped the public understanding of them in this period is Rob Sindall, *Street Violence in the Nineteenth Century: Media Panic or Real Danger?* (Leicester: Leicester UP, 1990).

16. The English language may narrowly have escaped a more permanent reminder of Speke's escapade in the form of a new verb. If the word had caught on, the *OED* would probably now cite the *London Journal* 42 (1 July 1868): 462: "SPEKED.—The following dialogue occurred between a lady and her husband, on the gentleman's returning home unusually late one night, and reproaching his wife with unnecessary anxiety at his absence:—'I was almost afraid that you had spoken.'—'Spoken, my dear! What can you possibly mean?'—'Well, I suppose it is ungrammatical to say so; but it occurred to me, dearest Alfred, that you had *Speked.*'"

6. The Scholars' Tales

1. Mark Turner, for example, is on record as being skeptical about the value of genre studies for cultural studies in general and periodicals research in particular; see the section titled "The Limits of Genre" (especially 119–20) in his essay "A Cultural Critique of Victorian Periodicals" (1995).

2. The conclusion of Heather Dubrow's popular 1983 overview *Genre* proposed in general terms that "one of the most fruitful ways to examine the nature of particular periods and the changes from one era to another" would be to study "how a particular genre interacts with the other literary forms and aesthetic attitudes of its day" (113–14), although virtually no specific research into interactions between genres, or between a genre and its culture, had been done at that date.

3. Carolyn Williams noted in a 1999 article in *Victorian Literature and Culture* that "genre theory has not been fashionable in cultural studies" (518), but suggests that "now is a good time to rework the concept of 'genre' as a fully cultural as well as a literary category. . . . It might well be that in the play of genres we can find one perfect place to study the way culture takes *form*" (520). Tilottama Rajan and Julia M. Wright's collection *Romanticism, History, and the Possibilities of Genre: Re-forming Literature, 1789–1837* (Cambridge: Cambridge UP, 1998) includes a number of intriguing readings of genre in the Romantic era, including Judith Thompson's chapter on John Thelwall, which makes an argument for the significance of the Romantic period that I would claim should be applied more broadly to the Victorian period as well, and indeed has always applied to the world of discourse: that "when all laws, systems, and hierarchies are under pressure, the true historical dynamics of genre—the processes by which and reasons for which generic laws, systems, and hierarchies are constructed and deconstructed—are revealed, and genre itself appears less like an orderly courtroom or hierarchical house of lords than an open-air political forum or speaker's corner in which competing voices engage in discussion, debate, and harangue" (123).

4. There is reason to hope that literary scholarship is entering a phase of sophisticated and creative reconsideration of theories and methods. Recent moves to rethink the

major theoretical assumptions of the field (some of which one might wish to have had ten or twenty years ago) include Peter D. McDonald's "Ideas of the Book and Histories of Literature: After Theory?" in *PMLA* 121.1 (Jan. 2006): 214–28. Caroline Levine has recently proposed a "strategic formalism" as a promising method by which cultural studies could recognize that there is "a force to forms themselves: a historical potential that inheres in techniques rather than persons" ("Strategic Formalism" 636), and Marjorie Levinson has critiqued the "new formalism" and reviewed its rise and progress in *PMLA*. Formalist tools have also seemed attractive to some historians; for thoughtful remarks on the way literary tools of investigation can be used to read textual sources, see Martin Weiner's "Treating 'Historical' Sources as Literary Texts: Literary Historicism and Modern British History," *Journal of Modern History* 70 (1998): 619–38.

5. See ch. 1, n. 20, and n. 12 below.

6. In what looks like a good insight searching for an equally good metaphor, Pavel proposes that seeing genre as "a set of good recipes, or good habits of the trade, oriented towards the achievement of definite artistic goals," might make "the instability of generic categories less puzzling and less threatening" (210).

7. At least notionally. Habermas remarks, "Not that this idea of the public was actually realized in earnest in the coffee houses, the salons, and the societies; but as an idea it had become institutionalized and thereby stated as an objective claim. If not realized, it was at least consequential" (36).

8. A shorter version of the core thesis of Hampton's book, and one that fully acknowledges its Habermasian origins, is "Liberalism, the Press, and the Construction of the Public Sphere: Theories of the Press in Britain, 1830–1914," *Victorian Periodicals Review* 37.1 (Spring 2004): 72–92. Habermas is almost impossible to avoid in the last decade of periodicals studies, having had major or minor theoretical influence on Pearson's *Thackeray and the Mediated Text* (2000), Drew's *Dickens the Journalist* (2002), and Schroeder's "'Better Arguments': The *English Woman's Journal* and the Game of Public Opinion" (2002), among many others.

9. Anderson's remarks in *Imagined Communities* about the intellectual structure— or lack thereof—of newspapers are intriguingly similar to Anthony Trollope's remarks about American journalism in his *North America* (1862). Anderson calls the organization of news on the front page of the *New York Times* "arbitrary" (33), and says that reading a newspaper is "like reading a novel whose author has abandoned any thought of a coherent plot" (33 n. 54). Trollope, though a brilliant analyst of British newspapers, was puzzled by the newspapers he saw on his visit to America, and similarly accused them of lacking organizing principles.

That a modern national newspaper's front page stories are chosen and juxtaposed in ways that are anything but arbitrary is shown, of course, by the substantial similarity between the front pages of national papers—all independently created—on any given day. The decisions that form a given front page are a compound of sophisticated judgments about relative "newsworthiness" of stories, the current semiotics governing page layout (levels of importance indicated by placement to the left or right, and above the newspaper's fold or below), market-driven estimates of the interests of particular sets of readers, and internal negotiations between competing section editors. What the remarks of Trollope (and Anderson) actually reveal is not an absence of generic organization in the texts they read, but their own lack of the genre tools that would enable them to decode the text successfully. An American newspaper of the 1860s seems disorganized only to someone who expects a British-model paper; a modern newspaper appears to be a badly made novel only to the reader who expects it to be a novel.

10. For Bourdieu's most specific remarks on the field of journalism in particular, see the short essay collected in *On Television and Journalism* (London: Pluto, 1998).

11. One scholar who has recently applied Bourdieu's concept of the literary field to Victorian literary history in ways that might have surprised Bourdieu is Mary Poovey, who hypothesizes an alternative set of norms the British literary field might have adopted in "Forgotten Writers, Neglected Histories."

12. Michael Schudson has also analyzed the points of conflict between Anderson and Habermas in particular. "There is all the difference in the world between a community (Anderson's focus) and a public (Habermas's concern)," he writes in a 2002 review essay: "The former tends to imply a common emotional identity, the latter only a common set of norms for public conversation. The former indicates fellow feeling on the basis of interaction (even if it is mediated interaction), the latter suggests civil interaction around a common political subject even in the absence of fellow feeling. Where Anderson examines social membership, Habermas looks to criticism of the state and the formation of liberal institutions. Anderson's 'imagined communities' have nothing to do with liberalism but everything to do with national consciousness; the Habermasian 'public sphere' has everything to do with liberalism, both its achievements and its limitations" ("News, Public, Nation" 484).

13. "There exists a great chasm between those, on one side, who relate everything to a single central vision . . . and, on the other side, those who pursue many ends, often unrelated and even contradictory. . . . The first kind of intellectual and artistic personality belongs to the hedgehogs, the second to the foxes" (Berlin 436–37).

14. It is striking that Habermas's original 1962 *Structural Transformation of the Public Sphere,* which uses the nineteenth-century British periodical press as its paradigmatic case, does not even attempt to adduce evidence for its analysis *from* nineteenth-century British periodicals; the sources it relies on as primary are contemporary and subsequent commentators *on* the primary texts of the press, including John Stuart Mill and Karl Marx.

15. Laurel Brake has observed that "methodology is the problem that haunts study of the press" (166), Ann Parry that "study of the periodical press is, and has been bedeviled, by the lack of generally accepted investigative procedures that satisfactorily connect institutional studies with social and political structures" (18). Lyn Pykett has commented on "the double problem of defining the object of study, and devising an

appropriate methodological framework within which to conduct that study" (3–4), and Brian Maidment has noted the "startling absence of any well-developed corpus of work studying the generic issues specific to periodicals" (143).

Probably the second most common observation, closely related to the first, is that rigorous study of periodicals is only now just beginning in earnest—a motif with a distinguished history that seems to begin with James Mill's 1824 *Westminster Review* remark that "it is indeed a subject of wonder, that periodical publications should have existed so long . . . without having become subject to a regular and systematic course of criticism" (206). Mill's attempt at an inaugural essay did not prevent Edward Lytton Bulwer from restarting the subfield from scratch again a decade later; Bulwer wrote that he was "not aware of any essay on the subject which seems written with a view rather to examine than declaim" (232). New beginnings and methodological dawns for the study of the periodical press have been announced so often since, and especially in the past fifty years, that despite the clear good faith of all such programs, it is hard not to sense (or hope for) deadpan comedy in Sean Latham and Bob Scholes's 2006 observation in *PMLA* that "to address periodicals as typologically distinct and historically coherent objects, we may have to develop new scholarly methodologies adequate to the task" (529).

16. The one-note analyses of reading in each of these theories are reminiscent of Richard Altick's comparison, in *The English Common Reader,* of similarly one-note theories about reading held in the nineteenth century by conservatives such as S. T. Coleridge, who thought the spread of reading to the people would lead directly to underclass rebellions, and by liberal optimists such as Charles Knight, who considered reading a panacea.

17. Both articles are reprinted in revised and expanded form in Brake, Jones, and Madden's *Investigating Victorian Journalism.* My page references are to the revised versions.

18. Cynthia Bandish, for example, has claimed that it is possible to extrapolate from Bakhtin and "view the composite of texts in a literary magazine as an extended dialogue" (241), and that this composite nature creates "a text comparable to Bakhtin's dialogic novel" (242).

19. It was not always a duty they were able to fulfill, however. "Promoting an ideology" is second and "Giving the periodical a distinctive character" is seventh on Patten and Finkelstein's valuable list of What Editors Do, but their discussion emphasizes how variable were actual editors' degrees of successful agency in determining the ideology and voice of their periodicals, and how powerful was the influence of "a congeries of forces, including the proprietors, stable of contributors, subscribers, advertisers, the importance of continuity, changing political circumstances and markets, and new commercial opportunities" (170).

20. Alastair Fowler comes to a parallel conclusion that "only variations or modifications of convention have literary significance" (18).

21. Although these examples are outside my mid-century period, the early novels of Grant Allen contain compelling scenes of later-Victorian novice journalists learning

their craft by absorbing the conventions of particular genre forms. The protagonist of *The Scallywag* (1893) becomes a skilled specialist in "middle" articles, and one of the characters in *Philistia* (1884) gets employment as a newspaper leader writer after laboriously learning to recreate the genre using purchased examples. Interestingly, what its author claims as the first book-length "how-to" on British press writing, John Dawson's *Practical Journalism,* organizes itself mainly by discourse genre and subgenre, with separate chapters for "Leader-Writing," "Reviewing," "Descriptive Writing," and various sub-specialties of writing about art, theater, and war.

Epilogue

1. Alastair Fowler, although he resists the idea that genre change may be caused by external forces, nonetheless discusses in *Kinds of Literature* the challenges posed by evaluating genres and their exemplars when the genres have substantially changed over time. The work is delicate, he notes: "It is a matter of tact in deciding where a historical accommodation is required, or when the broad generic outline may be treated as unchanged" (49).

2. For a particularly earnest and well-meaning version of the argument that journalistic discourse was called into existence by a universal human need for certain kinds of information, see the introduction of Bill Kovach and Tom Rosenstiel's *Elements of Journalism* (New York: Crown, 2001), often assigned as a textbook in American journalism classrooms.

3. Other scholars have been here before me, of course, to note that the traditional account of a New Journalism arriving full-grown to displace Old Journalism cannot be reconciled with the historical record. In neatly complementary essays in the collection *Papers for the Millions* (1988), Laurel Brake and Joel Wiener have shown that Old Journalism was not so stable, New Journalism not so new. Brake points out that earlier changes in press discourse seem as important as those later dubbed New Journalism: "The entire history of the press is characterized by markers, or transformations, of equal significance to the changes in the newspaper press of the 1880s to which Arnold attached the epithet *new*" ("Old Journalism and New" 4). Wiener performs a similar revision from the point of view of the newer forms, noting that most of the innovations now considered "New Journalism" had been invented and put into practice piecemeal well before the 1880s. "It is clear that the New Journalism had a more secure pedigree than Arnold and many of his contemporaries and subsequent writers were prepared to concede," wrote Wiener. "Perhaps the most tenable conclusion is that additional work needs to be done before definitive judgments about Victorian journalism can be made" ("How New" 65).

4. In this light, it seems significant that the effectiveness of the most famous journalistic forms that have influenced Western national politics, including the anonymous "Junius" political letter, the "yellow press" editorial of William Randolph Hearst, the muckrakers, and the anonymously sourced Washington political story of the last decades of the twentieth century, all had perceptible half-lives. It's tempting to wonder

if new journalisms may not be like new antibiotics—only capable of working for so long, even in theory, before antagonist forms adapt.

5. Alastair Fowler also recommends that "to reconstruct the original genre, we have to eliminate from consciousness its subsequent states" (261), though he acknowledges how difficult this can be to do in practice.

6. *Society* was Robertson's breakthrough success as a playwright, and in George Rowell's classic account of Victorian theater, its debut is significant enough to mark a change of chapters, to "The Return of Respectability" (75). The play is sometimes seen as liminal in theater history, a precursor of the theater of realistic acting and bigger ideas that developed under Shaw and through the inspiration of Ibsen. Robertson, born into a theatrical family, had been struggling as an actor, journalist, and would-be playwright since his early twenties. Rowell notes that his plays reflect his early-Victorian theatrical training, and that their characterizations and situations are sometimes contrived and melodramatic. He did move the stage in the direction of realism, however. William Archer calls Robertson "a pre-Raphaelite of the theatre" for his attention to detail, and W. S. Gilbert apparently considered Robertson the man who "invented stage-management" (quoted in Rowell 80, 81).

7. We remember that it was also in 1865 that Trollope's Quintus Slide told Phineas Finn that a young politician should cultivate a newspaper as a "horgan" for his views.

8. Fitzjames Stephen remarked in his 1862 *Cornhill* article "Journalism" the degree to which journalism lends itself to composition via this sort of free improvisation: "The faculty of composing leading articles is merely a form of technical skill, like the handiness of a mechanic, the fluency and readiness of a barrister, or the delicate touch of a musician. . . . At any odd time—whilst taking a walk, or in reading the newspaper, or smoking a cigar—he gets into his head the point of the article, and one or two of the main topics which are to illustrate and enforce it in a paragraph a piece, and when this is once satisfactorily done, it flows from the end of his pen with perfect and almost unconscious ease" (56–57).

9. Desmond McUsquebaugh, a former Irish MP, "might have been chancellor of the Exchequer if he'd chosen," Stylus tells Chodd, "but he didn't." Olinthus O'Sullivan, a Doctor of Civil Laws, is "one of the finest classical scholars in the world; might have sat upon the woolsack if he'd chosen, but he didn't." Bill Bradley was once a successful novelist, whose romance "Time and Opportunity" went through ten editions and brought him £2,000, "which was his ruin. . . . He's never done anything since. We call him 'One book Bradley.'" Other Owls include an expatriate German statesman, an "eminent tragedian," and a medical doctor named Scargil who "discovered the mensuration of the motive power of the cerebral organs. . . . How many million miles per minute thought can travel. He might have made his fortune if he'd chosen." All are now decidedly down on their luck, however, and when Sidney needs five shillings for a cab, the request becomes an occasion for stage business in which Stylus, Scargil, O'Sullivan, Bradley, and McUsquebaugh, to help him, all attempt to borrow the amount from each other.

10. Maynard Savin notes that London theater managers initially considered the "Owl's Roost" scenes "such a daring lampoon on the bohemian set that they shuddered at the thought of the antagonism the play might arouse" (65). In the event, however, newspaper critics at all levels of the press from the *Times* and *Athenaeum* to the *Daily Telegraph* and on down were more than cordial, and their positive reviews of the play were enhanced by the goodwill many in both the theater community and the London press felt for the previously unlucky Robertson (Savin 61, 69–70).

11. Accounts of the Victorian press in the 1860s and 1870s in the press itself tend to describe it in the same terms used for the press of Tom Towers and the *Times* of the 1850s—an authoritative and omniscient source of political opinions, an authoritative public guide and instructor. By its own account, the press throughout this period cultivated a discursive voice that remained stable, authoritative, and mostly quite responsible—maybe even a bit too responsible. The article "An Age of Lead" (*Macmillan's* 24 [1871]: 63–68), and T. H. S. Escott's "English Journalism in 1832 and 1874" (*Belgravia* 28 [1876]: 39–49), both complain about the pervasive dull, sensible gravity of the 1870s daily newspaper.

12. The value of *Society* as a representation of current beliefs about journalism seems to be confirmed by the reception accorded the play by newspaper critics. The reviewer in the *Times*, probably John Oxenford (Savin 69), warmly praised this portrait of a daily newspaper's short life, social-climbing owners, Bohemian population, and spectacular death. The reviewer was particularly delighted with the Owls, "a picture of the rank and file of literature and art, with all their attributes of fun, generosity, and esprit de corps, painted in a kindly spirit" (14 Nov. 1865: 7). Considering that Anthony Trollope's portrayal of a newspaper proprietor in *The Warden* ten years before had drawn sneers from the *Times,* this is interesting, but not surprising, since Robertson's "Earthquake" was not a picture of the *Times,* as "The Jupiter" had been, but of one of the cheap penny papers with which the *Times* of 1865 competed. The reviewer in the more middle-class *Illustrated London News* found more to like in the journalistic characters of Shirley Brooks's *Sooner or Later* (1868), who have nothing of the Owl's Roost about them: "We have a high-class editor, moving in the best circles, and decidedly an honour to our craft (Mr. Brooks never makes his authors Bohemians, and he is loyal to his calling)" (11 Jan. 1868: 35).

13. There are, of course, novelist-journalists who write in this period as if journalism's cultural power is still at full 1850s levels. Eliza Lynn Linton makes a hardworking woman journalist her heroine for *Sowing the Wind* (1867), and the character is proud of the political power she exerts. Shirley Brooks's serial *Sooner or Later* (1868) ends with a fulsome tribute to the power of modern journalism, although Brooks's reviewer in the *Illustrated Times* thought the passage "might as well have been omitted" (25 Jan. 1868: 59).

14. Leighton and Surridge's fine paper "Illustrated Serial Fiction in the 1860s: Martineau and Eliot" was given at "Speaking with Authority," the British Women Writers Conference at the University of Kentucky, 12–15 April 2007.

15. Even one of the earliest historians of mid-Victorian culture, Walter Besant, could see when looking back at the newspaper of 1837 in *Fifty Years Ago* (1887) that two major transformations had occurred over that interval, not just one: the leading article genre had risen from relative unimportance in 1837 to a peak of influence in 1855, then returned again to relative unimportance by 1887. "As to the changes which have come over the papers, the leading article, whose influence and weight seems to have culminated at the time of the Crimean War, was then of little more value than it is at present" (212).

Works Cited

Primary Sources

[Ainsworth, W. H.]. "The Present State of Literature." *Bentley's Miscellany* 49 (1861): 215–19.

Allen, Grant. *The Scallywag.* 3 vols. London: Chatto and Windus, 1893.

[Aytoun, W. E.]. "A Lecture on Journalism: By an Old Stager." *Blackwood's* 68 (Dec. 1850): 691–97.

Bagehot, Walter. *Physics and Politics.* 1872. Introd. Roger Kimball. London: Ivan R. Dee, 1999.

[Bagehot, Walter]. "The First Edinburgh Reviewers." *National Review* 1 (Oct. 1855): 253–82.

Beresford Hope, A. J. B. "Newspapers and Their Writers." *Cambridge Essays.* Vol. 3. London: John W. Parker, 1858. 1–27.

Besant, Walter. *Fifty Years Ago.* Rev. ed. London: Chatto and Windus, 1892.

Braddon, Mary. *Lady Audley's Secret.* 1862. Ed. and introd. Jennifer Uglow. New York: Viking Penguin/Virago, 1987.

Browning, Elizabeth Barrett. *Aurora Leigh.* 1857. Ed. Margaret Reynolds. Athens: Ohio UP, 1992.

———. *The Letters of Elizabeth Barrett Browning.* Ed. Frederic G. Kenyon. 2 vols. New York: Macmillan, 1898.

———. *Letters of Elizabeth Barrett Browning Addressed to Richard Hengist Horne.* London: Richard Bentley and Son, 1877.

Browning, Robert. "Bishop Blougram's Apology." *The Poetical Works of Robert Browning.* Ed. Ian Jack and Robert Inglesfield. Vol. 5. Oxford: Clarendon P, 1995. 212–55.

Bulwer, Edward Lytton. *England and the English.* 1833. Chicago: U of Chicago P, 1970.

[Capes, J. M.]. "Compton Hall: or, the Recollections of Mr. Benjamin Walker." *Rambler* 3 (1855): 26–44.

Catling, Thomas. *My Life's Pilgrimage.* Introd. Lord Burnham. London: John Murray, 1911.

Collins, Wilkie. *The Woman in White.* 1859–60. Harmondsworth: Penguin Classics, 1985.

Conybeare, Rev. W. J. *Perversion: or, the Causes and Consequences of Infidelity. A Tale for the Times.* New York: Wiley and Halsted, 1856.

Copleston, Edward. *Advice to a Young Reviewer: With a Specimen of the Art.* 1807. Oxford: Blackwell, 1927.

[Dallas, E. S.]. "Popular Literature: The Periodical Press." *Blackwood's* 85 (Jan.–Feb. 1859): 96–112, 180–95.

Dawson, John. *Practical Journalism: How to Enter Thereon and Succeed.* London: L. U. Gill, 1885.

Dickens, Charles. *Bleak House.* 1852–53. Harmondsworth: Penguin, 1971.

———. *David Copperfield.* 1849–50. Harmondsworth: Penguin, 1966.

"Doing a 'Leader.'" *Press* 1 Dec. 1855: 1145.

Eliot, George. *Essays of George Eliot.* Ed. Thomas Pinney. London: Routledge and Kegan Paul, 1963.

———. *The George Eliot Letters.* Ed. Gordon Haight. 9 vols. New Haven: Yale UP, 1954–55.

———. *The Mill on the Floss.* 1860. Ed. Carol T. Christ. Norton Critical Edition. New York: Norton, 1994.

———. *Scenes of Clerical Life.* 1857. World's Classics. Oxford: Oxford UP, 1985.

Escott, T. H. S. "English Journalism in 1832 and 1874." *Belgravia* 28 (Feb. 1876): 39–49.

"The Fourth Estate." *Rambler* (3 Mar. 1849): 471–77.

[Greg, W. R.]. "The Newspaper Press." *Edinburgh Review* 102 (Oct. 1855): 470–98.

———. "The Relation between Employers and Employed." *Westminster Review* 57 (Jan. 1852): 61–95.

Guest, G. H. "Writing for Money." *Belgravia* 8 (1869): 273–75.

Hazlitt, William. *The Letters of William Hazlitt.* Ed. Herschel Moreland Sikes. New York: New York UP, 1978.

———. "The Periodical Press." *The Complete Works of William Hazlitt.* Ed. P. P. Howe. Vol. 16. London: J. M. Dent, 1933.

Hughes, Thomas. "Anonymous Journalism." *Macmillan's Magazine* 5 (Dec. 1861): 157–68.

Kemble, Frances Anne. *Further Records, 1848–1883.* New York: Henry Holt, 1891.

Kinnear, J. Boyd. "Anonymous Journalism." *Contemporary Review* 5 (1867): 324–39.

Knight, Charles. *Passages of a Working Life.* 1865. New York: AMS, 1973.

Lewes, George Henry. *Principles of Success in Literature.* 1865. Westmead: Gregg International, 1969.

———. *Ranthorpe.* 1847. Athens: Ohio UP, 1974.

"The London Daily Press." *Westminster Review* 64 (July 1855): 492–521.

Macaulay, T. B. "History." *Edinburgh Review* 47 (May 1828): 331–67.

Martineau, Harriet. *Autobiography.* 1877. Ed. Linda H. Peterson. Peterborough: Broadview, 2007.

———. "Female Writers on Practical Divinity." *Monthly Repository* 17 (Oct. 1822): 593–96.

[Masson, David]. "Present Aspects and Tendencies of Literature." *British Quarterly Review* 21 (Jan. 1855): 157–81.

[Meynell, Wilfrid]. "John Oldcastle." *Journals and Journalism: With a Guide for Literary Beginners.* 2nd ed. London: Field and Tuer, 1880.

Mill, James. "Periodical Literature: Edinburgh Review." *Westminster Review* 1 (Jan. 1824): 206–49.

Mill, John Stuart. *Autobiography.* 1873. Harmondsworth: Penguin, 1989.

———. *On Liberty.* 1859. Harmondsworth: Penguin Classics, 1985.

Miller, Mrs. Florence Fenwick. *Harriet Martineau.* London: W. H. Allen, 1889.

"The Modern Newspaper." *British Quarterly Review* 55 (1872): 348–80.

Morley, John. "Anonymous Journalism." *Fortnightly Review* 8, ns 2 (Sep. 1867): 287–92.

———. "Memorials of a Man of Letters." *Fortnightly Review* 29, ns 23 (Apr. 1878): 596–610.

———. *Recollections.* 2 vols. London: Macmillan, 1917.

———. "Valedictory." *Fortnightly Review* 38, ns 32 (Oct. 1882): 511–21.

Nicoll, W. Robertson. *James Macdonell, Journalist.* New York: Dodd, Mead, 1897.

"Our Leading Columns." *Chambers's Journal* 44 (20 July 1867): 449–51.

"Our Newspaper Institutions." *Saturday Review* 3 Nov. 1855: 2–3.

Paget, Francis. *Lucretia; or, the Heroine of the Nineteenth Century.* London: Joseph Masters, 1868.

[Parkes, Bessie Raynor]. "The Profession of the Teacher." *English Woman's Journal* 1 (1 Mar. 1858): 1–13.

"Philosophy of Journalism." *Chambers's Edinburgh Journal* ns 13 (29 June 1850): 404–6.

"Rules for the Conduct of Newspaper Editors with Respect to Politics and News." *Examiner* 6 Mar. 1808: 145–46.

Saintsbury, George. *History of Nineteenth Century Literature (1780–1895).* New York: Macmillan, 1896.

———. "Journalism Fifty Years Ago." *Nineteenth Century* 107 (Mar. 1930): 426–36.

"Sayings and Doings of the Day." *Critic* 15 Sep. 1851: 428–29.

[Stephen, James Fitzjames]. "Journalism." *Cornhill* 6 (July 1862): 52–63.

[Stephen, Leslie]. "Anonymous Journalism." *Saint Pauls Magazine* 2 (May 1868): 217–30.

———. "The Evolution of Editors." *Studies of a Biographer.* Vol. 4. New York: Knickerbocker, 1907. 35–68.

———. "The First Edinburgh Reviewers." *Hours in a Library.* New ed. 3 vols. London: Smith, Elder, 1892. 2: 241–69.

———. *Some Early Impressions.* 1903. Burt Franklin Research and Source Work Series 172. New York: Burt Franklin, 1968.

Thackeray, William Makepeace. *Pendennis.* 1848–50. Oxford: Oxford World's Classics, 1994.

"'Tis Eighty Years Since." *Chambers's Journal of Popular Literature, Science and Art* 30 Oct. 1869: 689–91.

Trollope, Anthony. *An Autobiography.* 1883. World's Classics. Oxford: Oxford UP, 1980.

———. *Dr. Thorne.* Everyman's Library. New York: Knopf, 1993.

――――. *An Editor's Tales*. 1870. Penguin Trollope. Harmondsworth: Penguin, 1993.

――――. *The Eustace Diamonds*. 1873. Oxford: Oxford UP, 1973.

――――. *He Knew He Was Right*. 1869. Oxford: Oxford UP, 1985.

――――. *The Last Chronicle of Barset*. 1867. Everyman's Library. New York: Knopf, 1995.

――――. "Mr. Robert Bell." *Pall Mall Gazette* 13 Apr. 1867: 11.

――――. *The New Zealander*. 1856. Oxford: Clarendon P, 1972.

――――. "On Anonymous Literature." *Fortnightly Review* 1 (1 July 1865): 491–98.

――――. *Orley Farm*. 1862. New York: Dover, 1981.

――――. *Phineas Finn*. 1869. Oxford: Oxford UP, 1973.

――――. *Phineas Redux*. 1874. Oxford: Oxford UP, 1973.

――――. *The Three Clerks*. 1857. Penguin Trollope. Harmondsworth: Penguin, 1993.

――――. "The Trade of Journalism." *Saint Pauls* 1 (Dec. 1867): 306–18.

――――. *The Warden*. 1855. Harmondsworth: Penguin, 1984.

――――. *The Way We Live Now*. 1874. Harmondsworth: Penguin, 2002.

"The Way We Live Now." Rev. *Saturday Review* 17 July 1875: 88–89.

Whitefoord, Caleb. *Advice to Editors of Newspapers*. London: Printed for Alexander Mac Pherson, 1799.

[Wynter, Andrew]. "Advertisements." *Quarterly Review* 97 (June 1855): 183–225.

Secondary Sources

Altick, Richard. *Deadly Encounters: Two Victorian Sensations*. Philadelphia: U of Pennsylvania P, 1986.

――――. *The English Common Reader: A Social History of the Mass Reading Public, 1800–1900*. 2nd ed. Columbus: Ohio State UP, 1998.

――――. *Victorian Studies in Scarlet*. New York: Norton, 1970.

Anderson, Amanda. *The Powers of Distance: Cosmopolitanism and the Cultivation of Detachment*. Princeton: Princeton UP, 2001.

Anderson, Benedict. *Imagined Communities: Reflections on the Origin and Spread of Nationalism*. 1983. London: Verso, 2006.

Arbuckle, Elisabeth Sanders. *Harriet Martineau in the London "Daily News": Selected Contributions, 1852–1866*. New York: Garland, 1994.

Aspinall, A. *Politics and the Press, c. 1780–1850*. London: Home and Van Thal, 1949.

Avery, Simon, and Rebecca Stott. *Elizabeth Barrett Browning*. London: Longman, 2003.

Bakhtin, M. M. *The Dialogic Imagination: Four Essays*. Ed. Michael Holquist. Trans. Caryl Emerson and Michael Holquist. Austin: U of Texas P, 1981.

――――. *Problems of Dostoevsky's Poetics*. Ed. and trans. Caryl Emerson. Minneapolis: U of Minnesota P, 1984.

――――. *Speech Genres and Other Late Essays*. Ed. Caryl Emerson and Michael Holquist. Trans. Vern W. McGee. Austin: U of Texas P, 1986.

Bandish, Cynthia. "Bakhtin's Dialogism and the Bohemian Meta-narrative of Belgravia: A Case Study for Analyzing Periodicals." *Victorian Periodicals Review* 34.3 (Fall 2001): 239–62.

Berlin, Isaiah. "The Hedgehog and the Fox." 1953. *The Proper Study of Mankind.* New York: Farrar, Straus and Giroux, 1998.

Boardman, Kay. "'Charting the Golden Stream': Recent Work on Victorian Periodicals." *Victorian Studies* 48.3 (Spring 2006): 505–17.

Bourdieu, Pierre. "The Field of Cultural Production, or: The Economic World Reversed." *Poetics* 12 (1983): 311–56.

———. *Language and Symbolic Power.* Ed. John B. Thompson. Trans. Gino Raymond and Matthew Adamson. Cambridge: Harvard UP, 1991.

———. *The Logic of Practice.* Stanford: Stanford UP, 1990.

Boyle, Thomas. *Black Swine in the Sewers of Hampstead.* New York: Viking Penguin, 1989.

Brake, Laurel. "The Old Journalism and the New: Forms of Cultural Production in London in the 1880s." *Papers for the Millions: The New Journalism in Britain, 1850s to 1914.* Ed. Joel H. Wiener. Westport: Greenwood, 1988. 1–24.

———. "Production of Meaning in Periodical Studies: Versions of the *English Review.*" *Victorian Periodicals Review* 24.4 (1991): 163–70.

———. *Subjugated Knowledges: Journalism, Gender and Literature in the Nineteenth Century.* New York: New York UP, 1994.

Brake, Laurel, and Anne Humpherys. "Critical Theory and Periodical Research." *Victorian Periodicals Research* 22.3 (Fall 1989): 94–95.

Brake, Laurel, Aled Jones, and Lionel Madden, eds. *Investigating Victorian Journalism.* New York: St. Martin's, 1990.

Brantlinger, Patrick. "What Is 'Sensational' about the 'Sensation Novel'?" *Nineteenth Century Fiction* 37 (June 1982): 1–28.

Brown, Lucy. *Victorian News and Newspapers.* Oxford: Clarendon P, 1985.

Butler, Marilyn. "Culture's Medium: The Role of the Review." *The Cambridge Companion to British Romanticism.* Ed. Stuart Curran. Cambridge: Cambridge UP, 1993. 120–47.

Calé, Luisa. "Periodical Personae: Pseudonyms, Authorship, and the Imagined Community of Joseph Priestly's *Theological Repository.*" *19: Interdisciplinary Studies in the Long Nineteenth Century* 3 (2006). www.19.bbk.ac.uk.

Campbell, Kate, ed. *Journalism, Literature and Modernity: From Hazlitt to Modernism.* Edinburgh: Edinburgh UP, 2000.

Chalaby, Jean. *Invention of Journalism.* New York: St. Martin's, 1998.

Clive, John. *Scotch Reviewers: The "Edinburgh Review," 1802–1815.* London: Faber and Faber, 1956.

Cohen, Ralph. "Introduction: Notes toward a Generic Reconstitution of Literary Study." *New Literary History* 34 (2003): v–xvi.

Conboy, Martin. *Journalism: A Critical History.* London: SAGE, 2004.

Cross, Nigel. *The Common Writer: Life in Nineteenth-Century Grub Street.* Cambridge: Cambridge UP, 1985.

Culler, A. Dwight. "Method in the Study of Victorian Prose." *Victorian Newsletter* 9 (1956): 1–4.

Dahl, Christopher C. "Fitzjames Stephen, Charles Dickens, and Dougle Reviewing." *Victorian Periodicals Review* 14.2 (Summer 1981): 51–58.

Darnton, Robert. "What Is the History of Books?" *Daedalus* (Summer 1982): 65–83.

David, Deirdre. "George Eliot's 'Trump': Recent Work on Harriet Martineau." *Victorian Studies* 47.1 (2004): 87–94.

———. *Intellectual Women and Victorian Patriarchy: Harriet Martineau, Elizabeth Barrett Browning, George Eliot.* Ithaca: Cornell UP, 1987.

Davis, Lennard. *Factual Fictions: The Origins of the English Novel.* New York: Columbia UP, 1983.

Davis, Lloyd. "Journalism and Victorian Fiction." *Victorian Journalism: Exotic and Domestic.* Ed. Barbara Garlick and Margaret Harris. St. Lucia: U of Queensland P, 1998. 197–211.

Davis, William A., Jr. "'This is my theory': Macaulay on Periodical Style." *Victorian Periodicals Review* (Spring 1987): 12–22.

Delaney, Paul. *Literature, Money and the Market, From Trollope to Amis.* Basingstoke: Palgrave, 2002.

Demoor, Marysa. *Their Fair Share: Women, Power and Criticism in the Athenaeum, from Millicent Garrett Fawcett to Katherine Mansfield, 1870–1920.* Aldershot: Ashgate, 2000.

Denison, Patrica D. "Victorian and Modern Drama: Social Convention and Theatrical Invention in T. W. Robertson's Plays." *Modern Drama* 37 (1994): 401–20.

Drew, John M. L. *Dickens the Journalist.* New York: Palgrave Macmillan, 2003.

Dubrow, Heather. *Genre.* London: Methuen, 1982.

Dudek, Louis. *Literature and the Press: A History of Printing, Printed Media, and Their Relation to Literature.* Toronto: Ryerson, 1960.

Easley, Alexis. *First-Person Anonymous: Women Writers and Victorian Print Media, 1830–1870.* Aldershot: Ashgate, 2004.

———. "Victorian Women Writers and the Periodical Press: The Case of Harriet Martineau." *Nineteenth-Century Prose* 24.1 (Spring 1997): 39–50.

Edwards, P. D. *Dickens's "Young Men": George Augustus Sala, Edmund Yates and the World of Victorian Journalism.* Aldershot: Ashgate, 1997.

Eliot, Simon. *Some Patterns and Trends in British Publishing, 1800–1919.* Occasional Papers 8. London: Bibliographical Society, 1994.

Elwin, Malcolm. *Thackeray: A Personality.* London: Jonathan Cape, 1832.

Erickson, Lee. *The Economy of Literary Form: English Literature and the Industrialization of Publishing, 1800–1850.* Baltimore: Johns Hopkins UP, 1996.

Errico, Marcus. "The Evolution of the Summary News Lead." *Media History Monographs* 1.1. 4 Aug. 1998. www.scripps.ohiou.edu/mediahistory/mhmjour1-1/htm.

Escott, T. H. S. *Anthony Trollope: His Work, Associates and Literary Originals.* London: John Lane, 1913.

Feather, John. *A History of British Publishing.* 2nd ed. London: Routledge, 2006.

Finkelstein, David, and Alastair McCleery. *An Introduction to Book History*. New York: Routledge, 2005.

Foucault, Michel. "What Is an Author?" *Language, Counter-Memory, Practice: Selected Essays and Interviews*. Ed. Donald F. Bouchard. Trans. Donald F. Bouchard and Sherry Simon. Ithaca: Cornell UP, 1977. 113–38.

Fowler, Alastair. *Kinds of Literature: An Introduction to the Theory of Genres and Modes*. Cambridge: Harvard UP, 1982.

Fowler, Roger. *The Languages of Literature: Some Linguistic Contributions to Criticism*. London: Routledge and Kegan Paul, 1971.

Frawley, Maria. "Harriet Martineau, Health, and Journalism." *Women's Writing* 9.3 (2002): 433–44.

Frow, John. *Genre*. London: Routledge, 2006.

Frye, Northrup. *Anatomy of Criticism: Four Essays*. Princeton: Princeton UP, 1971.

Frus, Phyllis. *Politics and Poetics of Journalistic Narrative: The Timely and the Timeless*. Cambridge: Cambridge UP, 1994.

Garlick, Barbara. "'The true principle of Biographical delineation': Harriet Martineau's 'Biographical Sketches' in the *Daily News*." *Victorian Journalism: Exotic and Domestic*. Ed. Barbara Garlick and Margaret Harris. St. Lucia: U of Queensland P, 1998. 46–61.

Garrett, Martin. *A Browning Chronology: Elizabeth Barrett and Robert Browning*. New York: St. Martin's, 2000.

Glendinning, Victoria. *Anthony Trollope*. New York: Knopf, 1993.

Gross, John. *The Rise and Fall of the Man of Letters: Aspects of English Literary Life since 1800*. London: Weidenfeld and Nicolson, 1969.

Habermas, Jürgen. "The Public Sphere." *New German Critique* 1.3 (Fall 1974): 49–55.

———. *Structural Transformation of the Public Sphere*. 1962. Ed. Thomas McCarthy. Trans. Thomas Burger and Frederick Lawrence. Cambridge: MIT P, 1989.

Hagan, John. "The Divided Mind of Anthony Trollope." *Nineteenth-Century Fiction* 14 (1959): 1–26.

Haight, Gordon. *George Eliot: A Biography*. 1968. New York: Penguin, 1985.

———. *George Eliot and John Chapman*. 2nd ed. New York: Archon, 1969.

Hall, N. John. *Trollope: A Biography*. New York: Oxford UP, 1991.

Hampton, Mark. *Visions of the Press in Britain, 1850–1950*. Urbana: U of Illinois P, 2004.

Hardman, Sir William. *The Hardman Papers, a Further Selection (1865–1868) from the Letters and Memoirs of Sir William Hardman*. Ed. S. M. Ellis. London: Constable, 1930.

Hardy, Barbara. *Particularities: Readings in George Eliot*. London: Peter Own, 1982.

Hartley, John. *Popular Reality: Journalism, Modernity, Popular Culture*. London: Arnold, 1996.

Hawkins, Angus. *Parliament, Party, and the Art of Politics in Britain, 1855–59*. Stanford: Stanford UP, 1987.

Haywood, Ian. *The Revolution in Popular Literature.* Cambridge: Cambridge UP, 2002.

Heyck, T. W. *The Transformation of Intellectual Life in Victorian England.* London: Croom Helm, 1982.

History of "The Times": The Tradition Established, 1841–1884. London: Times, 1939.

Houghton, Walter E. "Periodical Literature and the Articulate Classes." *The Victorian Periodical Press: Samplings and Soundings.* Ed. Joanne Shattock and Michael Wolff. Toronto: U of Toronto P, 1982. 3–27.

————, ed. *The Wellesley Index to Victorian Periodicals, 1824–1900.* Toronto: U of Toronto P, 1966–79.

Huett, Lorna. "Among the Unknown Public: *Household Words, All the Year Round,* and the Mass-Market Weekly Periodical in the Mid-Nineteenth Century." *Victorian Periodicals Review* 38.1 (Spring 2005): 61–82.

Hughes, Winifred. *The Maniac in the Cellar: Sensation Novels of the 1860s.* Princeton: Princeton UP, 1980.

Innis, H. A. "The English Press in the Nineteenth Century: An Economic Approach." *University of Toronto Quarterly* 15 (1945–46): 37–53.

Jenkins, Simon. "Jupiter's Thunder." *Trollopiana* 17 (May 1992): 17–23.

Jones, Aled. *Powers of the Press: Newspapers, Power and the Public in Nineteenth-Century England.* Aldershot: Scolar, 1996.

Kent, Christopher. "The Editor and the Law." *Innovators and Preachers: The Role of the Editor in Victorian England.* Ed. Joel H. Wiener. Westport: Greenwood, 1985. 99–119.

————. "Higher Journalism and the Mid-Victorian Clerisy." *Victorian Studies* 13 (1969): 181–98.

King, Andrew, and John Plunkett, eds. *Victorian Print Media: A Reader.* Oxford: Oxford UP, 2005.

Knelman, Judith. "Trollope's Journalism." *Library* 5.2 (June 1983): 140–55.

Koss, Stephen. *The Rise and Fall of the Political Press in Britain: The Nineteenth Century.* Chapel Hill: U of North Carolina P, 1981.

Latham, Sean, and Robert Scholes. "The Rise of Periodical Studies." *PMLA* 121.2 (Mar. 2006): 517–31.

Leader, Zachary. "Coleridge and the Uses of Journalism." *Grub Street and the Ivory Tower: Literary Journalism and Literary Scholarship from Fielding to the Internet.* Ed. Jeremy Treglown and Bridget Bennett. Oxford: Clarendon P, 1998. 22–40.

Leary, Patrick. "Googling the Victorians." *Journal of Victorian Culture* 10.1 (Summer 2005): 72–86.

Leckie, Barbara. *Culture and Adultery: The Novel, the Newspaper, and the Law, 1857–1914.* Philadelphia: U of Pennsylvania P, 1999.

Lee, Alan J. *The Origins of the Popular Press in England, 1855–1914.* London: Croom Helm, 1973.

Levine, Caroline. "Scaled Up, Writ Small: A Response to Carolyn Dever and Herbert F. Tucker." *Victorian Studies* 49.1 (Autumn 2006): 100–105.

———. "Strategic Formalism: Toward a New Method in Cultural Studies." *Victorian Studies* 48.4 (Summer 2006): 625–57.

Levine, George. *Dying to Know: Scientific Epistemology and Narrative in Victorian England.* Chicago: U of Chicago P, 2002.

Levine, George, and William Madden, eds. *The Art of Victorian Prose.* New York: Oxford UP, 1968.

Levinson, Marjorie. "What Is New Formalism?" *PMLA* 122.2 (Mar. 2007): 558–69.

Loesberg, Jonathan. "Bourdieu and the Sociology of Aesthetics." *ELH* 60 (1993): 1033–56.

———. "The Ideology of Narrative Form in Sensation Fiction." *Representations* 13 (1986): 115–38.

Maidment, B. E. "Victorian Periodicals and Academic Discourse." *Investigating Victorian Journalism.* Ed. Laurel Brake, Aled Jones, and Lionel Madden. New York: St. Martin's, 1990. 143–54.

Matthew, H. C. G. "Rhetoric and Politics in Great Britain, 1860–1950." *Politics and Social Change in Modern Britain: Essays Presented to A. F. Thompson.* Ed. P. J. Waller. New York: St. Martin's, 1987. 34–58.

McCormack, Kathleen. "The Saccharissa Essays: George Eliot's Only Woman Persona." *Nineteenth-Century Studies* 4 (1990): 41–59.

McDonald, Peter D. *British Literary Culture and Publishing Practice, 1880–1914.* Cambridge: Cambridge UP, 1997.

Montwieler, Katherine. "Marketing Sensation: *Lady Audley's Secret* and Consumer Culture." *Beyond Sensation: Mary Elizabeth Braddon in Context.* Ed. Marlene Tromp, Pamela K. Gilbert, and Aeron Haynie. Albany: State U of New York P, 2000. 43–61.

Morson, Gary Saul. "Bakhtin, Genres, and Temporality." *New Literary History* 22 (1991): 1071–92.

Morson, Gary Saul, and Caryl Emerson. *Mikhail Bakhtin: Creation of a Prosaics.* Stanford: Stanford UP, 1990.

Mullen, Richard, and James Munson. *The Penguin Companion to Trollope.* New York: Penguin, 1996.

Nevill, John. *Harriet Martineau.* London: F. Muller, 1944.

Noble, Thomas. *George Eliot's "Scenes of Clerical Life."* Yale Studies in English 159. New Haven: Yale UP, 1965.

———. Introduction. *Scenes of Clerical Life.* By George Eliot. New York: Oxford UP, 1985. vii–xvii.

North, John. "Overview." *The Waterloo Directory of English Newspapers and Periodicals, 1800–1900.* www.victorianperiodicals.com/Contents/Overview.asp. Accessed 4 May 2007.

Orwell, George. *George Orwell: The Collected Essays, Journalism and Letters.* Vol. 4: *In Front of Your Nose, 1946–1950.* Ed. Sonia Orwell and Ian Angus. Boston: David R. Godine, 2000.

Parry, Ann. "Intellectuals and the Middle Class Periodical Press: Theory, Method, Case Study." *Journal of Newspaper and Periodical History* 4.3 (Autumn 1988): 18–32.

Patten, Robert L., and David Finkelstein. "Editing *Blackwood's*; or, What Do Editors Do?" *Print Culture and the Blackwood Tradition, 1805–1930.* Ed. David Finkelstein. Toronto: U of Toronto P, 2006. 146–83.

Pavel, Thomas. "Literary Genres as Norms and Good Habits." *New Literary History* 34.2 (2003): 201–10.

Pearson, Richard. *W. M. Thackeray and the Mediated Text: Writing for Periodicals in the Mid-Nineteenth Century.* Aldershot: Ashgate, 2000.

Pemberton, T. Edgar. *The Life and Writings of T. W. Robertson.* London: Richard Bentley and Son, 1893.

Perkin, J. Russell. *A Reception-History of George Eliot's Fiction.* Ann Arbor: UMI Research Press, 1990.

Peterson, Linda. "Harriet Martineau: Masculine Discourse, Female Sage." *Victorian Sages and Cultural Discourse.* Ed. Thais Morgan. New Brunswick: Rutgers UP, 1990. 171–86.

———. "Reinventing Authorship: Harriet Martineau in the Literary Marketplace of the 1820s." *Women's Writing* 9.3 (2002): 337–49.

Pichanick, Valerie Kossew. *Harriet Martineau: The Woman and her Work, 1802–1876.* Ann Arbor: U of Michigan P, 1980.

Pinney, Thomas. Introduction. *Essays of George Eliot.* London: Routledge and Kegan Paul, 1963. 1–10.

Poovey, Mary. "Forgotten Writers, Neglected Histories: Charles Reade and the Nineteenth-Century Transformation of the British Literary Field." *ELH* 71 (2004): 433–53.

Pykett, Lyn. "Reading the Periodical Press: Text and Context." *Investigating Victorian Journalism.* Ed. Laurel Brake, Aled Jones, and Lionel Madden. New York: St. Martin's, 1990.

Reynolds, Margaret. "Critical Introduction." *Aurora Leigh.* By Elizabeth Barrett Browning. Athens: Ohio UP, 1992. 1–54.

Rose, Jonathan. "Rereading the English Common Reader: A Preface to a History of Audiences." *Journal of the History of Ideas* 53.1 (1992): 47–70.

Rosmarin, Adena. *The Power of Genre.* Minneapolis: U of Minnesota P, 1985.

Rowell, George. *The Victorian Theatre: A Survey.* Oxford: Clarendon P, 1956.

Sanders, Valerie. "Absolutely an Act of Duty: Choice of Profession in Autobiographies by Victorian Women." *Prose Studies* 9.3 (Dec. 1986): 54–70.

Savin, Maynard. *Thomas William Robertson: His Plays and Stagecraft.* Providence: Brown UP, 1950.

Schoch, Richard. "Performing Bohemia." *Nineteenth Century Theatre and Film* 30.2 (Winter 2003): 1–13.

Schroeder, Janice. "'Better Arguments': The *English Woman's Journal* and the Game of Public Opinion." *Victorian Periodicals Review* 35.3 (Fall 2002): 243–71.

Schudson, Michael. "News, Public, Nation." *American Historical Review* 107.2 (Apr. 2002): 481–95.

———. "The Politics of Narrative Form: The Emergence of News Conventions in Print and Television." *Daedalus* 111.4 (1982): 97–112.

———. *The Power of News.* Cambridge: Harvard UP, 1995.

Scott, J. W. Robertson. *"We" and Me.* London: W. H. Allen, 1956.

Seitel, Peter. "Theorizing Genres—Interpreting Works." *New Literary History* 34 (2003): 275–97.

Shattock, Joanne, and Michael Wolff. *The Victorian Periodical Press: Samplings and Soundings.* Toronto: U of Toronto P, 1982.

Sindall, Rob. *Street Violence in the Nineteenth Century.* Leicester: Leicester UP, 1990.

Skilton, David, ed. *The Early and Mid-Victorian Novel.* London: Routledge, 1993.

Smalley, Donald, ed. *Trollope: The Critical Heritage.* London: Routledge and Kegan Paul, 1969.

Smith, Anthony. *The Politics of Information: Problems of Policy in Modern Media.* London: Macmillan, 1978.

Smith, K. J. M. *James Fitzjames Stephen: Portrait of a Victorian Rationalist.* Cambridge: Cambridge UP, 1988.

Srebrnik, Patricia Thomas. "Trollope, James Virtue, and *Saint Pauls Magazine.*" *Nineteenth-Century Fiction* 37.2 (Dec. 1982): 443–63.

Stange, Robert. "The Voices of the Essayist." *Nineteenth-Century Fiction* 35 (Dec. 1980): 312–30.

Summers, Kathryn. "Epideictic Rhetoric in the *Englishwoman's Review.*" *Victorian Periodicals Review* 34.3 (Fall 2001): 263–81.

Surridge, Lisa. *Bleak Houses: Marital Violence in Victorian Fiction.* Athens: Ohio UP, 2005.

Sutherland, John. Introduction. *He Knew He Was Right.* By Anthony Trollope. Oxford: Oxford UP, 1985. vii–xxiii.

———. *The Stanford Companion to Victorian Fiction.* Stanford: Stanford UP, 1989.

Thomson, Clive. "Bakhtin's 'Theory' of Genre." *Studies in Twentieth-Century Literature* 9.1 (Fall 1984): 29–40.

Tuchman, Gaye. *Making News: A Study in the Construction of Reality.* New York: Free Press, 1978.

Tucker, Herbert. "Tactical Formalism: A Response to Caroline Levine." *Victorian Studies* 49.1 (Autumn 2006): 85–93.

Turner, Mark. "Toward a Cultural Critique of Victorian Periodicals." *Studies in Newspaper and Periodical History. 1995 Annual.* Ed. Michael Harris and Tom O'Malley. Westport: Greenwood, 1997.

———. *Trollope and the Magazines: Gendered Issues in Mid-Victorian Britain.* New York: St. Martin's, 2000.

Turner, Paul. *Victorian Poetry, Drama, and Miscellaneous Prose, 1832–1890.* Oxford History of English Literature 14. Oxford: Clarendon P, 1989.

Tusan, Michelle Elizabeth. *Women Making News: Gender and Journalism in Modern Britain.* Urbana: U of Illinois P, 2005.

Uglow, Jennifer. *George Eliot.* New York: Virago/Pantheon, 1987.

VanArsdel, Rosemary T. "Victorian Periodicals: Aids to Research: A Selected Bibliography." Victorian Research Web. Ed. Patrick Leary. http://victorianresearch.org/periodicals.html.

Vernon, James. *Politics and the People: A Study in English Political Culture, c. 1815–1867.* Cambridge: Cambridge UP, 1993.

Vos, Tim P. "News Writing Structure and Style." *American Journalism: History, Principles, Practices.* Ed. W. David Sloan and Lisa Mullikin Parcell. Jefferson, NC: McFarland, 2002. 296–305.

Wakeham, John. "Trollope and the Press." *Trollopiana* 37 (May 1997): 11–16.

Watson, George. *Never Ones for Theory? England and the War of Ideas.* Cambridge: Lutterworth, 2000.

Webb, R. K. *Harriet Martineau: A Radical Victorian.* London: Heinemann, 1960.

Weedon, Alexis. "SHARP Distinguished Achievement Award Winners." 5 Sep. 2006. SHARP-L Archives. https://listserv.indiana.edu.

Wellek, Rene, and Austin Warren. *Theory of Literature.* 3rd ed. New York: Harcourt, Brace, 1956.

Wheatley, Vera. *The Life and Work of Harriet Martineau.* London: Secker and Warburg, 1957.

Wiener, Joel H. "How New Was the New Journalism?" *Papers for the Millions: The New Journalism in Britain, 1850s to 1914.* Ed. Joel H. Wiener. Westport: Greenwood, 1988. 47–71.

———, ed. *Innovators and Preachers: The Role of the Editor in Victorian England.* Westport: Greenwood, 1985.

———, ed. *Papers for the Millions: The New Journalism in Britain, 1850s to 1914.* Westport: Greenwood, 1988.

Willey, Basil. *Nineteenth Century Studies: Coleridge to Matthew Arnold.* London: Chatto and Windus, 1949.

Williams, Carolyn. "'Genre' and 'Discourse' in Victorian Cultural Studies." *Victorian Literature and Culture* 27.2 (1999): 517–20.

Wolff, Michael. "Charting the Golden Stream: Thoughts on a Directory of Victorian Periodicals." *Victorian Periodicals Newsletter* 13 (Sept. 1971): 23–38.

Woods, Oliver, and James Bishop. *The Story of The Times.* London: Michael Joseph, 1983.

Index

Eliot, George (*continued*)
  names used by, 201n3; rejection of
  journalism by, 100, 115–16, 120–21,
  162; as theorist of journalism, 167–
  68. Works: *Adam Bede,* 99, 120;
  *Essays and Leaves from a Note-
  Book,* 114; "Janet's Repentance,"
  102, 115–20, 168, 202n9; *The Mill on
  the Floss,* 120; "The Sad Fortunes
  of the Reverend Amos Barton,"
  99; *Scenes of Clerical Life,* 115. *See
  also* Evans, Marian
Eliot, Simon, 19–20
Emerson, Caryl, 40, 192n15
English Woman's Journal, 100
Erickson, Lee, 26, 191n12
Errico, Marcus, 187n2
Escott, T. H. S., 76, 211n11
essay, familiar, 26. *See also* review essay
Evans, Marian, 10, 39, 98, 100–115; cri-
  tique of journalism by, 107–9; dis-
  like of slashing criticism, 103–4;
  editorship of *Westminster Review,*
  101, 102–3, 104–5; motives for writing, 105–6; names used by, 201n3;
  relationship with G. H. Lewes, 105.
  Works: "Evangelical Teaching: Dr.
  Cumming," 107, 109–10, 116; "Lord
  Brougham's Literature," 107, 108;
  "Poetry and Prose, from the Note-
  book of an Eccentric," 104; "The
  Poet Young," 101–2; "Silly Novels
  by Lady Novelists," 107, 110–11;
  "Worldliness and Other-Worldliness: The Poet Young," 111–14. *See
  also* Eliot, George
Examiner, 8, 139, 179

Fenves, Peter, 202n9
field, literary. *See under* Bourdieu,
  Pierre

Finkelstein, David, 87, 191n10, 199n18,
  200n21, 208n19
Forster, W. E., 47
Fortnightly Review, 77, 102, 120, 180
Fowler, Alastair, 6, 8, 153, 155, 196n17,
  208n20; on generic change, 26,
  209n1; on genre content, 188–
  89n10; on genre families, 192n17;
  on genre interaction, 189n15; on
  genre maps, 197n1; on genre systems, 191n9; on historical genres,
  73–74, 210n5; on Victorian genres,
  8, 189–90n16
Fraser's Magazine, 62
Froude, J. A., 103
Frow, John, 6
Frye, Northrop, 40

Galilean discourse, 7–8. *See also*
  Bakhtin, Mikhail; genres
Galt, John, 167
Gaskell, Elizabeth, 111
Geake, Charles, 62
genres, 5–9, 35, 39–41, 66–67, 73–74,
  153–59, 161–64; acquisition of, 30–
  31, 71, 191n13, 196n17; as aids to
  composition, 6, 142, 153–54, 164,
  171, 189nn13–14, 210n8; change in,
  26, 162, 209n1; history of, 8, 27, 28–
  31, 70, 175; interaction of, 9, 16–17,
  32–33, 40, 43–44, 157, 168; of journalism, 16–17, 27, 30, 31, 153, 155; —,
  cataloguing of, 4; —, as job qualification, 157–58; —, quality of, 164;
  —, standardization of, 6, 29–31;
  and language, 5, 7, 40; in literary
  history, 1, 156; maps of, 71, 73,
  197n1; repertoires of, 155, 157; as
  reserves of meaning, 5, 35, 40, 84,
  154, 193n23; scholarship and, 4,
  40–41, 141–42, 153–54, 175, 187n2,

205n3; struggle of, 7, 17, 18–29, 34; as technologies, 153; as world-views, 9, 35, 40, 66–67, 83, 154, 157; writers as theorists of, 167; writers' use of, 6–7, 157. *See also* Bakhtin, Mikhail; inverted pyramid; leading articles (editorials); novel(s); novelization, review essay; slashing articles
Gilbert, W. S., 210n6
Gissing, George, 167
Glendenning, Victoria, 199n19
Greg, W. R., 36, 103, 192n18; on the newspaper press, 36, 201n4
Gross, John, 17

Habermas, Jürgen, 11, 142–43, 145, 146, 147, 149–50, 155–56, 158, 206n7, 207n14; Schudson on, 207n12
habitus. *See* Bourdieu, Pierre.
Hagan, John, 197n6
Haight, Gordon, 102, 201n2, 201n6
Hampton, Mark, 143, 206n8
Hardman, William, 130, 137
Hardy, Barbara, 98
Hartley, John, 149, 187n1
Hawkins, Angus, 192n19
Hazlitt, William, 27, 28, 162–63, 190n5
Hennell, Sara Sophia, 104, 105, 114
heteroglossia, 7, 152–53. *See also* Bakhtin, Mikhail
Heyck, T. W., 17
historiography, 2, 28–29, 69
history of the book, 10, 11, 75, 93, 175; social sciences and, 146
Holloway, John, 188n9
Hope, A. J. Beresford, 8, 60
Horne, Richard, 63
Houghton, Walter, 88, 166, 193n20, 199–200n20
Household Words, 74, 93

Huett, Lorna, 91
Hughes, Thomas, 102
Hughes, Winifred, 204n10
Humpherys, Anne, 151, 152
Hunt, Frederick Knight, 52, 58
Hunt, John, 8, 28
Hunt, Leigh, 8, 28
Hunt, Thornton, 105
Hutton, R. H., 130, 138
Huxley, T. H., 103

identity, in sensation novels, 133, 204n10
Illustrated London News, 130–31, 138
Internet Library of Early Journals (ILEJ), 2, 148
inverted pyramid, 30

Jameson, Anna, 16
Jeffrey, Francis, 25, 28, 102, 164
Jenkins, Simon, 75, 197n7
Jewsbury, Geraldine, 108–9, 114
Johnson, Samuel, 26, 87, 106
journalism: as apprenticeship, 18, 98–99; attacks on, 60, 83; Elizabeth Barrett Browning on, 14–16, 18; change in, 39, 162, 166; compared to other genres, 16, 41, 82; competition with other genres, 41, 82, 161–62, 166; contemporary theories of, 43, 60, 62, 63, 84, 166; genre forms of, 2, 16–17, 25, 26, 27, 30, 31, 37, 153, 155; history of, 165, 192–93n19; ideology of, 64, 65, 101, 140, 196n15; limited repertoire of, 155; as literary subject, 37–38; rates of pay for, 23, 29, 105, 191n12, 201–2n6; reputation of, 37, 41, 161, 170–72, 174; in Robertson's *Society*, 170–72; scholarship of, 2, 16–18, 142–47, 158, 187n1; sensational, 10–11, 122–

Recent Books in the VICTORIAN LITERATURE AND CULTURE SERIES